Racism a...

SOCIOLOGY FOR A CHANGING WORLD
Series Editors: Graham Allan and Mary Maynard
Consultant Editor: Janet Finch

This series, published in conjunction with the British Sociology Association, evaluates and reflects major developments in contemporary sociology. The books will focus on key changes in social and economic life in recent years and on the ways in which the discipline of sociology has analysed those changes. The books will reflect the state of the art in contemporary British sociology, while at the same time drawing upon comparative material to set debates in an international perspective.

Published

Rosamund Billington, Annette Fitzsimons, Lenore Greensides and
    Sheelagh Strawbridge, *Culture and Society*
Lois Bryson, *Welfare and the State*
Frances Heidensohn, *Crime and Society*
Glenn Morgan, *Organisations in Society*
John Solomos and Les Back, *Racism and Society*
Mike Savage and Alan Warde, *Urban Sociology, Capitalism and Modernity*
Andrew Webster, *Science, Technology and Society*

Forthcoming

Gordon Causer and Ray Norman, *Work and Employment in
    Contemporary Society*

Series Standing Order

If you would like to receive future titles in this series as they are published, you can make use of our standing order facility. To place a standing order please contact your bookseller or, in case of difficulty, write to us at the address below with your name and address and the name of the series. Please state with which title you wish to begin your standing order. (If you live outside the United Kingdom we may not have the rights for your area, in which case we will forward your order to the publisher concerned.)

Customer Services Department, Macmillan Distribution Ltd
Houndmills, Basingstoke, Hampshire RG21 6XS, England

RACISM AND SOCIETY

John Solomos

and

Les Back

First published 1996 by
MACMILLAN PRESS LTD
Houndmills, Basingstoke, Hampshire RG21 6XS
and London
Companies and representatives
throughout the world

ISBN 0–333–58438–4 hardcover
ISBN 0–333–58439–2 paperback

A catalogue record for this book is available
from the British Library.

10 9 8 7 6 5 4 3 2 1
05 04 03 02 01 00 99 98 97 96

Printed in Malaysia

For Kyriacou Solomou, Nikolas Solomou, Joan Back and Bob Back with much love, for the support they have provided over the years

Contents

List of Figures

Acknowledgements

The author and publisher wish to thank the following who have kindly given permission for the use of copyright material:

The Robert Opie Collection, for Britannia and the domestic: Vinolia advertisement, 1915 (p. 162);

The Robert Opie Collection, for John Bull as an English champion: England's Glory Matches tin sign, 1905 (p. 165);

A Rhodes *Propaganda: The Art of Persuasion in World War II* – Angus Robertson, for a Nazi cartoon representing the black Allied soldier (p. 173);

'Greetings from England: The Coming Invasion' Nazi pamphlet circulated in Holland, 1944 (p. 175);

Monstrous Regiment: Nazi poster portraying the GI as a jitter-bugging marauder: Poster in Holland, 1944 (p. 177);

Benetton Publicity, for United Colors? Benetton billboard poster, 1991 (p. 188);

Benetton Publicity courtesy of *Colors* Magazine, for Altered Image: Toscani's portrait of a black Queen Elizabeth, spring 1993 (p. 198).

Every effort has been made to trace all the copyright-holders but if any have been inadvertently overlooked the publisher will be pleased to make the necessary arrangements at the first opportunity.

Preface

It is impossible in the present environment to ignore the role of ideas about race in shaping and determining the social and political relations of societies all over the globe. Whether one looks at the popular media or at the changing research agendas of the social sciences and humanities, there is no escaping the realisation that questions about race and related social issues are at the heart of a whole range of debates. If we take the situation in Britain and other European societies as a case in point, there seems little doubt that *immigration* and *race relations* have come to occupy an important space in political debates about many aspects of social and economic policy (Balibar and Wallerstein, 1991; Miles, 1993; Wrench and Solomos, 1993). As a number of commentators have noted an underlying theme in American debates about a whole range of social issues is the question of race. Studs Terkel, a perceptive commentator on American culture and society, captures a key aspect of contemporary trends when he talks of the 'obsession' with race in all sectors of urban America (Terkel, 1992).

A good example of this process is the debate that has taken place in numerous advanced industrial societies about the issue of the *underclass*. Although it is clear that this subject cannot be seen easily through a racial lens in all national and localised social and economic environments, there is a clear racial theme in much of the policy debate about both the causes and the solutions to this phenomenon (Smith, 1992; Weir, 1993). Another instance of the increasing salience of race can be found in the wave of political mobilisations about immigration, national identity and related issues across Europe during the 1990s. These have served above all else to highlight the importance of racism as a social and political force. But these new forms of mobilisation have also raised important questions about what it is exactly that we mean when we refer to racism in contemporary societies, and how we conceptualise the differences and similarities between the present and the past. Over the past few years there has been much journalistic writing and speculation about these topics, but as yet there has been little systematic analysis of the underlying historical and conceptual issues.

It is partly as a result of such developments that we have seen an unprecedented explosion of academic interest in the study of race and racism as social, cultural and political phenomena. Without too much exaggeration one can say that the study of the history and contemporary expressions of racism has come to the fore in a wide range of academic disciplines. Whilst perhaps even a decade ago the study of racism was a highly specialised field in such disciplines as history, sociology and politics, there is a hardly any branch of the social sciences and humanities which has not witnessed a resurgence of interest in the study of various aspects of racism. This is reflected in the wide range of monographs and edited collections about race and racism that have come out over the past few years, as well as in the changing research agenda in universities and research institutes. Indeed, it is clear that questions about race, ethnicity and identity have come to occupy a key role within contemporary debates about postmodernism and globalisation (Kristeva, 1991; Hall, 1992; Kristeva, 1993; Rattansi and Westwood, 1994; Winant, 1994).

It is against this background that we began work on *Racism and Society*, and in this sense it is a book of its time. It is a contribution to the ongoing discussion of the role of race and ethnicity in contemporary societies. But it is also worth emphasising that is also the result of our long-standing concern with the analysis of the role and changing contours of racial ideologies and practices in contemporary societies. We have worked on various aspects of this question for over a decade and felt it appropriate to try to provide an overview of what we see as some of the key issues and main trends in this field of social analysis. Additionally, we felt unhappy with the ways in which existing texts dealt with the complex range of issues raised by the study of race and racism in contemporary societies. In this sense this volume is an attempt to outline the broad contours of the study of the role that race and racism play in shaping social relations and institutions, and to encourage further debate and analysis. We do not see this book as a text that provides the final word on this subject. Indeed, what makes the study of contemporary forms of race and racism such an interesting and challenging area at the present time is the complex range of social and political relations researchers have sought to explore and the variety of theoretical perspectives that have been developed to provide the conceptual tools for this research. What we seek to provide, therefore, is a critical overview of some of the key issues as we see them.

Given recent developments in Europe, the United States and elsewhere, we hardly need reminding that the boundaries of the study of the relationship between racism and society are by no means fixed and unchanging. Indeed, in writing this volume we became even more aware than we were at the beginning of our endeavours of the complexity of the issues we were attempting to analyse and of the need to utilise perspectives from a range of theoretical and historical research in order to provide a useful and critical intervention in current debates. This has become particularly clear in the context of recent developments in both Western and Eastern Europe, where in quite diverse social and political contexts we have seen the emergence of new forms of racism and ethnic nationalism that have had a devastating impact at both a personal and a collective level (Žižek, 1993). It is also clear that in contemporary societies ideas about the social relevance of *race* are by no means uniform and unchanging. Hence the tendency of many commentators to use notions such as *new racism* and *cultural racism* in order to talk about the changing morphology of racial ideas and practices in societies such as Britain, the United States of America and other Western societies.

The changing meaning and social role of race and racism in the present social and political environment makes it inherently difficult to provide a comprehensive account of this field of study. Yet this is what we are attempting to do, with the clear understanding that our account of key issues and processes is both provisional and limited in its objectives. Rather than retracing familiar theoretical and historical territory the main concerns of the book will be to concentrate on how sociologists and other social researchers have attempted to provide conceptual frameworks for the analysis of racialised social relations and how they have applied these frameworks to the analysis of specific social phenomena. We hope that in exploring the interplay between theory and historical analysis we can see how far we have moved towards a better understanding of the ways in which *race* is used in particular social and historical contexts, what it signifies and its impact on social, political, economic and cultural processes in contemporary societies.

Rather than focus on the rather narrow issue of whether or not race is a social scientific category as such, we shall explore the ways in which it becomes a form of collective social identity in particular social and historical circumstances. It should be clear from the tenor of the arguments to be found in this volume that we do not see race as a natural category in any sense, though it is often used as such. Race and ethnic categories are ideological entities that are made and remade through struggle. In this sense race can be seen as a discursive category through which differences are accorded social significance. But it is also more than just a discursive category since it carries with it material consequences for those who are included within, or excluded from, a particular racial identity.

We hope also to show the value of dialogue between researchers who are working within a variety of disciplines and theoretical perspectives. What we shall suggest is that it is necessary to evaluate radically the contribution of all the main paradigms in this field. While it may be beyond the scope of a single volume to attempt to discuss all of the important theoretical and historical contributions that we have seen in this field over the past few decades, we have attempted to provide a sharply focused overview of these debates that ranges across narrow disciplinary boundaries. This is partly because we have seen in recent years an explosion of interest in the study of race and racism from within a variety of disciplines. There have been important contributions from sociology, politics, geography, cultural studies and literary theory, psychology and related fields. This growth of interest in the study of race and racism has led to an expansion of the research agenda to take account of key aspects of racialised relations in contemporary societies. Quite apart from the traditional focus on studies of communities and institutions, we have seen a growing number of studies that look at issues such as political mobilisation, policing and socio-legal processes, youth, popular culture, race and gender, sexuality and the history of racial ideas. Additionally, we have seen important political debates about the role of policy change and state policies in this field, including the role of initiatives that are predicated on the construction of *multi-cultural* and *anti-racist* strategies for dealing with the role of racist ideologies and racial discrimination.

Our main aim in writing this book is to examine two key dimensions of contemporary racial relations. The first may be broadly seen as covering the social and political aspects of the analysis of race and racism in contemporary societies. The analysis in this part of the book is intended to provide the basis of a theoretical and conceptual framework for analysing contemporary forms of racism and the social relations that arise on the basis of racial categorisation. The second dimension is an exploration of how ideas about *race* mobilise social and cultural processes that help shape our understandings of what racial relations are in contemporary societies. This means, above all, that we are concerned to show how and why in particular contexts social and cultural discourses about race and ethnicity converge and help to shape policies and practices around specific social groups and 'problems'. In this part of the book we shall also explore the variety of ways in which racialised minorities themselves have mobilised notions of race, ethnicity and culture in organising themselves both socially and politically.

These concerns explain the way in which the various chapters are organised. The first two concentrate on the analysis of the theoretical and historical context of the study of race and racism as aspects of contemporary social relations. Taken together they are intended as a brief, and critical, analysis of research and scholarship about race and racism in contemporary societies. In Chapter 1 we consider the changing terms of theoretical debates concerning the ways in which the social category of race is used and what it is supposed to signify. This involves an exploration of the changing terms of debate about the role of the processes through which the category of race is attributed social significance, and their consequences for social structures and institutions. Chapter 2 then takes the analysis further by looking at some of the key historical aspects of the uses of race in specific contexts and their impact on the emergence and significance of ideas about race in contemporary societies. This is an area of much heated debate over the years and we provide a critical account of the main perspectives that have resulted from research on the history of racial ideas and of their impact on specific social contexts.

The main concern of the first two chapters can be seen as laying the foundations for the analysis to be found in the rest of the book. Chapter 3 extends this account by exploring the question of racial inequalities and how they have been analysed. We look specifically at the interface between racialised inequalities and inequalities deriving from class, gender and wider sets of social relations. This is followed in Chapter 4 by an analysis of the relationship between race and forms of political action, focusing on the complex ways in which ideas about race have influenced and continue to influence political institutions and the channels through which both majorities and minorities mobilise politically. Chapter 5 then deals with the continuing debate about the nature of *racism* and *anti-racism*. This is a thorny problem, as the range of interventions in recent years about the question of what some writers call 'new racism' shows.

In Chapters 6 and 7 we shift focus somewhat and look at the ethnic and cultural dimension of contemporary racial relations. Chapter 6 takes up the question of the relation between race, culture and ethnicity in shaping what one might term the cultural forms of mobilisation around these signifiers. This requires a critical analysis of the increasingly complex and ambivalent forms of racialised identities which are to be found in contemporary societies and the ways they are understood and analysed. We seek to go beyond the limits of recent debates by exploring the changing expressions of ethnic and cultural identity in the present socio-political environment. In Chapter 7 there follows the analysis of the role played by race and racism in constructions of popular cultural forms. This is an arena which has been much discussed in recent years, particularly in relation to the renewed interest in the study of the role that culture plays in shaping our understandings of race and ethnicity in the modern environment. What recent debates have tended to do, however, is to look at these processes from a largely ahistorical perspective. In order to remedy this gap we have attempted to situate more recent developments within a broader historical account. This is most evident in our depiction of race and popular culture in British society and in the discussion of the role of racial symbols in Nazi popular culture.

Finally, in Chapter 8 we consider the consequences of the shifting meanings of race and racism in the present socio-political environment. This allows us to return to some of the thorny theoretical questions that we touched on in the first part of the book. In particular we take up the suggestion made by some writers that we need to develop a conception of racism that takes as its starting point the existence of complex and multifarious *racisms* in specific historical contexts. Additionally, we take an exploratory look at some of the issues that are likely to confront us in the coming period in thinking through the question of what can be done to tackle the rise of racism in its various forms, with its consequent costs for humanity.

Over the years we have been aided in exploring and analysing these questions by colleagues and friends. We were able to present some of our arguments to the varied and friendly groups of people that regularly attended the *Workshop on the Politics of Racism* at Birkbeck College from 1988 to 1993. We would like in particular to express our gratitude for the help and encouragement of Clive Harris and Michael Keith, who kindly commented on aspects of the argument as it developed. We hope that they agree that we listened to at least some of their comments. Parminder Bhachu provided us with kind words of encouragement from a distance, which were much appreciated. Our respective academic institutions provided the space and environment for us to work on this volume, at a time of increasing pressure on academic research time. For that we are grateful. Paul Moody was kind enough to provide us with some of the illustrations we have used in Chapter 7. Our publishers, Frances Arnold and Catherine Gray, provided the right balance between critical suggestions and encouragement to keep us going and made sure that we did not forget the nature of our audience. The editors of this series, Graham Allan and Mary Maynard, provided valuable comments which were of great assistance during the revision of a number of chapters. The Baggies offered a very different but no less important source of inspiration, sustenance and exasperation, while that intoxicating victory over the Wolves in March 1995 came at a particularly important point during completion of the final version, and helped us along. Further encouragement was provided by the Economic and Social Research Council which funded our joint research on *Race, Politics and Social Change in Birmingham* (Award No. R000231545). This funding has resulted in a study of contemporary forms of racialised politics and social change, in which we attempted

among other things to provide an analysis of new forms of political mobilisation and the changing terms of discourses about race
in the present environment (Solomos and Back, 1995).

It was while working on this study that we also became conscious of the need to explore some of the conceptual and theoretical issues arising from our writing and discussions in more detail.
Another source of inspiration in producing this volume came
from our own students. They helped to make us conscious of the
need for a critical text that explores the changing dynamics of the
relationship between racism and social relations in the contemporary global environment. Although in recent years there has been
a flood of edited collections and monographs on key features of
contemporary racism many of these texts have looked at only
some of the theoretical debates, particularly those arising from the
engagement with postmodernism and cultural studies. It seems to
us that there is at the present time a clear need for a text that
engages with these recent debates but at the same time provides a
rounded, accessible and historically informed account of the interrelationship between racism and social relations. This book is
our attempt to produce such a text, though it represents very
much work in progress. We hope that all the above, in their different ways, find our endeavours of interest, though we take final
responsibility for the product.

JOHN SOLOMOS
LES BACK

1 Theoretical Perspectives

During the past two decades theoretical and political debates have raged over the status of race and racism as social and analytical concepts. There has been much debate about why the notion of race is still widely used in both popular and social scientific discourses when it is widely accepted that 'races' as such do not exist. This has reached the stage where some writers argue vehemently that the notion of 'race' must be bracketed every time it appears in social scientific discussion. At the same time, much heated debate has taken place about how to theorise racism as a social phenomenon, and how to evaluate its consequences. We have seen the development of the sociology of race relations as an established subdiscipline, of Marxist and neo-Marxist approaches and more recently of postmodernist studies of race and racism. Additionally, of course, during this same period it is undoubtedly true that the question of race has been at the heart of numerous political and policy debates. In a number of advanced industrial societies the 'question of race' or the 'immigration issue' has in one way or another come to occupy a key place in debates about a variety of issues, ranging from social policy, employment and policing to welfare provision. Quite apart from the situation in Britain and the United States, which has long been commented upon, one can refer to the debates going on in countries such as France, Germany and Holland by way of example (Brubaker, 1992; Wrench and Solomos, 1993).

One indicator of the impact of these debates on academic discourse and research is that race and racism has become an established field of study in a number of social science disciplines, most notably in sociology, political science, economics, anthropology, cultural studies and geography. This is a development that has happened relatively quickly. From a situation in the late 1960s

1

where the study of race was a minor concern in the mainstream of sociology, as well as other social science disciplines, it is now clear that aspects of race and racism are an established part of the teaching curriculum and of the research agenda of a number of social science and humanities disciplines. There has also been a noticeable increase in both undergraduate and postgraduate courses which specialise in this field. This has led in way or another to the establishment of race and ethnic studies as a 're-spectable' field of study and research. This is not to say that the meanings attached to notions such as race and ethnicity are the same across the whole spectrum of academic disciplines. What is clear is that they have taken on so many different connotations that sometimes it is obvious that people are not even talking about the same thing.

Along with the evident growth of research in this field, however, it is also clear that there has been a fragmentation into entrenched theoretical paradigms. This has in turn resulted in a profusion of theoretical claims and counter-claims which have not necessarily helped to shed new light on the interrelationship between race, class and gender in specific social situations. At the same time, there has been noticeable confusion about the question of what role so-called 'multicultural perspectives' should have on university curricula. The ongoing debate about 'political correctness' and 'multiculturalism' on university campuses in the United States, and to a lesser extent in Britain, is one of the more politicised aspects of this debate and it is noticeable that a key area of concern has been with the question of how issues of race and ethnicity are covered or not covered within higher and other educational institutions (Graff, 1992; Hughes, 1993; Jacoby, 1987, 1994; Goldberg, 1994).

Rather than retrace all these debates our concern in *Racism and Society* is to attempt to go beyond them somewhat by taking a broader perspective. We begin the task in this chapter by an examination of the central aspects of contemporary theoretical debates. In the course of this critical analysis we shall argue that it is necessary to move beyond inflexible theoretical certainties in order to develop an adequate framework for analysing the role that race and racism play in contemporary social relations. We begin, therefore, by examining some of the key theoretical concerns around which debate has taken place in recent years. In particular we will focus on the role of what is sometimes called the *race relations problematic* and the criticisms and alternatives that have been suggested from a variety of theoretical and conceptual frameworks. Our aim is to position and evaluate these debates within particular historical and political contexts, rather than viewing them in isolation. We will argue that a series of political strategies are encoded within these academic debates, and that it is necessary to untangle some of the conceptual and political issues in order fully to understand the reasons why these theoretical perspectives are strictly limited in their ability to comprehend and explain both historical and contemporary aspects of racism.

Race and sociological theory

The study of race as a field of social scientific inquiry and research originated in the earlier part of this century in the work of a number of American sociologists and anthropologists, most notably during the 1920s and 1930s. They were influenced by the work of Robert Park, one of the key early journalistic and sociological writers in this field and a founder of the Chicago school of sociology. During the period from the 1920s to the 1950s the works of these scholars helped to establish what came to be defined as the study of race relations, particularly through their studies of segregation, immigration and race consciousness in the United States (Park, 1925; Stanfield, 1985, 1993). During the inter-war period the works of these authors helped to develop a body of sociological concepts which were later to be refined into a sociology of race relations in other societies, including Britain. Their studies of the specific contexts within which ideas about race became socially meaningful remain some of the classics of this field, and in fact it is interesting to note that in recent years there has been some renewed interest in the work of Park and others, and its implications for the analysis of contemporary situations.

As we shall see in Chapter 2 popular and scientific discourses about race had become a theme in anthropological, medical and political writings some time before questions about race and ethnicity were taken up by the emerging social sciences. By the late nineteenth and early twentieth century, however, social scientific attempts to analyse the question of race were evident both in the United States and Europe. Given the intellectual and political environment of the time it is perhaps not surprising that these early sociological studies were influenced to some extent by Social Darwinism. This was evident, for example, in some of the writings of American sociologists in the period from the late nineteenth century to the First World War (Stanfield, 1985, 1993; Drake and Cayton, 1993). But by the early twentieth century sociological theorising on race in the United States encouraged the first sustained attempts to analyse the ways in which race became a relevant social category where cultural and social meanings were attached to the physical traits of a particular social group. This in turn helped to popularise notions about the origins of racial conflicts and prejudice which concentrated on situations of cultural contact. The emphasis in sociological studies of the 'race problem' during these decades was on the origins of race prejudice, the interplay between prejudice and conflict, the impact of assimilation on the life of African Americans and the processes through which racial conflicts could be mediated or overcome.

These early studies of race did not concern themselves with the study of racism as a doctrine. The usage of the term racism in both political and social scientific discourses was linked to the rise of Nazism in Germany. As the Nazis came to power and articulated and put into practice their ideas about racial superiority, the term racism came to be used to refer to ideas which defined some racial or ethnic groups as superior and others as inferior (Barzun, 1938; Barkan, 1992; Mosse, 1966). This usage of the term was first suggested by Ruth Benedict in her book *Race and Racism* which defined racism as 'the dogma that one ethnic group is condemned by nature to congenital inferiority and another group is destined to congenital superiority' (1943: 97). In this context racism was seen as referring to those sets of ideas that defined ethnic and racial groups on the basis of claims about biological nature and inherent superiority or ability.

In the post-1945 period a number of developments outside the United States encouraged interest in the study of race and racism in other societies. An important development in this context was the emergence of migrant labour as an important social group in many West European societies. Migration from the ex-colonies and southern Europe led to the creation of racial and ethnic minorities in countries such as Britain, France, Germany and Holland. Another important development was the entrenchment of the Apartheid system in South Africa, a process which aroused the interest of both social scientists and political activists, particularly in relation to the role of the political and legal system in enforcing racial segregation and the 'separate development' of different racial groups.

In Britain, and other European societies, the growth in the theorisation of race and racism ran parallel to these developments. This work has provided a number of important and sophisticated analyses of the politics and ideology of racism. There were two central concerns in these early European attempts to theorise racial and ethnic relations. First, the patterns of immigration and incorporation in the labour market of black and other ethnic communities. Second, the role of colonial history in determining popular conceptions of colour, race and ethnicity in European societies.

A number of early studies of what came in Britain to be called *race relations* were carried out in the 1950s and 1960s by scholars such as Michael Banton, Ruth Glass, John Rex and Sheila Patterson. Most studies of this period concentrated on the interaction between minority and majority communities in employment, housing and other social contexts. What is interesting in hindsight, given the virulence of some of the theoretical debates of the past decade, is the relative absence of a clear theoretical perspective about (i) what constituted the object of analysis of these specific studies and (ii) the absence of a wider socio-political perspective about the interplay between *race relations* and other kinds of social relations.

By the 1960s, however, there was a noticeable growth of interest in the theorisation of the study of both the new forms of migration and settlement as they were being experienced in Britain and elsewhere and other types of *race relations*. Michael Banton's book on *Race Relations* represents a good example of texts from this period. It looked at race relations from a global and historical perspective, concentrating particularly on situations of cultural contact, beliefs about the nature of race, and the social relations constructed on the basis of racial categories. By looking at the experience of changing patterns of interaction historically Banton argued that six basic orders of race relations could be delineated:

namely institutionalised contact, acculturation, domination, paternalism, integration and pluralism (Banton, 1967). It was during the period of the 1960s that what Banton and others have called the *race relations problematic* became the dominant approach in this field (Banton, 1991).

While utilising racial classifications this literature also incorporated anthropological perspectives on ethnicity and social boundaries. This became evident in the development of studies of particular ethnic communities that came to occupy such a prominent role in research in this field. We shall return to this dimension more fully in Chapter 6. Suffice it to say here that the study of racial minorities came to be heavily influenced both by approaches which focused on ethnicity as well as race relations situations.

Another major influence on the development of a sociology of race and ethnic relations can be found in the work of John Rex. Rex has made the most sustained effort to bring a class perspective to the study of ethnic relations. Rex's text on *Race Relations in Sociological Theory* has exercised a major influence over this field since its appearance and it remains one of the most ambitious attempts to provide a theoretical grounding for research in this field. According to Rex's analytic model the definition of social relations between persons as race relations is encouraged by the existence of certain structural conditions: for example, frontier situations of conflict over scarce resources, the existence of unfree, indentured, or slave labour, unusually harsh class exploitation, strict legal intergroup distinctions and occupational segregation, differential access to power and prestige, cultural diversity and limited group interaction, and migrant labour as an underclass fulfilling stigmatised roles in a metropolitan setting (Rex, 1970). From this perspective the study of race relations is concerned with situations in which such structured conditions interacted with actors definitions in such a way as to produce a racially structured social reality.

These are the concerns which Rex articulated clearly in two studies of race relations in Birmingham during the 1960s and the 1970s. In the study conducted by Rex and his associates in Handsworth during the mid 1970s (Rex and Tomlinson, 1979) the basic research problem was to explore the degree to which immigrant populations shared the class position of their white neighbours and white workers in general. The substance of the analysis goes on to outline a class structure in which white workers have been granted certain rights which have been won through the working-class movement via trade unions and the Labour Party. The result was that in the 1970s a stasis or truce was established between the interests of dominant status and class groups and the white working class. The position of migrant workers and their children is located outside the negotiation that had taken place between the white workers and capital. They experience discrimination in all the areas where the white workers had made significant gains, that is employment, education and housing. It follows from this that the position of migrant workers placed them outside the working class in the position of an *underclass*:

> The concept of underclass was intended to suggest ... that the minorities were systematically at a disadvantage compared with their white peers and that, instead of identifying with working class culture, community and politics, they formed their own organisations and became effectively a separate underprivileged class. (Ibid., p. 275)

From this point Rex and Tomlinson develop a model of political action and even a political agenda for black populations as they become a 'class for themselves'. Immigrant minorities are forced into a series of reactive–defensive political strategies. This process takes on different forms within Asian and West Indian communities. Within Asian communities this results in a concentration on capital accumulation and social mobility. In the West Indian community it takes the form of withdrawal from competition altogether with an emphasis on the construction of a black identity. This all leads to what Rex refers to elsewhere as the 'politics of defensive confrontation' (Rex, 1979).

Neo-Marxism and racism

The early 1980s saw the emergence of a number of substantial criticisms of the research agenda on *race relations*, written largely from a neo-Marxist perspective. Such criticisms were influenced both by theoretical and political considerations, and they helped to stimulate new areas of debate. One of the first attempts to provide a theoretical critique of the approaches of both Banton and Rex is to be found in the work of Robert Miles since the early 1980s. The starting point of Miles's critique was his opposition to the existence of a sociology of race, and his view that the object of analysis should be racism, which he viewed as integral to the process of capital accumulation (Miles, 1982; 1986). His analysis was first articulated in *Racism and Migrant Labour* and it is perhaps the most sustained attempt to include the study of racism within the mainstream of Marxist social theory. His empirical research has focused specifically on the situation in Britain and the rest of Europe, and has looked at the role of political, class and ideological relationships in shaping our understandings of racial conflict and change in these societies.

For Miles the idea of race refers to a human construct, an ideology with regulatory power within society. Analytically race constitutes a paper tiger (Miles, 1988) that may be a common term of reference within everyday discourse, but which presents a serious theoretical problem. It is here where Miles diverges from what he sees as the race relations problematic. While Rex is concerned with models of social action (i.e. for Rex it is enough that race is utilised in everyday discourse as a basis for social action), Miles is concerned with the analytical and objective status of race as a basis of action (Miles, 1984a, p. 42). Race is thus an ideological effect, a mask which hides real economic relationships (Miles, 1984). Thus the forms of class consciousness which are legitimate for Miles must ultimately be seen as the product of socio-ec nomic relations which are hidden within the regulatory process of racialisation. In one of his most famous formulations he argues: '[Race is] an idea that should be explicitly and consistently confined to the dustbin of analytically useless terms' (Miles, 1989, p. 72). Rather than accepting any notion of race as given he develops the idea of a process of *racialisation* as the key analytical tool of his approach: 'I therefore employ the concept of racialisation to refer to those instances where social relations between people have been structured by the signification of human biological characteristics in such a way as to define and construct differentiated social collectivities' (Miles, 1989, p. 75). For Miles the process of racialisation is interrelated with the conditions of migrant labourers. Its effects are the result of the contradiction between 'on the one hand the need of the capitalist world economy for the mobility of human beings, and on the other, the drawing of territorial boundaries and the construction of citizenship as a legal category which sets boundaries for human mobility' (Miles, 1988, p. 438). Within the British setting this ideological work conducted primarily by the state acts as a means of crisis management and results in racialising fragments of the working class. Race politics are thus confined to the forces of regulation. For Miles the construction of political identities which utilise racial consciousness plays no part in the development of a progressive politics.

Miles raises some fundamental questions about the nature of political action within communities of migrant labour. The most important of these is the degree to which black and minority politics are really distillations of class conflict. If this is true any movements away from class-based political action (i.e. movements towards any notions of black community politics) are doomed to failure (Miles, 1988, 1989). If one takes this argument further, class-based political action is ultimately in opposition to any sort of sustained political organisation around a notion of race. For Miles the politics of race is narrowly confined to the struggle against racism. This is neatly captured in the way he uses Hall's (1980, p. 341) statement on the relationship between class and race. He concludes that it is not race but racism which is 'the modality in which class is lived and fought through' (Miles, 1988, p. 447).

Miles's insistence that racial differentiations are always created in the context of class differentiation (Miles, 1989a) is a core feature of his critique of the work of Banton and Rex. However, his position results in a kind of class reductionism which ultimately limits the scope of theoretical work on conceptualising racism and racialised social relations. For example, in some contexts class exploitation may be incidental to the construction of situations of racial dominance (Goldberg, 1992). However, the greatest contribution that Miles makes is his insistence that *races* are created with the context of political and social regulation. Thus *race* is above all a political construct. It is within this context that the concepts of *racial categorisation* and *racialisation* have been used to refer to what Robert Miles calls 'those instances where social relations between people have been structured by the signification of human biological characteristics in such a way as to define and construct differentiated social collectivities' (Miles, 1989a, p. 75). His work constitutes an attempt to reclaim the study of racism from an apoliticised sociological framework and locate it squarely in a Marxist theorisation of social conflict.

Another influential critique of the sociology of race in the early 1980s emanated from the Centre for Contemporary Cultural Studies in Birmingham. The work of the CCCS Race and Politics Group during this period was particularly concerned with the changing nature of the politics of race during the 1970s and the development of new forms of racial ideology. The theoretical approach of the CCCS Group was influenced was influenced by the work of Stuart Hall in particular (Hall, 1980). They were critical of the arguments of both established sociologists of race and the more radical writers such as Miles.

The work of the Group resulted in the publication of *The Empire Strikes Back* (CCCS, 1982). This volume attracted widespread attention at the time and it still remains a point of reference in current debates. Two of the contributors to this volume have subsequently attempted to develop substantive studies derived from it (Gilroy, 1987, 1993a, 1993b; Solomos, 1988, 1993). A major concern of the CCCS Group was the need to analyse the complex processes by which race is constructed as a social and political relation. They emphasised that the race concept is not simply confined as a process of regulation operated by the state but that the meaning of race as a social construction is contested and fought over. In this sense they viewed race as an open political construction where the political meaning of terms like black are struggled over. Collective identities spoken through race, community and locality are for all their spontaneity powerful means to coordinate action and create solidarity (Gilroy, 1987). This work shares Rex's concern with social action but rejects his sociological framework as being at best ill founded and at worst politically spurious.

Within this model of political action a multiplicity of political identities can be held. An inclusive notion of black identity can prevail and at the same time allow heterogeneity of national and cultural origins within this constituency (ibid., p. 236). Gilroy, for example, argues that the crucial question here is the extent to which notions of race can be reforged into a political colour of opposition. He holds little hope that this process can be developed within the arena of representative democracy. Instead he views pressure group strategies which have evolved out of community struggles that utilise a specifically black political vernacular as the way forward. Gilroy argues for a radical revision of class analysis in metropolitan contexts. He suggests that political identities which are spoken through race can be characterised as social movements which are relatively autonomous from class relations.

In exploring these issues *The Empire Strikes Back* acted as a catalyst to a politicisation of debates about the role of research in relation to race relations. In a sense the political struggles that were occurring within black communities during the 1980s were being echoed in the context of the production of knowledge about racism. The sociology of race relations stood accused of being implicitly conservative and unable to articulate the theorisation of racism with the nature of a class divided and structural inequalities in power. On the other hand, the sociologists of race and ethnic relations were also criticised for letting their theoretical imaginations be coloured by an implicit Eurocentrism. The result was that the sociological literature demonstrated an inability to record the experiences of the black people in Britain in a sympathetic way (Lawrence, 1981). These challenges marked an attempt to articulate the theoretical debates about how to understand racism with the political urgencies of economic crisis and the ideological challenge of the Conservative New Right. The point that we want to emphasise here is that this debate needs to be situated within the political conjuncture of the early 1980s. It is quite clear that the preoccupation with prioritising the analysis of racism was linked to a concern to fix the theoretical debate on questions of power and inequality. However, in making the conceptualisation of racism a priority, these critiques failed to develop a theoretical framework for an elaborated analysis of wider social and cultural processes. It is this issue which has become one of the central theoretical questions of recent years.

Feminism, race and ethnicity

During the past decade some of the most important contributions to the analysis of racism have come from writers whose work can be seen as deriving from feminism, though often also influenced by some of the perspectives we have touched upon already. From the early 1980s a growing number of studies, chiefly from the United States and Britain, have sought in one way or another to place questions about sexism, gender and sexuality on the agenda of the study of racial relations. This has led to some valuable insights into the everyday social processes which helped to shape the interrelationship between race and gender in particular historical contexts (Hall, 1992; Ware, 1992). It has also produced a wealth of theoretical interventions by black and minority feminist writers into debates about contemporary racisms and their sociopolitical contexts (Carby, 1982, 1987; Minh-ha, 1989; Williams, 1991).

This interest in the issue of gender and sexism is a relatively recent development. In the British context, for example, *The Empire Strikes Back* which was published in 1982 was one of the first books on race relations in Britain to look in any depth at the question of gender and the role of sexism in the context of racialised relations. The contributions of Hazel Carby and Pratibha Parmar to this volume provided a point of reference and debate in the literature about the interplay between race, class and gender during the 1980s (CCCS, 1982). They also highlighted the relevance of looking at this dimension of racial relations in a context where the bulk of research remained gender blind. Carby's contribution in particular is a point of reference in discussions within feminism about racism, and led to some heated debates in *Feminist Review* among other journals. At the same time, a vibrant and critical discussion about the position of black and other minority women in relation to feminism was emerging in the United States. This took a number of forms. The work of writers such as bell hooks addressed the limits of feminist theory in dealing with questions of race and class. The work of other writers questioned the limitations of black nationalist politics when dealing with questions of gender. A particularly controversial example of this trend was the book by Michele Wallace *Black Macho and The Myth of the Superwoman* which was originally published in 1979 and which sought to explore key aspects of the relationship between black men and women (Wallace, 1990a). Another key and influential text was *Ain't I A Woman: Black Women and Feminism* by bell hooks, originally published in 1981, and which was concerned with both establishing the possibility of a dialogue between black women and feminism and with a critical analysis of the limits of feminism in relation to the question of race (hooks, 1981).

In the aftermath of these debates a growing number of studies have began to explore the interrelationship between racism and sexism, racial inequality and gender inequality and the position of African–Caribbean, Asian and other migrant women in British society. This has helped to overcome the gender blind approach of many studies of racial relations, though there are still many aspects of the position of black and ethnic minority women which have received little attention. Most attention has focused on: (i) the role of women in the migration process; (ii) the employment and social position of black women; (iii) family relations; and (iv) the links between racial and gender equality. All these studies have contributed to a growing awareness of the complex sets of interrelationships that take place between racial, class and gender relations in specific socio-economic contexts (Anthias and Yuval-Davis, 1992). They have also helped to shed light on often neglected but nevertheless crucial aspects of racialisation.

Perhaps one of the most controversial areas of debate has been the issue of whether feminists have overconcentrated on patriarchy, and neglected race and ethnicity as sources of women's oppression. This is certainly a theme which pervades many of the early black feminist critiques of the mainstream of feminist politics, and it has continued to be a key area of debate. It is certainly the case that many feminist texts from the 1960s and 1970s showed little or no awareness of the historical background and contemporary context of racial inequalities. Whatever the merits of the specific debates that have taken place over this issue it is worth emphasising that contemporary feminism has had to take on board questions about race and ethnicity in a systematic manner. The mainstream of contemporary feminism has been forced in one way or another to come to terms with questions about race and racism. There is now a wealth of literature which has arisen out of the ongoing debates between white and black feminists over the past decade. What is more important, however, is that this dialogue has encouraged the development of grounded research on the position of black and minority women (Mohanty et al., 1991).

One interesting example of this is the growth of research on the position of migrant women in various societies. In the past studies of migration have tended to make assumptions which have either excluded or underplayed the position of women in the migration process. But more recently an increasing amount of research has focused either directly or indirectly on the position of migrant women. A number of important studies have explored the impact of immigration and nationality legislation on black and ethnic minority women, their employment patterns, the impact of racism on their lives, and their struggles to improve their social and economic situation.

The social and employment position of black and minority women has become another focus of much recent writing. Part of this interest has been concerned with the history of black women's employment, but most attention has concentrated on the actual jobs which black women do, their changing employment patterns, comparisons with the position of white women, the impact of unemployment and likely future trends in the employment status of young black women. A number of studies have looked at the actual environments in which black and ethnic minority women actually work, their relationship with their employers, and their interactions with white workers. Important work in this field has been carried out in a number of European countries, particularly in the light of recent transformations in the process of migration itself.

One of the most controversial issues in both research and political debate has been the historical patterns and contemporary forms of black family relations. In the United States, the black family has often been seen as 'weak' and therefore as one of the key causes of the social and economic problems suffered by blacks there. This view was expressed in the famous Moynihan Report during the 1960s and has recently been taken up by ideologues of the new right on both sides of the Atlantic. Partly in response to these views, a number of black writers have attempted to argue that the black family represents one of the strengths of black communities, providing a channel for black men and women to tackle the effects of racism. This view was supported to a degree by some black feminist writers, and indeed it can be said that some of them reified the 'black family' as a source of resistance against slavery, colonialism and racism. Yet such views did not receive universal support and became the subject of much critical debate (Bhatt, 1994a).

Aspects of these debates about black family structures and racism have now become current in Britain, where increasing attention has been given to the role of marital patterns and family relations in some black communities. One example of this is the issue of single mothers among West Indian communities, and the ways in which this has become a subject of public and policy debate.

Quite apart from the academic research that has taken up the question of race and gender, over the past decade we have seen a massive growth in writings by and about black and minority women. The works of novelists such as Toni Morrison have explored key aspects of the experience of black women in America through the form of the novel and have become another important contribution to current debates. A good example of the impact of Morrison's work is her novel *Beloved* whose narrative provides a powerful and chilling account of the experience of black Americans during and after slavery (Morrison, 1988). As Morrison herself comments about the contemporary situation in America: 'For both black and white American writers, in a wholly racialised society, there is no escape from racially inflected language, and the work writers do to unhobble the imagination from the demands of that language is complicated, interesting, and definitive (Morrison, 1992, pp. 12–13). In this context it is not surprising that literary texts such as those of Morrison have come to occupy an important and vibrant role in contemporary debates about the historical interface between race and gender. This is perhaps because more than traditional sociological studies they have done much to give voice to the experience of black women and to highlight the lived realities of racial ideologies and practices.

Another important area in recent research concerns the role that ideas about the sexuality of minority women has played in racial ideologies. There is a wealth of studies which have shown that at various historical conjunctures sexuality has played a major role in the fantasies which make up the world of racism. This research has tended to have a historical focus and to be concerned specifically with slavery and colonialism. But it is also clear that aspects of contemporary popular culture and advertising involve the reproduction of images of black female sexuality and sensuality. The role that such images play in the articulation of racialised culture in the context of contemporary societies remains to be fully investigated.

Some writers, however, tend to argue for a somewhat essentialist view of the position of black women in contemporary societies. The influential work of Patricia Hill Collins, a black American feminist, is a case in point. A key theme in her work is the need to understand the 'individual uniqueness' of the position of black women and she emphasises the role of a 'distinctive Afrocentric epistemology', 'a core African value system', that informs the thinking and political mobilisation of black women today. The work of writers such as Collins tends to construct an almost mystical view of what is called an 'Afrocentric feminist consciousness', and it specifically seeks to differentiate black feminism from other forms in an absolutist manner (Collins, 1990).

Perhaps the main achievement of the debates outlined above has been that they have helped to establish the complex historical linkages between racism and sexism and encouraged theoretical debate about the interrelationship between the two (James and Busia, 1993). Despite important contributions, however, questions about gender and sexism have remained a neglected aspect of the mainstream of studies of racial and ethnic relations. The main research centres in this field have been largely unaffected by the debates discussed above and they have done little or no substantive research with a clear gender dimension. Even where issues of race have been looked at there has been an implicit assumption that 'the three worlds of inequality' (race, class and gender) are somehow separate from each other. There is a long way to go before the gender dimension is fully integrated into the study of race and racism, but as we shall see in other parts of this book it would be impossible to analyse key aspects of contemporary racism without serious consideration of the changing social relations which shape the position of minority women.

New ethnicity, new racism

In many ways the terms of the debates that we have looked at above reached their high point during the 1980s, though they continue to influence research agendas and teaching. However, a number of recent developments have meant that the neo-Marxist critiques of the early 1980s have not been able to cope with the complexities of theorising racism in the 1990s. The first of these is the crisis within Marxism itself. In this context some have called for a radical revision of class analysis (Castells, 1983; Gilroy, 1987; Anthias, 1992) in order to incorporate political movements which mobilise around forms of identity other than class. Others have suggested a need for a move away from Marxism as a framework of analysis and have taken on board some of the concerns of post-structuralism and postmodernism (Gates, 1986; Goldberg, 1990, 1993).

One of the results of this shift is the growing concern with the status of cultural forms and a return to an analysis of the nature of ethnicity in metropolitan settings. The political naiveté of the early work on ethnicity meant that for much of the 1980s the analysis of cultural processes and forms were rejected in favour of a focus on the politics of racism. The rejection of 'culture' was tied up with the notion that the culturalist perspective of the 1970s did little more than blame the victims of racism (Lawrence, 1982). However, the question of cultural production and the politics of identity are fast becoming an important area of contemporary debate. New perspectives are being developed which examine the ways in which cultural forms are being made and remade, producing complex social phenomena (Hewitt, 1991). These new syncretic cultures are being plotted within the global networks of the African and South Asian diaspora (Gilroy, 1987, 1993a; Bhachu, 1991).

The process of reclaiming 'culture' in critical debate has simultaneously involved a re-examination of how racism is conceptualised. These contributions engage in one way or another with the arguments of post-structuralism and postmodernism and they point to the need to avoid uniform and homogeneous conceptualisations of racism. Although not yet part of the agenda of mainstream research on race relations, a range of studies of racialised discourses in the mass media, literature, art and other cultural forms have begun to be produced. Reacting against what they see as the lack of an account of cultural forms of racial discourse a number of writers have sought to develop a more rounded picture of contemporary racial imagery by looking at the role of

literature, the popular media and other cultural forms in representing changing images of race and ethnicity (Chambers, 1990,
1994; Hall, 1991b, 1992; Cohen, 1992, 1993; Brah, 1993).

As David Goldberg has pointed out, 'the presumption of a
single monolithic racism is being displaced by a mapping of the
multifarious historical formulations of *racisms*' (Goldberg, 1990, p.
xiii). In this context it is perhaps not surprising that a key concern
of many recent texts in this field is to explore the interconnections between race and nationhood, patriotism and nationalism
rather than analyse ideas about biological inferiority. This broadening out of the analytical focus of recent debates has had a
number of positive consequences, not least because it has forced
on the research agenda a dialogue between researchers working
on a variety of theoretical and empirical concerns. It has also
ensured that questions about race are seen as closely linked to
issues such as ethnicity and nationalism.

In the British context this shift has coincided with the ascen-
dancy of the political right in Britain during the 1980s and 1990s.
This has prompted commentators to identify a new period in the
history of English racism. The *new racism*, or what Fanon (1967a)
referred to as *cultural racism*, is seen as having its has its origins in
the social and political crisis afflicting Britain (Barker, 1981;
Gilroy, 1990a). Its focus is the defence of the mythic
'British/English way of life' in the face of attack from enemies
outside ('Argies', 'Frogs', 'Krauts', 'Iraqis') and *within* ('black communities', 'Muslim fundamentalists'). As Gilroy points out one
alarming consequence of this new racism is that blackness and
Englishness tend to be reproduced as mutually exclusive categories (Gilroy, 1987, pp. 55–6).

The new cultural racism points to the urgency of comprehending racism and notions of race as changing and historically situated. As David Goldberg has pointed out it is necessary to define
race conceptually by looking at what this term signifies at different times (Goldberg, 1992). From this perspective the question of
whether *race* is an ontologically valid concept or otherwise is side-
stepped in favour of an interrogation of the ideological quality of
racialised subjectivities. The writing on new racism shows how
contemporary manifestations of race are coded in a language
which aims to circumvent accusations of racism. In the case of
new racism race is coded as culture. However, the central feature

of these processes is that the qualities of social groups are fixed, made natural, confined within a pseudo-biologically defined culturalism (Barker, 1981). What is clear from these writings is that a range of discourses on social differentiation may have a metonymic relationship to racism. The semantics of race are produced by a complex set of interdiscursive processes where the language of culture and nation invokes a hidden racial narrative. The defining feature of this process is the way in which it naturalises social formations in terms of a racial–cultural logic of belonging.

With the widening of theoretical concerns has come a literature which looks at the aesthetic elements of the culture of racism. This is an area which has been neglected within the discussions of race and social theory in the field of race relations. Equally, with a number of notable exceptions (Cohen, 1988a, 1988b, 1991; Cohen and Bains, 1988) the emerging discipline of cultural studies has also been curiously silent on the issue of how to understand the cultural dynamics of racism. There is an important intellectual and theoretical project in interrogating the historical, cultural, literary and philosophical roots of ideologies of race.

The role of the press and other popular media in shaping social images about racial and ethnic minorities has been a particular focus. A number of detailed studies have, for example, looked at how press coverage of racial questions can help to construct images of racial minorities as outsiders and as a threat to social cohesion (Hall *et al.*, 1978; van Dijk, 1991). One important example of this process was the furore about Salman Rushdie's *The Satanic Verses* and the response of some Muslim political leaders to its publication (Al-Azmeh, 1993). The attempt by some Muslim community leaders to use the affair as a means of political mobilisation received wide coverage in the media and led to a wide-ranging debate about the 'future of race relations' in British society (Asad, 1990). Sections of the press used the events surrounding the Rushdie affair to question the possibility of a peaceful transition towards a multiracial society. Hostile media coverage of the events surrounding the political mobilisations around the Rushdie affair thus served to reinforce the view that minorities who do not share the dominant political values of British society pose a threat to social stability and cohesion. The affair also gave added impetus to debates about the multiple cultural and political identities that have been included in the broad categorisation of 'black and ethnic minority communities'.

One of the weaknesses of the literature which looks at media and political discourses is that it has not attempted to look at how these ideological forms manifest themselves within specific social and political contexts. The question remains as to how pervasive is the 'new racism'? Or, how do these national discourses relate to the particularities of a specific social context? Gilroy, for example, alludes to a new kind of cultural politics which defines new racism and develops a political and cultural aesthetic that is both black and English (Gilroy, 1993b). Stuart Hall, returning to the flag metaphor, refers to a shift in his own thinking: 'Fifteen years ago we didn't care, or at least I didn't care, whether there was any black in the Union Jack. Now not only do we care but we must (Hall, 1988, p. 30). From this starting point Hall has argued forcefully for the need to conceptualise the complex ways in which black minority communities in Britain have managed to construct and reconstruct notions of 'ethnicity' and 'cultural identity' which have meaning in the present socio-political environment (Hall, 1988, 1990). Within the context or this 'new ethnicities' framework there are no essential racial, ethnic national identities outside the social, political and historical processes which shape understandings of what race and ethnicity mean in particular societies.

What is interesting to note is that parallel to these theoretical debates a series of empirical studies have attempted to provide evidence for these trends. A particular area of interest has been the changing morphology of youth cultures, where a number of key studies have shown that significant dialogues are taking place within multiethnic communities of working-class youth (Hewitt, 1986; Jones, 1988; Back, 1995). In the encounter between black young people and their white inner city peers: 'Black culture has become a class culture ... as two generations of whites have appropriated it, discovered its seductive forms of meaning for their own' (Gilroy, 1990a, p. 273). The result is that it is impossible to speak of black culture in Britain separately from the culture of Britain as a whole. These processes have important implications for developing an analysis of racism which is socially, politically and even geographically situated. The local context has important effects resulting in complex outcomes where particular racisms may be muted while others flourish (Back, 1993a).

Another focus within the emerging literature on the cultural politics of racism has been the social construction of race and difference in literature and the cinema. This has been a neglected area of research but in recent years it has been remedied by the publication of a number of important studies of race, culture and identity. Originating largely in the United States such studies have looked at a number of areas, including literature, the cinema and other popular cultural forms. They have sought to show that within contemporary societies our understandings of race, and the articulation of racist ideologies, cannot be reduced to economic, political or class relations.

This type of approach is in fact more evident outside sociology. The work of literary and cultural theorists in the United States and Britain has in recent years begun to explore seriously the question of race and racism, and has led to a flowering of studies which use the debates around post-structuralism and postmodernism as a way of approaching the complex forms of racialised identities in colonial and post-colonial societies (Gates, 1986, 1988; Goldberg, 1990, 1993). There has also been a growth of interest in historical research on the origins of ideas about race and in the dynamics of race, class and gender during the colonial and post-colonial periods (Ware, 1992). This has been reflected in important and valuable accounts of the changing usage of racial symbols during the past few centuries and in accounts of the experiences of colonialism and their impact on our understandings of race and culture.

One influential trend in these recent debates is the emergence of studies of the role of colonial and post-colonial discourses in constructing images of the 'other'. Influenced partly by Edward Said's classic study of *Orientalism* (1985) and by post-structuralism and deconstructionism there have been numerous studies in recent years of the genealogy of colonial discourses about race and gender. The work of writers such as Gayatri Spivak, Homi Bhabha and Trinh Minh-ha represents some key features of this trend. These scholars have sought to provide a critique of both the discourses of colonialism and of the 'West' and modernity. Perhaps the main achievement of their work is that it has highlighted the complex processes of racial and gender identification experienced by the colonised during the colonial and post-colonial periods (Spivak, 1987, 1993; Minh-ha, 1989; Bhabha, 1990, 1994; Williams and Chrisman, 1993).

With the recent development of postmodernism and of deconstruction theory in relation to issues of race and gender, we have seen an explosion of studies which have sought to explore various aspects of colonial and post-colonial discourses (Young, R., 1990, 1995). One noticeable gap in these studies, however, is that they have based themselves almost exclusively on textual analysis and they have almost totally ignored the analysis of both colonial and post-colonial social relations of politics and power. At best these theoretical approaches work with rather limited and historically limited histories of colonialism (Lowe, 1991). It is also ironic, as some commentators have recently noted, that such critiques of colonial discourses and of the 'West' can be used for a variety of political purposes. The example of the ways in which the critique of 'Orientalism' has been taken up in right-wing Islamic and Hindu nationalist political movements is a case in point (Ahmad, 1992; Bhatt, 1994a).

Racism and 'whiteness'

Another key issue in recent research about the contemporary social and political impact of race and racism is the question of how ideas about 'whiteness' are constructed and reconstructed. It has become clear that there is a need to shed the narrow confines of the race relations problematic and develop a more sophisticated analysis of the impact of various racisms on the 'white majority'. An embryonic literature exists on the politics of whiteness which is attempting to develop such a focus of inquiry (Roediger, 1991, 1994; Frankenberg, 1993; Allen, 1994). However, there are immediate difficulties with this endeavour as Richard Dyer (1988) has shown in his discussion of film representations. Dyer contends that white ethnicity in the cinema is implicitly present but explicitly absent and as a result it has 'an everything and nothing quality'. In these representations whiteness is equated with normality and as such it is not in need of definition. Thus 'being normal' is colonised by the idea of 'being white'. From a different perspective bell hooks has graphically discussed the terrorising effect that 'whiteness' has on the black imagination. Writing on her experience of growing up as a black woman in the American South she comments: 'whiteness in the black imagination is often a representation of terror' (hooks, 1992, p. 342). Clearly there is a need for a research agenda which looks at the way white subjectivities are racialised, and how 'whiteness' is manifested in discourse, communication and culture.

This turn within critical writing has important implications. One of the fundamental criticisms of the sociology of race and ethnic relations is that it has too often focused on the victims rather than the perpetrators of racism. Prioritising whiteness as an area of critical endeavour has the potential to disrupt the sociological common sense which equates the discussion of racism with the empirical scrutiny of black communities. Toni Morrison in her analysis of whiteness in American novels comments: 'My project is an effort to avert the critical gaze from the racial object to the racial subject; from the described and imagined to the describers and imaginers; the serving to the served' (Morrison, 1992: 90). Stuart Hall has pointed out the urgency of deconstructing the meanings of whiteness, not just in order to counter racism but also important for the well-being of the African and Asian diaspora living in Britain:

> I think for black people who live in Britain this question of finding some way in which the white British can learn to live with us and the rest of the world is almost as important as discovering our own identity. I think they are in more trouble than we are. So we, in a curious way, have to rescue them from themselves – from their own past. We have to allow them to see that England is a quite interesting place with quite an interesting history that has bossed us around for 300 years [but] that is finished. Who are they now? (Hall, 1989)

There is already an emerging literature which is trying to answer the rhetorical question which Hall has asked (Jones, 1988; Back, 1993a; Gilroy 1993b). However, the connection between race and nation may well be eclipsed in the 1990s by the spectre of an integrated and racialised Europe.

In the present political environment we have seen a wide-ranging political debate about the changing role of national identity in the context of a unified Europe. Margaret Thatcher's famous speech in Bruges in 1988 represents an interesting example of this trend:

> Too often the history of Europe is described as a series of interminable wars and quarrels. Yet from our perspective today surely what strikes us most is our common experience. For instance, the story of how Europeans explored and colonised and – yes, without apology – civilised much of the world is an extraordinary tale of talent, skill and courage. (Thatcher, 1988, p. 2)

While much of the debate on racism in the 1980s focused on the relationship between nationhood and racism, it may be that in the 1990s racialised discourses will focus on the 'natural Europe home' and attempt to define who belongs there.

Theoretically comprehending 'whiteness' is certainly an important intellectual project. However, there are a number of possible shortcomings. In the hurry to shift the critical gaze there is always a danger of suspending reflection on the analytical terms of this project. Like many of the debates on the ontological status of culture, there is a danger of reifying whiteness and reinforcing a unitary idea of 'race'. In order to avoid this it is crucial to locate any discussion of 'whiteness' in a particular empirical and historical context. Equally, one must insist that whiteness is a political definition which regulates the consent of white subjects within the context of white supremacy. Additionally, any discussion of whiteness must incorporate an appreciation of how gendered processes are inextricably articulated with the semantics of race (Ware, 1992).

The need to comprehend the social construction of whiteness as a form of identity and a political discourse must (i) focus on decolonising the definition of 'normal', and (ii) simultaneously prohibit the reification of whiteness as a social identity. An interesting example of recent research on this issue is the work of Ruth Frankenberg (1993), which focuses on the ways in which white women in the United States experience questions about race. Frankenberg's study is particularly useful because of the way she uses in-depth accounts by white women of their views and experiences about race in order to shed light on the changing dynamics of race, gender and class in the United States. Other important studies about this issue have looked at the situation in South Africa and the ways in which racial and gender relations were fashioned by state policies during the Apartheid period (Cock, 1989).

Conceptualising racisms and racial discourse

In many ways the turn towards the conceptualisation of culturally defined racisms and the politics of identity has been led by political events and their impact on the role that racial symbols play in political debate. In particular the continuing hegemony of the Conservative right in Britain has challenged theorists to reappraise the usefulness of Marxist orthodoxy. This is perhaps best exemplified by the debate over the *New Times* thesis (see Hall and Jacques, 1989 and Sivanandan, 1990a) which suggests that a range of sites for social antagonism and resistance exists within contemporary Britain which cannot be conceptualised within a conventional class analysis. Equally, in the context of the complex forms of identity politics the semantics of race cannot be confined to the politics of regulation (Miles, 1989). The controversy over the publication of Salman Rushdie's book *The Satanic Verses* has provided a warning that the politics of culture cannot be appreciated within theoretical frameworks which assume that 'race' and its complex manifestations can be seen as unchanging and monolithic.

Questions of cultural production and change must be integrated within contemporary conceptualisations of racism. Thus we are suggesting that these theoretical debates need to be contextualised within a shifting political context. The certainties of the critique of the race relations problematic are no longer tenable. What seems to characterise the contemporary period is, on the one hand, a complex spectrum of racisms, and, on the other the fragmentation of the definition of blackness as a political identity in favour of a resurgence of ethnicism and cultural differentiation. At the same time, and perhaps paradoxically, new cultures and ethnicities are emerging in the context of dialogue and producing a kaleidoscope of cultural syncretisms. There may well be contradictory trends emerging, but neither the *race relations problematic* nor the *racism problematic* are equipped to deal with the contemporary situation. In the final section we want to make some suggestions as to how these conceptual problems might be resolved. We shall return to this issue throughout the book, but at this point we want to sketch out the broad contours of our argument.

The politics of race and racism has undergone numerous transformations in recent decades. Debates about the ontological status of race, the object of investigation and the agenda for research in this field are partly the result of these transformations. While some authors writing in the tradition of race and ethnic relations studies have been careful to separate the research process from political action, such a separation is in some ways impossible and even undesirable. This is why the political agendas involved in conceptualising racism need to be made explicit.

It is perhaps because analytical debates necessarily involve political disputes, that no one theoretical perspective is dominant at the present time. Indeed much of the mainstream research in this field is not theoretically informed in any substantial way. There is a need for greater theoretical clarity on key concepts and a broadening of the research agenda to cover issues that have been neglected, such as the politics of culture and identity. In this sense Banton may well be right in his contention that different theoretical paradigms may be able to contribute their own distinctive accounts of the processes which involve the attribution of specific meanings to racial situations (Banton, 1991). However, the point that Banton misses is that the various paradigms which are adopted within this area of research contain an implicit or explicit political position *vis-à-vis* the politics of knowledge production. In this case it is not a matter of choosing appropriate analytical tools from some diverse theoretical bag, but rather it is necessary to situate these paradigms in relation to each other and political debates over what could or should be the focus of analysis.

In a very real sense the question of how to conceptualise racism has never been purely an academic matter. From its very origins the study of racism has been intimately connected to issues such as the rise of fascism, the holocaust and the destructive consequences of racist political mobilisations. In this sense the analysis of racism cannot be easily separated from the wider political culture in any given historical conjuncture. Indeed it is clearly the case that the manipulation of racial symbols and the development of racist movements has involved a politicisation of racial signifiers through political discourse and state policies.

Racialised political discourses therefore need to be located, as we shall argue in subsequent chapters, within processes of social regulation and identity formation. Racism manifests itself in plural and complex forms. In this situation the logic of racism needs to be appraised in what we shall call *metonymic elaborations*. This means that racisms may be expressed through a variety of coded signifiers. We have already discussed one such elaboration, that is the coding of race as culture. Contemporary racisms have evolved and adapted to new circumstances. The crucial property of these elaborations is that they can produce a racist effect while denying that this effect is the result of racism. For example, the new racisms of the 1980s and 1990s are coded within a cultural logic. As a result the champions of this racism can claim that they are by no means racist but merely interested in protecting their way of life and that the issue of colour or phenotype is irrelevant to their arguments.

In this context unitary or simplistic definitions of racism become hard to sustain. However, it seems clear that contemporary racisms share some central features. They attempt to fix human social groups in terms of *natural* properties of belonging within particular political and geographical contexts. The assertion that racialised subjects do not belong within, say, British society is then associated with social and cultural characteristics designated to them within the logic of particular racisms.

It follows from the above argument that racist discourses need to be rigorously contextualised. This means that racisms need to be situated within specific political, cultural, social and economic moments. The effect of a particular racist discourse needs to be placed in the conditions surrounding the moment of its enunciation. This means irrevocably crossing the analysis of racism with other social relations surrounding gender and sexuality or the culture of institutional politics. We need to break with simplistic notions of race as a fixed transhistorical category whose meaning is the same in all social contexts.

We found an interesting example of the complexities of contemporary ideas about race and ethnicity in the context of our own research on the politics of race in Birmingham (Solomos and Back, 1995). During the course of this research we identified particular elaborations of racism which were being mobilised against black politicians within the context of specific political debates and conflicts. During the 1980s and 1990s there was a significant increase in black political participation in the Labour Party, and in particular participation by Muslims originating from Kashmir and Pakistan. In this changing context black politicians were often accused of fostering duplicitous political affiliation. It was asserted that an 'Asian Mafia' existed within the context of Birmingham's Labour Party. This was underscored by a construction of 'subcontinent politics' as corrupt, violent and incompatible with Britain's democratic process. This construction demonstrated a moment where the political mobilisation of black communities was racialised. In this context the truth or falsehood of particular events or assertions became irrelevant. What was significant was that these discourses made accusations of impropriety believable with regard to all people designated as 'Asian politicians'. The claim that a 'white mafia' exists simply does not resonate with racialised discourse in the same way as what we have described above. What this particular form of political racism does is (i) undermine the political struggles for representation being waged within 'Asian' communities, and (ii) legitimate resistance to political representation in terms of cultural incompatibility of 'subcontinent culture' with 'British culture'. This is an example of the metonymic elaboration of race where race is coded as culture. When people utilising these ideas are challenged they claim that this is not racism, but merely reflects and provides 'evidence' of deficiencies within the political culture of black and minority communities.

What this example suggests to us is that the meanings of race and racism need to be located within particular fields of discourse and articulated to the social relations found within that context. It is then necessary to see what kinds of racialised identities are being formed within these contexts. We are suggesting a position which builds into any analysis a rigorous scrutiny of racialised definitions, whether they are operated by the local state or the range of political mobilisations that are occurring around racial and ethnic identities within black communities. This approach seeks to decipher the meanings of racialised identities without attempting to prioritise one classification as more legitimate than another.

There is a need to develop a model for conceptualising racisms which is (i) sensitive to local and contextual manifestations of racist discourse and (ii) able to connect local manifestations with wider or national public discourses. As yet theoretical debates have produced accounts of racism which derive contemporary forms of racism from public political discourse. This evidence is then used to generalise about broad trends within society as a whole. We are suggesting that there is a need to move away from this rather generalised approach and to situate racisms within particular settings and social contexts, before moving towards a more general account of their wider significance. This is the approach we have adopted in this book, and our main concern is to explore the ways in which specific racisms are situated in particular social and political contexts.

In this chapter we have explored the development of some key approaches to the study of race and racism in contemporary societies. In the rest of the book we want to move on to see how the issues we have explored here can help us to understand key features of racialised social relations and their impact on particular social philosophies and social programmes. In developing this narrative we hope to show that the theoretical framework we have outlined above can be a useful analytic tool. In particular we shall argue that the analysis of contemporary racisms needs to be situated within particular discursive contexts. Racism cannot be reduced to economic or class relations but neither can it be seen as completely autonomous from wider social relations such as gender and sexuality. This is why there is need for a more rigorous analysis of the interactions between racism and social, economic, political and cultural relations. The implications of this analytic framework will be explored further in the rest of this volume. This will take us to the concluding chapter, where we shall again take up the question of how we can conceptualise the changing usages of race and racism in the present political environment.

2 Historical Perspectives

What do we mean when we talk of racism as shaping the structure of particular societies? What role have race and racism played in different historical contexts? Is it possible to speak of racism in the singular or racisms in the plural? These questions are at the heart of many of the theoretical and conceptual debates we explored in the previous chapter, and yet what is interesting about much of the literature relating to the sociology of race and racism is its lack of historical perspective concerning the positioning of race and racism within social relations. It has to be said also that there have been differing accounts of the history of racism over the past two centuries or so. While there has been a wealth of historically specific accounts of racialised social relations in different societies, much of the contemporary literature on racism continues to be written from a view which either ignores the complex histories of modern racisms or simply interprets specific historical situations from within the narrow confines of contemporary theoretical frameworks. This lack of historical perspective has meant that there are major lacunae in recent sociological studies of racial relations, with the exception of a few attempts to rethink the role that historical processes and ideas about race have played in shaping contemporary social relationships and institutions. There have also been a number of studies of the origin and changing usage of the idea of race in different societies. Good examples of these are the work of Michael Banton (1977, 1987a), George Mosse (1985a), Tzvetan Todorov (1993) and David Goldberg (1993).

In this chapter we want to explore some aspects of the rich historical literature on the background to our modern ideas about the social significance of race and racism. We hope that by looking at some key features of the historical background we shall

30

Can't isolate the current situation from the past

be able to uncover the range of factors and processes that have gone into the making of specific racist discourses, practices and effects. This will allow us to explore in more detail than we have been able to do so far the complex ways in which ideas about race have been shaped by historically specific sets of social relations, for example, by relations of domination in colonial and imperial settings, by class, gender and other sets of power relations. It is not our intention here to reduce the contemporary situation to historical factors alone. But at the same time we want to warn against the dangers, all too common in much of the recent social science literature in this field, which ignore the history of racism and see contemporary forms in almost complete isolation from the past.

We shall concentrate on six key themes for the purposes of analytical clarity. First, the emergence of ideas about race and their impact on the development of racist discourses. Second, the role of slavery in shaping racial ideas and social relations. Third, the development of 'scientific' ideas about race and the usages of scientific discourses in the development of racist ideas. Fourth, the role of imperialism and colonialism in the articulations of racism through forms of domination. Fifth, the role of the Nazi racial state in the development of ideas and practices which aimed to preserve 'racial purity'. Finally, we shall look at the role that migration and the movement of labour across the globe has played in the development of contemporary ideas about race in advanced industrial societies. In addition to the accounts to be found in this chapter, it is important to note that we shall return to some of these themes later in the book. This is because at certain points in our analysis we shall need to focus on specific examples in order to illustrate and explain the processes we are looking at.

Changing ideas about race

As we have already argued in Chapter 1, from a theoretical perspective, it is clear that the concepts of race and racism have no fixed and unchanging meaning. From a broader historical view, it is clear from research on the usages of the notion of race over the past two centuries that it has taken on various forms in different national contexts (Barzun, 1938; Montagu, 1964; Biddiss, 1979; Benedict, 1983). As regards the rise of racism in European societies two key themes have preoccupied many writers. First, a number have located the rise of modern racism within the processes of intellectual and social transformation that characterised European societies in the period of the late eighteenth and nineteenth centuries. Although the notion of race is sometimes taken to have existed from time immemorial it is in practice relatively recent, with most historians agreeing that it came into common usage in the period from the mid to the late eighteenth century. This period is commonly seen as the high point of the Enlightenment, yet it is during this era that doctrines about race came to be articulated in a consistent manner. A clear statement of this periodisation is provided by George Mosse:

> Racism has its foundations both in the Enlightenment and in the religious revival of the eighteenth century. It was a product of the preoccupation with a rational universe, nature, and aesthetics, as well as with the emphasis upon the eternal force of religious emotion and man's soul. It was part, too, of the drive to define man's place in nature and of the hope for an ordered, healthy, and happy world. (Mosse, 1985a, p. 3)

It is certainly from the eighteenth century that we can trace the emergence in Europe of writings about race and what we now call racism. The idea that races existed involved the affirmation in popular, scientific and political discourses that humanity could be divided into distinct groupings whose members possessed common physical characteristics (Todorov, 1993, pp. 90–3). In addition to this basic idea, however, the belief in the existence of races of humankind involved both the attribution of different origins to human groupings and cultural and social significance to racial boundaries.

A second and equally important theme has been the impact of European exploration, expansion, slavery, colonisation and imperial domination on ideas about race. These processes have been going on in one way or another since the fifteenth and sixteenth centuries (Pieterse, 1992). The interest in them lies in the fact that they are seen as being at the root of racial ideas and values, for example in relation to the supposed 'inferiority' of black Africans. Indeed, in much of the contemporary literature on race relations in the United States and Britain the development of racism is seen as related in one way or another to the historical experience of slavery, colonialism and other institutions of 'white supremacy' (Fredrickson, 1981).

From a longer term perspective, of course, the awareness of phenotypical and cultural differences cannot be seen as simply the product of the period since the mid eighteenth century. Quite apart from the impact of European expansion and exploration in the period from the sixteenth century onwards, which we shall discuss in more detail later, it seems clear from research about ancient societies, ranging from Egypt, Greece and Rome, that ideas about differences on the basis of colour and phenotypical features were to be found, though they cannot by any means be compared to out modern notions about what is now called 'race'. Rather, such research as has been done tends to emphasise the differences between ancient and modern views of Africans, for example (Snowden, 1970, 1983; Bernal, 1987, 1991; Thompson, 1989). Snowden argues that the 'dark' or 'black skinned' Africans mentioned most often in the records of ancient Mediterranean societies frequently came from the Nile valley. Egyptians had been in contact with the black kingdoms of the Nile valley long before other ancient peoples did so. He mentions that in some Egyptian records the issue of colour is not always mentioned, although features such as curly hair are. Egyptians only rarely differentiated the black people within their country or in neighbouring kingdoms on the basis of colour. Awareness of colour increased, however, when Nubians or Kushites came into contact with peoples outside Africa. In ancient Greek and Roman records there are detailed descriptions of black Africans. Terms used to describe them included the word Ethiopian, which literally meant 'burnt faced person'. For Snowden, such an awareness of colour differences did not necessarily have important social consequences: 'Though obviously aware of the Nubians colour, however, neither writers of the Old Testament nor classical authors attached any basic significance to it' (Snowden, 1983, p. 74). To support this argument he and other writers give examples of favourable images of blacks to be found in poems, writings of the time and philosophical works (Finley, 1980, 1983). This is not to say that it is not possible to find instances of negative views and stereotypes about Africans and others in ancient writings, but it is difficult to reduce such ideas to modern notions of race.

Whatever the longer term history of images of the 'other' in various societies and historical periods it does seem clear that only in the late eighteenth century and early nineteenth century does the term race come to refer to supposedly discrete categories of people defined according to their physical characteristics. In short, the concept as we understand it today came into being relatively late in the development of modern capitalist societies. Although usages of the term race have been traced somewhat earlier in a number of European languages, the development of racial doctrines and ideologies begins to take shape in the late eighteenth century, and reached its high point during the nineteenth and early twentieth centuries.

During the late eighteenth century the early attempts at racial classification involved a variety of ideas. For example, a number of anatomists, including most famously Pieter Camper, sought to measure the 'facial angles' of members of different races, in order to categorise them according to corporal stature and beauty. The German physician Franz Joseph Gall employed cranial measurement to classify races in terms of intelligence, morality and beauty, while the German theologian Johann Kaspar Lavater believed that physical appearance was a reflection, or even a determinant, of moral and intellectual character. The French anatomist Georges Cuvier argued for the existence of different types of mankind, namely the Caucasian, Mongolian and Ethiopian. Using these methods, besides devising new and ingenious ones, biologists and anthropologists set out to document 'racial types'. It was but a short step from the conceptualisation of race as type to the articulation of ideas about the relationship between race and national character.

During this period writings on race began to exhibit an awareness of the existence of distinct races of humankind. In various European countries, including England, there developed a racial categorisation of both European and other societies, whereby races were defined as being culturally, psychologically and physically distinct. This obsession with measurement and statistics generated a conception of race founded upon the idea of difference and inequality. People could be conveniently divided and classified not merely in terms of geographical origin or colour but equally by virtue of cranial capacity or shape.

These discourses about race can be seen as reflecting an ongoing debate seeking to resolve the origin of differences between different human groups. Two broad schools of thought developed. The older more established of these was that of monogenism, the belief that all humankind, irrespective of colour or other characteristics, was directly descended from Adam and from the single and original act of God's creation. Monogenism was promulgated by the Church and was universally accepted until the eighteenth century when opposition to theological authority began to fuel the rival theory of polygenism, which held that the different 'racial' communities had different origins. Monogenism had always sought to substantiate the idea of human unity by proposing that 'racial' variations were the consequence of divine intervention or, more commonly, of the differences in the environment in which people lived. Black-skinned Africans, it was argued, were simply the product of climatic conditions, a branch of the original human family having migrated to the equatorial zone and thereby developed a protective pigment. This, the monogenists claimed, in no way implied a different species, but rather confirmed either God's intervention or a degeneration from the norm. In contrast the polygenists believed that ethnic features were innate and permanent, undergoing no significant modifications through environmental change. They were therefore confident that Europeans who lived in Africa would continue to display the same somatic characteristics irrespective of the change in environment. They constantly cited instances of Africans who had been brought to Europe and who, in the course of several generations had shown no evidence of physiological change.

Michael Banton, among others, has shown in some detail how the usage of the term race has changed over time, particularly in the context of British and European society (Banton and Harwood, 1975; Banton, 1977, 1987b). He agrees with the periodisation of the usage of the idea of race which locates the late eighteenth century as the key period. But he also seeks to locate the growth in the usage of race within a broader social context: 'Physical differences between peoples have been observed throughout human history; all over the world people have developed words for delineating them. "Race" is a concept rooted in a particular culture and a particular period of history which brings with it suggestions about how these differences are to be explained' (Banton, 1980, p. 39). Banton's account provides valuable insights into the variety of usages of race over the past two hundred years or so. He shows how writers from Britain, France and Germany began to use the notion of race to refer to the existence of racial types. If we accept the above argument it follows that we have to go beyond the notion that race and racism are fixed transhistorical categories. What is clear from recent scholarship and research is that the usage of the category of race to classify various types of human beings is relatively recent, and indeed that the widespread use of the language of race is a phenomenon of the post Enlightenment period. This is, of course, not to say that the category of race was not used in earlier times. The concept of race became part of philosophical and popular language in Europe during the seventeenth and eighteenth centuries.

Moreover, it is clear that from the end of the eighteenth century onwards the meanings attached to the notion of race began to change quite significantly. Michael Biddiss notes:

> Before 1800 it [race] was used generally as a rough synonym for 'lineage'. But over the first half of the nineteenth century 'race' (and its equivalents in a number of other European languages) assumed an additional sense that seemed, initially, tighter and more scientific. This usage was evident, at its simplest, in the growing conviction that there were a finite number of basic human types, each embodying a package of fixed physical and mental traits whose permanence could only be eroded by mixture with other stocks. (Biddiss, 1979, p. 11)

The attempt to classify human races according to physical and mental attributes was to become a key concept in the social and political debates of the nineteenth century. In this sense ideologies of race are as much a product of modernity as are socialism and liberalism. Although the location of the origins of modern racism in the eighteenth century has become a commonly accepted argument in the literature, the attempt to construct a linkage between racism and the Enlightenment has proved more controversial. Tzvetan Todorov, for one, has sought to challenge the attempts by others to construct a simple linkage between racism and the philosophical modes of thought encouraged by the Enlightenment (Todorov, 1986, 1993). Todorov sees the view of racism as a consequence of Enlightenment philosophy and humanism as both inaccurate and simplistic, since in his view there has been a tendency to underplay the universalist and egalitarian values which were at the heart of Enlightenment philosophy (Todorov, 1986, pp. 372–3). There is much of value in Todorov's warning against too simplistic a linkage between the Enlightenment and racism. For although racism and nationalism may be 'the underside of the Enlightenment', he is surely correct to point to the inadequacy of seeing racism as the inevitable product of the Enlightenment. It is worth emphasising that racial ideologies have been essentially contested in the period since 1800. Over the past two centuries the idea of race has been the subject of intense political debate and has been constructed and reconstructed around other related sets of ideas and social values.

Racism, slavery and capitalism

To summarise the argument so far, we have argued that it is important to situate the development of ideas about race within the specific set of social and philosophical debates that took place in European societies during the seventeenth and eighteenth centuries. More broadly, we pointed out that the emergence of discourses about race and the development of racist ideologies need to be contextualised within the particular intellectual and philosophical environment of European societies during this period. This point, however, touches upon another theme which we have only hinted at so far: namely, the intertwining between the emergence of the language of race and the processes of economic expansion and capitalist development which were going on at the same time (Curtin, 1964; Jordan 1968; Todorov, 1984). How do ideas about the categorisation of human beings into 'races' link up to the development of new patterns of economic and social exploitation? In what sense can we see racial ideas as either the outcome or as integral element of wider economic and social transformations?

This is a theme which has been much discussed in the literature, though not always with much conceptual clarity. Yet it is clear that a recurrent theme in debates about the history of racism, as well as contemporary processes of racialisation, is the issue of the relationship between capitalist economic expansion and exploitation and the emergence of racism and racial ideologies. An important point of reference in this regard is Eric Williams's book on *Capitalism and Slavery*, originally published in 1944, and which sought to locate slavery as essentially an economic phenomenon which arose because of the need to exploit labour through coercion. In this sense Williams reacted against the argument that slavery, particularly in the forms developed in the Americas, was essentially racial in origin, and based on beliefs about racial inferiority. Rather, for Williams racism was a consequence, not the cause, of slavery: the product of the need to justify the institution of slavery and the means of coercion on which it relied (Solow and Engerman, 1987; Blackburn, 1988). Another important text of relevance to this debate is Oliver Cox's monumental *Caste, Class and Race*, which was originally published in 1948. Writing from within a broadly Marxist perspective, Cox located the origins of 'race prejudice' from the period of European expansion at the end fifteenth and beginning of the sixteenth centuries. He argued that racism arose from the need to exploit labour in the form of slave labour. 'Race prejudice' constituted a justification for the exploitation of the labour power of certain groups of workers, and was 'a social attitude propagated among the public by an exploiting class for the purpose of stigmatising some group as inferior in that the exploitation of either the group itself or its resources or both may be justified' (Cox, 1970, p. 393).

The arguments of Williams and Cox have been the subject of much controversy and debate over the years, both within sociology and history (Engerman and Genovese, 1975). Chief among the criticisms have been two fundamental points: first, it has been argued that it is far too simple to see slavery as an economic phenomenon; second, Williams and Cox have been criticised for viewing the development of racist ideologies in purely functionalist terms, that is as serving simply as a justification for the exploitation of labour power. These criticisms have been backed up by historical research which tends to question the usefulness of viewing either slavery or racist ideologies from a purely economic perspective. Interestingly enough, this research has been produced by writers influenced by Marxism as well as by non-Marxist historians. The outcome is that we now have a much more sophisticated analysis of the relationship between slavery and the process of capitalist development.

What seems clear from these debates is that any rounded account of the origins and transformation of racism needs to be contextualised within a broader historical analysis. A number of recent studies have highlighted the complex role that race and ethnicity played in the process of European expansion and domination. A good example of this mode of analysis is Eric Wolf's *Europe and the People Without History* (1982). This is one of the most challenging attempts to look at the extent to which the histories of Europe, Africa, the Americas and Asia were shaped from 1400 onwards by the experience of European expansion and the economic, social and political transformations that resulted. These processes of transformation inevitably involved complex constructions of the 'other' that went hand in hand with the changing patterns of economic, social and political interchange.

A more specific account of the role of race in European expansionism is provided by Winthrop Jordan's classic study *White Over Black* (1968). Jordan's account is particularly interesting because of the way he manages to capture in some detail the changing representations of Africans from the sixteenth to the nineteenth centuries within the context of America. Rejecting the view that there has been a uniform and unchanging view of Africans ever since the sixteenth century, Jordan provides a systematic and richly detailed account of the representations of Africans' skin colour, religions, relation to other human groups and sexuality. His account shows in some detail that the first impressions articulated by Europeans of Africans in the sixteenth century were transformed quite fundamentally by the experience of slavery and economic domination, by changing political and ideological environments and by cultural changes.

Slavery in its various historical forms, and specifically the Atlantic slave trade, did not have a purely economic rationale and its impact was as much on social and power relations as on economic institutions (Patterson, 1982). In relation to the Atlantic slave trade there is a wealth of historical evidence about the impact that the institution of slavery had on European images of Africans (Lovejoy, 1983; Manning, 1990). As Jordan and others have persuasively argued, these images did not remain fixed and unchanging across time and space, but it seems quite clear that during the seventeenth and eighteenth centuries the development of the slave trade was an important part of the wider process leading to the development of European images of Africans and other peoples.

The interrelationship between the institution of slavery and the social and political position of slaves was clear throughout this period. It is perhaps symptomatic of the way in which black slaves were treated as mere articles of commerce, as commodities, that the case of slave ship *Zong* could have arisen in 1781. The case arose because 131 slaves were jettisoned by the captain ostensibly on the plea that he had run out of water. He then entered an insurance claim for the loss of his 'cargo'. At the trial, the issue was not about murder but whether the throwing overboard of the 131 slaves was a true act of jettison for which the insurance company would have to pay but a case of fraud. According to the Solicitor-General, John Lee, who defended the owners of the slaves, it would have been 'nothing less than madness' to have brought a murder charge since the slaves thrown overboard 'were property' (Walvin, 1992, pp. 16–21).

Another example of the intertwining between the imagery of slavery and race during the late eighteenth and early nineteenth centuries can be found in the work of absentee Jamaican planter Edward Long. Long wrote his much quoted *History of Jamaica* in 1774 and in it he defended not only the slave trade but the argument that Europeans and blacks belonged to different species. For Long the slave trade was nothing but the 'healthy culling process' of an increasing African population. He saw the black slaves as not only lazy, they were lying, profligate, promiscuous, cowardly, savage, debased, ugly and demonstrably inferior to 'whites'.

We have to remember that plantation slavery in the Americas and the rest of the New World was held together and reproduced over time by vicious police laws designed to ensure that those who dominated at every level of society did so not only on the basis of holding property but because they were 'white'. In this social and political environment domination and subordination now appeared not only as the function of owning productive agrarian property but as the result of a 'natural' phenomenon (Davis, 1966). It is within this context that being black became the presumption of being slave. For the black slave, this was

underscored by the police laws which accorded slaves no existence in law as subjects having the ability to acquire property.
They were defined as a thing not a person, and could not bring a
civil action for any personal injury done to them. It remained for
owners to prosecute by indicating how the personal injury done
to their property deprived them of, or rendered less valuable, the
service of their slaves. Until the late 1820s the testimony of a
slave was not admissible in court as evidence unless accompanied
by a certificate of baptism. Bought and sold on the basis of physical stamina, it was perhaps inevitable that a racist folk system
should arise among plantation owners as to the stereotypical characteristics of the different slave peoples ranked exclusively in relation to their economic potential for the slave system: the Asanti
were reputedly physically strong but rebellious; the Ibo more
'docile' but cunning and deceitful. The convergence of despised
stereotypical characteristics into a popular type, and its conve-
nient availability as a stigmatised image whenever and wherever a
slave-owning class had, mentally, to conjure up an image of the
black peoples they were enslaving cannot be coincidental. Studies
of both the United Sates (Genovese, 1967, 1972) and Britain
(Walvin, 1982) have emphasised the role that stereotypes of the
'character' of slaves played in informing racial ideologies during
the eighteenth and nineteenth centuries. Yet, if, in the character
of Sambo, we undoubtedly see some of the results of enslave-
ment, we also recognise that such characteristics were deeply
contradictory (Fredrickson, 1971) – if Sambo was 'childish' but
also 'sly'; 'slavish' but 'cunning'; dependent like a lap-dog but
also 'vicious' like a wild animal. The stereotypes are resonant
with their ambivalence for the simple reason that they betray the
fact that the total submission and fawning flattery which the
slave-owning class constantly required, as a symptom that 'all was
well on the plantation', could never be procured. The numerous
rebellions are a living testimony of this (Craton, 1980; Harding,
1981).

What is interesting to note is that many of the popular images of
Africans produced during the eighteenth and early nineteenth centuries were also the product of the anti-slavery movement and not
merely of supporters of slavery (Drescher, 1987). It would be misleading to ignore the role and impact of anti-slavery organisations
in both questioning, and in other cases reproducing, some of the

dominant images of African slaves that were in circulation. Anti-slavery was in this sense very much a part of both popular and elite political discourses in this period and it played an important role in informing popular opinion about the issue of slavery.

It is important to note that it was in the crucible of these trans-formations that ideas about 'national identity' began to take a firm hold in European societies. In the case of Britain, for example, the idea of a unified national identity was very much an invention of the period from the mid eighteenth to the early nine-teenth century (Colley, 1992). Indeed, ideas about 'Englishness' or 'Britishness' were never fixed and unchanging and had to be reworked and fashioned around new values throughout the past two centuries (Samuel, 1989, vols 2, 3).

Race, science and society

Along with the broader philosophical, social and economic trans-formations that we have just looked at, the period of the late eighteenth and nineteenth centuries witnessed another important development of the usage of race: namely, the proliferation of scientific and pseudo-scientific theories of race. Such theories were to reach their high point in the nineteenth century, but it is important to note that in different forms the usages of scientific discourses in discussions about race continued to influence think-ing about this issue well into the twentieth century (Stepan, 1982; Barkan, 1992; Harding, 1993).

The emergence of scientific discourses about race cannot be seen in isolation from the wider philosophical ideas about racial types that we have outlined above. It was after all during the late eighteenth and nineteenth centuries that we saw the emergence and codification of ideas about race which were articulated around notions of 'good' and 'evil' races, of 'inferior races'. Ideals and myths that went to make up racial images were structured around ideals of beauty and classified 'races' according to whether they possessed certain virtues or not. It was largely on the basis of these ideas that during the early nineteenth century a concept of 'race' had emerged which went something like this: (i) the physi-cal appearance and behaviour of individuals was an expression of a discrete biological type which was permanent; (ii) cultural variation was determined by differences in biological type; (iii) biological variation was the origin of conflict both between individuals and nations; and (iv) 'races' were differentially endowed such that some were inherently superior to others.

These arguments drew upon and developed the popular concept of the *Great Chain of Being* which was to infuse the arguments of monogenists, polygenists and, later, Social Darwinists alike (Lovejoy, 1964). The concept was based on the metaphorical ladder from God to the lowest form of creation. Each 'race' represented a rung in the vertical construction with black people somewhere near the bottom and whites somewhere near the top. This intellectual structure satisfied a desire for order in society as well as in nature. Just as various forms of creation had their places in the Chain of Being, so society was properly ordered according to rank and status. A key concern of the time was with the use of methods of measurement of the intellectual, moral and external characteristics of a race, and manifested by their cultural and social achievements. Such attempts were partly based on the arguments about 'race' in the nineteenth century but they were given a new inflection by the scientific discourses of the mid nineteenth century.

In the context of Britain, Robert Knox's *Races of Men,* originally published in 1850, articulated some of the views that were current in racial thinking in Britain during this period. Knox was crucially concerned with the question of the existence of distinct 'races' of a relatively permanent kind. He was also interested in the moral and intellectual qualities of different races, and saw the Anglo-Saxon race as the most developed species of mankind. His influence on racial thinking in Britain during the mid nineteenth century was of some importance. As Nancy Stepan argues his analysis incorporated a number of elements:

> It incorporated many of the anti-environmentalist and polygenist arguments of racial thinking that had made their appearance in science between 1800 and 1850. Knox brought these elements together to create a racial fantasy in which Saxons, Celts, gypsies, Jews and the dark races of the world played out their biological destinies. (Stepan, 1982, p. 41)

Knox's ideas were in places somewhat unusual for their time, since for example he used his ideas about race to adopt a political stance against colonialism (Banton, 1977, pp. 46–8). But he was a key figure in attempts to develop a science of race at this time and his ideas played a role in scientific discourses for some while.

Another important text from this period is Comte Arthur de Gobineau's *Essay on the Inequality of the Human Races,* which was originally published in 1853. Although de Gobineau's work attracted little attention at the time it is commonly seen as one of the classic texts of racist thought, and played a role in racial thinking well into this century. In practice de Gobineau was essentially a synthesiser of ideas that were current in a broader social and political context (Biddiss, 1970, 1975). He conceived of humanity as divided into three races: white, yellow and black, and began by stating that 'the race question dominates all other problems of history'. His analysis became famous in latter times because of (i) the way he saw the Aryan race as the creators of civilisation and (ii) his view of the inevitability of racial degeneration through miscegenation. Such ideas were to prove an integral element of latter racial thinking in a number of countries, including France and Germany. They also provided the basis of some key elements of the racial philosophy of the Nazis, though not always in ways which he would have envisaged.

In the second half of the nineteenth century the work of Charles Darwin began to exercise an important role in the development of thinking about race. Darwin published his *On the Origin of Species* in 1859 and his *Descent of Man* in 1871. At one level his work resolved the problems of the monogenist–polygenist debate by making them irrelevant. His theory of evolution greatly extended the time-scale in which the life processes operated and thereby allowed time for the development of the diverse types of men from a common origin. Darwin was less concerned with the static nature of formal classification and more with the dynamic process of biological change. His theory of evolution described the origins of varieties by accidental or spontaneous changes in type and the maintenance or elimination of these varieties by natural selection. By natural selection Darwin referred to the process by which those members of a plant or animal population which are best adapted to their environment contribute more to subsequent generations than those less well endowed. In short, the survival of the fittest. In contradiction to the polygenists Darwin proved not only that the European was related to the African, but that all men were related to the ape. The theory of natural selection as such, however, describes the mechanics of the origin and perpetuation of varieties, but it did not state which 'racial' groups were stronger or lower in 'civilised' development. 'Racial' characteristics were therefore not placed on a comparative scale of value, but left to the operation of natural selection to decide their survival or extinction.

Thus the Darwinian arguments in favour of heredity and variation challenged the idea of the fixity of species, but during the late nineteenth and early twentieth centuries themes derived form Darwin were used in debates about race in a variety of national contexts. This was evident, for example, in the popularity of Social Darwinism and of Eugenics during this period (Mosse, 1985a; Dengler, 1991). Arguments about 'natural selection' and the 'survival of the fittest' were simplified and adopted as part of racist thinking, and indeed they became an important theme in writings about race throughout this period (Stocking, 1968, 1987; Jones, 1980). Some cited Darwin's work as proof that Africans were doomed eventually to disappear in favour of the 'stronger', European 'race'. In other words, Darwin's notion of struggle for existence was reworked as a confrontation between so-called 'races' and natural selection wedded to the existing ideas of 'racial' typology. This was perhaps not surprising in the wider context of colonial expansion and imperial domination that characterised the period of the late nineteenth and early twentieth centuries.

Imperialism, colonialism and race

In much of the literature on the development of racist ideologies and practices an important role is assigned to the methods by which colonialism and imperialism helped to construct images of the 'other' (Mannoni, 1964). In particular there have recently been numerous studies of the development of images of colonised peoples and the manner in which these were popularised and reproduced in British society. There have also been attempts to analyse the ways in which ideas about race were variously the result of formulating the 'differences' between coloniser and colonised. Such studies have certainly done much to shed light on an issue which has, by and large, been marginal to the study of

race and racism. But part of the problem in discussing the interplay between imperialism and colonialism with racism is the tendency to overgeneralise without exploring in any detail the
connections between the institutionalisation of imperial domination and colonisation and the emergence of racist ideas and practices. Mosse is surely right when he argues that 'Imperialism and
racism ... were never identical; their interrelationship was
dependant upon time and place' (Mosse, 1985a, p. x). But it is
precisely the nature of this relationship that remains to be fully
analysed, particularly if we are to understand how and why
common-sense images about race were influenced by the role
that countries such as Britain played as colonial and imperial
powers.

A variety of recent critical research on the politics of colonialism has shown that images of the 'other' played a key role in
colonial discourses (Parry, 1972; Ross, 1982; Pratt, 1992). Such
images were closely tied to racial stereotypes, but it was also clear
that they related to all aspects of the relationship between the
colonised and colonisers. Sander Gilman has made this linkage
clear when he argues: 'In the nineteenth century, in the age of
expanding European colonies, the black became the primitive
perse, a primitivism mirrored in the stultifying quality of his or
her dominant sense, touch, as well as the absence of any aesthetic
sensibility' (Gilman, 1991, p. 20). From this perspective the
linkage of colonised peoples with images of the 'primitive' was
the product of complex historical processes and it took different
forms in specific colonial situations. A case in point is the impact
of the 'scramble for Africa' on images of the peoples of the 'dark
continent', and the circulation of these images in metropolitan
societies. While, as we have shown above, European images of
Africa had taken shape over some centuries, it is also the case that
the expansion of colonial power during the nineteenth century
helped to invent new images and to institutionalise specific forms
of class, gender and racial relations (Mudimbe, 1988 and 1994;
Appiah, 1992; Coombes, 1994).

What of the impact of these images on racial ideas and values in
the colonial powers themselves? In the British context it seems
clear that in the Victorian era the experience of colonialism and
imperial expansion played an important role in shaping ideas about
race, both in relation to Africa and India (Bolt, 1971). It was also

during this period that the question of the Empire became an integral part of British politics and society in the earlier part of this century. Images of colonial peoples were not the outcome of any singular process. In the context of both Africa and Asia, for example, a number of interlinked processes were at work in the construction of images of both the 'natives' and the 'colonisers' (Kiernan, 1969; Brantlinger, 1988; Dirks, 1992; Sharpe, 1993; Spurr, 1993). We need to remember that most Victorians had no personal contact with the exotic peoples and places that they were assuming responsibility for. Their opinions were formed according to the sources of their information, and these sources were for the most part the popular press and literature. The linkages between colonialism and racism became evident throughout the late nineteenth and early twentieth centuries in the form of the articulation between nationalism and patriotism in the construction of the very definition of 'Englishness' and 'Britishness'.

It would be a mistake, however, to see such racial images in isolation from wider sets of social relations. As a number of commentators have forcefully argued, an important aspect of racial thinking during the nineteenth century was the similarity between discourses about race and those about class. This was evident in both Britain and the rest of the Empire. Douglas Lorimer's study of racial attitudes in Victorian society distinguishes the parallels between colour and class prejudice of middle-class Victorians very clearly. He notes the similarities between the attitudes of those middle-class travellers whose tourism took them to India, Egypt, and the East End of London, in order to view the strange, primitive and exotic creatures of the world (Lorimer, 1978).

Moreover, during the high point of imperialism in the late nineteenth and early twentieth centuries racialised notions of national identity were pertinent outside the colonial context. At this juncture imperialist ideologies had developed a racial notion of national identity to refer to other European nations as well as colonial people. During this period also nationalist movements and ideals began to gain a degree of influence in many European countries. As Michael Mann notes in his study of the period:

> Increasing social density, state infrastructures, and linguistic and sometimes also religious community now gave racism a national definition ... Ideologists for the Anglo-Saxon, the

Frank, the Teuton, the Slav 'race' developed a mythological history of common descent. In the 1900s, British politicians and popular writers used the word 'race' in a perfectly routine way to refer to the British people, in discussing problems of the empire, and in regard to economic rivalry with Germany-even with the United States. Thus racism was not unitary but split, as Europe had always been split, between the transnational and the national. (Mann, 1993, pp. 581–2)

What this process made clear is the variety of ways in which the idea of race could be used to refer to the putative 'racial' differences between competing nations and states. Interestingly enough, in the period before the First World War it was precisely such ideas about 'race' that gained an important role in political discourses of the time (Kennedy and Nicholls, 1981).

This is not to say that colonialism and imperialism did not also have an important impact on political ideologies, literature and popular culture. Certainly, if one looks at literary and cultural output at the end of the nineteenth century, and well into the twentieth, it is redolent with images of the role of Britain as an imperial power and as a source of civilised culture for the colonies. Some of the most interesting research in this field has been about the role that colonialism and imperialism played in influencing political discourses and values through popular culture at this time. In the British context, a number of valuable studies have illustrated the depth of the impact that imperialism had on popular cultural expressions throughout the late nineteenth and early twentieth centuries. John MacKenzie has indicated in his interesting studies both the complexity and the extent of imperial propaganda on popular culture, education, literature and other cultural forms (MacKenzie, 1984, 1986). Other studies of colonial societies have emphasized the depth of the cultural and political imagery of colonialism as well and its impact on Western societies (Miller, 1990; Dirks, 1992; Pieterse, 1992; Spurr, 1993). The important role of sexuality in constructions of the 'native' has been highlighted by recent research about imperial culture (Hyam, 1990; Parker *et al.*, 1992; Young, 1995)

Yet it has to be said that one of the major lacunae in the existing literature is that while much has been written about the impact of colonial expansion and imperial domination on racial attitudes, there has been surprisingly little comment on the role and impact of anticolonial ideas and movements. As Stephen Howe has astutely commented in his pioneering study of British anti-colonialism: 'Arguably, anticolonialism was the most ubiquitous international ideology from the 1950s to the 1980s, uniting the whole Communist world, almost all articulate opinion in the developing countries, and most left-wing thought in the Western world' (Howe, 1993, p. ix). Given the extent of its influence on political and social discourses during this period it is indeed surprising that we have little knowledge of both the nature of the anticolonialist movements and the role that anticolonialism had on the changing ideas about race in Britain and elsewhere. It is perhaps this absence that has helped to produce a rather monolithic view of the impact of the Empire on domestic British political culture.

It has to be noted here that in practice recent research has tended, if anything, to question the idea of a uniform and unchanging colonial view of 'race' that was prevalent at all stages of colonial history and European expansion. Rather, a number of scholars have shown that in practice colonial societies were by no means static and unchanging in their articulation of racial ideologies and social relations. In summary, while it is important in analysing the history of racism to include the role played by processes of domination and colonisation, it would be misleading to construct a simplistic one to one relationship between the two. It is perhaps understandable in the immediate aftermath of the decline of colonialism that much of the attention of researchers has focused on its role in fostering and spreading racial stereotypes and myths in metropolitan societies. The danger, however, is that in so doing we may lose sight of the complexity and diversity of colonial social relations and blame many of our contemporary mores on the 'experience' of colonial domination.

Anti-Semitism, Nazism and the racial state

From a present perspective it is an inescapable fact of recent history that the experience of the Holocaust and the genocidal policies of the Nazi state are an integral part of any contemporary discussion about 'race' and racism. Indeed, it is impossible to understand the history of both academic research in this field as well as political discourses without reference to the enormity of the impact of Nazi racial policies (Proctor, 1988; Weindling, 1989; Burleigh and Wippermann, 1991). Though the focus of our own study is not on anti-Semitism itself, it is quite clear that the history of contemporary racism has been influenced in one way or another by the experience of fascism and the anti-Semitic political mobilisations which were a key feature of fascist movements. As pointed out above the usage of the very term racism is in fact closely related to the rise of Nazism and the racial theories they advocated and put into practice.

The term anti-Semitism came into popular usage at the end of the nineteenth century, but it is widely accepted that as a term it captures the long history of resentment and hatred of Jews. Anti-Semitism can be seen, therefore, as referring to the conception of Jews as an alien, hostile and undesirable group, and the practices that derive from, and support, such a conception. The history of anti-Semitism is, of course, much more complex and of longer historical origin than the racial theories of the Nazis (Cohn, 1970; Poliakov, 1974a, 1974b; Gilman and Katz, 1991). It has existed in a variety of historical contexts and has been legitimised by a wide range of beliefs and folklore about Jews. Indeed it seems clear that if one looks at all the major European countries they all have quite specific histories of anti-Semitism, influenced both by sets of beliefs about Jews and by broader socio-political processes. In the British context, for example, there is evidence of anti-Semitism at different historical conjunctures. But it is perhaps in the late nineteenth century that the arrival of sizeable numbers of Jewish migrants from Eastern Europe became a focus of political debate, leading to the development of a political anti-Semitism in particular localities. The political influence of anti-Semitism in France towards the end of the nineteenth century can also be seen as related to the changing political and social relations in French society at the time (Wilson, 1982).

But perhaps the main focus of research on political anti-Semitism has been on the history of Germany. Although the history of anti-Semitism in Germany was by no means unique, it is certainly the case that in the aftermath of the Holocaust the German experience has been at the heart of most research (Pulzer, 1988; Rose, 1990; Gilman, 1991). Whatever the limitations of this focus on the German experience, the wealth of research on the social and political context within which various kinds of anti-Semitism developed in Germany has provided some important insights into the ways in which racial ideologies and practices are constructed by and through specific political movements.

Theodor Adorno's and Max Horkheimer's *Dialectic of Enlightenment* provided a valuable early account of the role that anti-Semitism played in the politics of fascism. Adorno and Horkheimer sought, on the one hand, to situate anti-Semitism in the broader context of class and political struggles in German society and, on the other, to underline its specific and unique characteristics. Although they sought to locate anti-Semitism in the broader framework of capitalist society they also highlighted the murderous consequences of the fascist construction of the Jews as a 'degenerate race': 'The fascists do not view the Jews as a minority but as an opposing race, the embodiment of the negative principle. They must be exterminated to secure the happiness of the world' (Adorno and Horkheimer, 1986, p. 168). The usages of racial theories by the Nazis thus provided not only a basis for the articulation of anti-Semitism but a means of justifying the 'final solution to the Jewish question' and the inevitability of a 'race war'. From this perspective the political consequences of Nazi racial theories, with their emphasis on race as a total criterion, provided the basis for the extermination of Jews. The Holocaust itself needs to be analysed in the context of what actually happened during the period of Nazi rule from 1933 to 1945. As a number of studies have shown, a key feature of the Nazi state was precisely its 'racial' nature (Gilbert, 1986).

A fascinating discussion of the role that anti-Semitism played in German society during the nineteenth and early twentieth centuries is provided by George Mosse's magisterial study on *The Crisis of German Ideology*. Mosse provides perhaps the best insight into the variety of factors that helped to shape the articulation between anti-Semitism and racism in the period from the second half of the nineteenth century to the rise of Adolf Hitler. He also illustrates the complex variety of processes which went into the transformation of latent anti-Semitism, including the role of educational institutions, youth organisations and political parties. Mosse's rich account of Volkish thought during the nineteenth century provides perhaps the best and most powerful account of the social and political roots of German anti-Semitism, highlighting the contrast in images of 'the uprootedness of the Jew' with those of the 'rootedness of the Volk' (Mosse, 1966, pp. 27–8). He also provides a detailed analysis of the linkages between the growth of anti-Semitism and the rise of national socialism as a mass political movement:

> That the Volkish ideology, wedded as it was to anti-modernity, could be absorbed by the modern mass movement techniques of National Socialism led to its final realisation. To be sure, if it had not been for very real grievances and frustrations, both on a personal level and on the national level, Germany's development in modern times might have taken a different turn. But the most important question is: Why did millions of people respond to the Volkish call? (Ibid., 317)

In some ways, of course, Mosse's question has not been fully answered, even when one takes into account the wealth of research on this question. But what is clear is that the fact that the Nazis used racial anti-Semitism as a key plank of their platform has cast a long shadow over subsequent debates about racism.

This has been underlined by one of the most challenging recent attempts to rethink the whole experience of the Holocaust, namely Zygmunt Bauman's *Modernity and the Holocaust*. Bauman seeks to reinterpret the meaning of the Holocaust and its role in contemporary history from the perspective of sociological theory. One of the ironies that he details is that anti-Semitism in Germany at the beginning of this century was weaker than in many other European countries. He points out that there were many more Jewish professionals and academics than in Britain, France and America. He also cites evidence that popular anti-Semitism was not very widespread in Germany, although it grew rapidly in the aftermath of the First World War. Perhaps most controversially, Bauman contends that the Holocaust was not an aberration but an integral feature of modernity: 'The Holocaust was born and executed in our modern society, at the high stage of our civilisation and at the peak of human cultural achievement, and for this reason it is a problem of that society, civilisation and culture' (Bauman, 1989, p. 13). From this perspective he argues that a key feature of Nazism was its

view of the need for 'social engineering' through its racial policies. The use of genocide by the Nazis was a means to an end, an
element in the construction of the 'perfect society' (ibid., p. 91).
In this sense Bauman is agreeing with the arguments articulated
by historians such as Mosse. But he also wants to go beyond such
historical accounts and explore more deeply the implications of
the Holocaust for how we think about our societies today.

The Nazi attempt to construct a 'racially pure' society and to
use state power to help bring this about has exerted a major
influence in discussions about race and racism in the post-1945
period. In particular it helped to emphasise and warn against the
destructive and genocidal consequences of racist theorising and
political mobilisation. It also served to highlight the complex
forms which racist ideologies can and do take at certain historical
conjunctures. We shall return to some of these points in Chapters
4 and 6.

Migrant labour, race and society

For most of the second half of the twentieth century perhaps the
key process that has shaped debates about race and ethnicity, especially in Europe, has been the phenomenon of new patterns of
international labour migration. In the period since 1945 the most
important pattern of labour migration has involved, in general,
the movement of workers from less developed countries, for
example from North Africa and the Mediterranean basin to
Western Europe, or from Latin America and Asia to North
America. Within this broad pattern there are, however, a number
of historically specific variations. In the case of Britain, most of
the migrants came from colonial and ex-colonial territories. In
other European countries the sources of migrants are far more
varied or have no direct colonial link as such. This process has
generally been seen as the outcome of both the demand for
labour in the advanced industrial economies as well as pressure on
migrants to move in search of employment and better living conditions. Although it is too easy to fall into the trap of seeing the
movement of migrant labour and the formation of settled minority communities as the cause of the growth of racism in a simple
fashion, it is quite clear from the experience of a number of

societies that the question of 'immigration' has become an inextricable and important element in the articulation of contemporary racial ideologies and practices. Migrants have become the main target of racist movements and organisations, though by no means the only ones.

In a general sense labour migration is not specific to the period after 1945. Eric Wolf's account of the complex processes involved in European expansion since the sixteenth century has shown quite clearly how the movement of labour has been at the core of the growth of capitalist economies. He makes the following telling point:

> Capitalist accumulation thus continues to engender new working classes in widely dispersed areas of the world. It recruits these working classes from a wide variety of social and cultural backgrounds, and inserts them into variable political and economic hierarchies. The new working classes change these hierarchies by their presence, and are themselves changed by the forces to which they are exposed. On one level, therefore, the diffusion of the capitalist mode creates everywhere a wider unity through the constant reconstitution of its characteristic capital–labour relationship. On another level, it also creates diversity, accentuating social opposition and segmentation even as it unifies. Within an ever more integrated world, we witness the growth of ever more diverse proletarian diasporas. (Wolf, 1982, p. 383)

In this sense the existence of what Wolf calls 'proletarian diasporas' is not in itself a new phenomenon. Indeed, different patterns of labour migration have been a feature of the economic development of various countries. One of the best examples is the migration to the United States during the latter part of the nineteenth century and the early part of the twentieth century, which involved approximately 30 million people in the period from 1860 to 1920. Migrations on a lesser scale were also a feature of a number of societies in Europe, including France, Britain and Germany. It is also clear that the political response to these earlier migrations played an important role in the development of racial ideologies. This pattern is apparent whereby the arrival of Jewish immigrants led to the development of an active political lobby against immigration, as well as a public discussion about the impact that the immigrants were likely to have on the purity of the 'racial stock' (Collinson, 1993). It was during this same period that similar debates about the politics of immigration took place in various societies.

It is clear, however, that in the period since 1945 international migration has involved new types of migration and a growth in volume. There is by now a wealth of accounts of how the complex forms of migration in the period since 1945, particularly to various European countries, have played an important role in the construction of new forms of racialisation. Castles and Miller (1993, pp. 196–201) have provided a useful comparative account of what they call processes of 'minority formation' and the their place in structuring societies' political debates and struggles.

Furthermore, a new politics of immigration has emerged in Europe as well as other parts of the globe. As Etienne Balibar notes in relation to the situation in France and other West European societies: "Immigration" has become, par excellence, the name of race, a new name, but one that is functionally equivalent to the old appellation, just as the term "immigrant" is the chief characteristic which enables individuals to be classified in a racist typology' (Balibar and Wallerstein, 1991, p. 222). This interlinkage between the politics of immigration and race has been evident in the context of Britain for some time. But during the late 1980s and 1990s this linkage became evident in France and Germany and a number of other European societies, partly in the context of the fundamental changes that took place in Eastern Europe at this juncture. However, it was also the result of both national and Europe-wide trends which have led to the politicisation of immigration and the rise of nationalist and openly racist social movements and political parties. While economic and social issues are an important aspect of these developments, it is also important to emphasise the role of ideological and cultural changes in shaping the changing politics of race and ethnicity in contemporary European societies. A case in point is the situation in France and Germany, where we have seen the growth of nationalist and racist movements which exert a growing influence on the public political debate about immigration.

The impact of immigration on the politics of race is likely to grow over the coming decade, since it seems likely that existing migratory processes are likely to continue and new patterns of global migration will emerge. In addition to traditional patterns of migration from developing countries to those industrial economies which provide an opportunity for an improved standard of living, there is, on the basis of current political trends, likely to be a significant increase in the number of refugees and displaced persons who will seek asylum in those countries who are willing to take them. On the basis of this scenario the issue of immigration is likely to remain closely intertwined with the politics of race.

Racism in comparative perspective

In this chapter we have focused in one way or another on the specificity of racism from the perspective of both time and place. What we have tried to show is that in order to place the role of racism in the contemporary social context, we need to situate the divergent historical processes that have shaped the understandings of race and racism that are current in our societies. There is, as we are fully aware, a much broader and deeper historical sociology of racism. As the work of a number of scholars has shown there have been a variety of both national and supranational processes at work in influencing the development of racist ideas and movements, and these cannot easily be subsumed under a monolithic category of racism. This key theme links up to some of the central problems which have arisen in recent attempts to contextualise racism within a historical perspective. Namely, it has allowed us to address some of the issues which we touched on from a theoretical angle in Chapter 1 from the perspective of historically specific research. Whatever the merits of the account we have given of specific processes, it seems clear that it is important not to lose sight of the historical moments and the wider context within which ideas about race emerge, develop and take on social significance.

A number of interesting attempts have been made to provide a comparative historical sociology of the workings of racism. The work of writers such as George Fredrickson provides an interesting and valuable model of this type of work (Fredrickson, 1981, 1988). Fredrickson's account in his classic study *White Supremacy: A Comparative Study in American and South African History* (1981) seeks to capture both the differences and similarities between these two societies through a richly contextualised analysis of the role of patterns of settlement, images of the 'natives', racial slavery, race mixture and the colour line and the changing social relationships of race in the twentieth century. He illustrates the value of contextualising the historical development of racial ideas and racialised social relations not only in specific contexts, but the need to challenge some common assumptions about the social history of both America and South Africa. Additionally, his account provides a useful reminder of the role of state institutions in shaping the constantly changing contours of the 'colour line'. In addition to Fredrickson, a number of other researchers have illustrated the importance of historically situated accounts of how ideas about race emerged and took shape in particular societies.

There is by now a rich body of historical work which has analysed the ways in which ideas about race have linked up with specific patterns of economic, social and political transformation. But much of the contemporary social science literature on race and racism remains largely uninformed by historical research or by more contemporary studies of the wider processes that have shaped racial institutions (Poliakov, 1982). This has resulted in a lack of historical reflexivity about the historical background to the emergence of modern racism and a failure to come to terms with the transformations of racial ideologies and practices over time and space. Yet what is also clear is that without a clear understanding of the historical context it is unlikely that we shall be able to come fully to terms with the question of how racial ideas have emerged out of and become an integral part of specific societies.

Part of the complexity of analysing the historical impact of racism is that it is often intertwined with other social phenomena, and indeed it can only be fully understood if we are able to see how it works in specific social settings. This is a theme we touched upon conceptually in Chapter 1, where we discussed some recent attempts to tackle aspects of this issue. In this chapter we have tried to explore some concrete historical examples and the ways they have impacted on processes of racialisation in specific societies. One interesting example of this process are the ways in which modern racial and nationalist ideologies rely on a complex variety of images of race, sexuality and nationhood (Mosse, 1985a, 1985b). The image of the 'other' as somehow sexually 'abnormal' has been a theme in racial discourses at various times, and in many ways continues to be to this day:

> The stereotype of the outsider filled with lust was a staple of racism, part of the inversion of accepted values said to characterise black or Jew who, at one and the same time, threatened society and by their very existence confirmed its standards. To Jews and blacks, the prime victims of racism, were joined others whose abnormal behaviour put them beyond the limits set by society. The insane, homosexuals, and habitual criminals were seen as sharing the stigma of being unable to control their passions, which ranged from sexual lust to murderous anger. (Mosse, 1985b, p. xiv)

This pattern has been noted by a number of other studies of specific historical situations (Ware, 1982; Parker *et al.*, 1992). This is but one example of the variety of ways in which racial ideologies and practices can and do interact in specific historical circumstances with other sets of ideas and values to produce the racialised social relations that we see around us.

Additionally, it is clear that racism is increasingly not an ideology which can be easily reduced to biological arguments as such. Contemporary racial thought invokes a range of markers of 'difference' in order to construct the stereotypes and images on which racism relies. On one level one can agree with Goldberg when he argues: 'Racists are those who explicitly or implicitly ascribe racial characteristics of others that they take to differ from their own and those they take to be like them. These characteristics may be biological or social' (Goldberg, 1990, p. 296). But even this definition seems to be a bit narrow when we look at the changing terms of racial discourses in contemporary societies. For what has become clear through comparative research is that only through a deeply contextualised account of the sources of racial ideas can we really grasp the variety of racisms that have emerged in specific historical environments.

In summary, the historical territory that we have mapped out in this chapter provides some of the background to the more specific and contemporary sets of issues that we cover in the rest of this book. In general, the key argument that we have sought to develop is that the development of the idea of race needs to be contextualised within specific social and historical relationships.

Although racial ideologies often appeal to primordial notions of kinship and myths of common ethnic origins to support their arguments, it is worth emphasising that the notion that there are races and racial relationships is relatively new (Guillaumin, 1980). This means breaking with the view that sees race and racism as transhistorical categories and as unchanging. More importantly, however, it implies that the ahistorical perspective which is still prevalent in much of the writing in this field needs to be challenged. There is still a wealth of issues about the history of racism that need to be explored. This is evident from recent research done within a range of disciplines and theoretical perspectives in the social sciences and humanities. In the present socio-political environment it is perhaps more clear than it has ever been that the analysis of racism and related phenomena, such as ethnic nationalism, cannot ignore the need for systematic comparative research in order to uncover the social, economic and political processes that have shaped the interrelationship between racism and contemporary social relations.

3 Social Relations and Racial Inequality

Up to this point we have concentrated our analysis on two themes: first, on how various theoretical paradigms have attempted to account for the phenomenon of racism and its role in shaping social and political relations in contemporary societies; second, on the various historical contexts within which ideas about race were developed and on the historically specific and transformative nature of racialised ideologies and racist exclusions. Both of these themes are closely interrelated to a somewhat broader question, namely the linkages between racism and forms of social inequality that have been characterised as either racial in origin or racial in character. In developing our account of the theoretical and historical dimension we have inevitably touched upon the ways in which racial ideologies and practices have helped to structure social and political relations in particular societies, and have in turn been shaped by specific sets of social relations or national political contexts. Indeed it is clear that much of the sociological literature on race and racism has been concerned with this question. At the same time, the question of racial inequality has been a core preoccupation in public policy debates about racism. This is evidenced in the whole panoply of policies and legislative measures concerned with racial inequality. We have not, however, discussed these issues in any detail so far. Yet it is clear that this is perhaps the most important question we confront when looking at both the historical background and contemporary political debates about race and racism.

It is to these issues that we now turn in order to analyse the changing morphology of racial inequalities in contemporary societies and the debates about what kind of policy initiatives are necessary in order to tackle them. While it is beyond the scope of this study to explore all aspects of these conceptual and policy debates we shall discuss at least some of the key issues raised by recent research in this field. Starting from an account of some of the themes of recent research on racial inequalities, we then move on to a discussion of the key features of exclusionary racial practices. This is perhaps the main area of concern to sociologists working in this field, and there has been a wealth of empirical research which has explored various aspects of this question. In addition to exploring the broader contours of racialised inequalities we also touch upon the interface between race and gender inequalities. This then leads into a critical overview of attempts to develop policies which aim to tackle racial inequality and ensure the integration of minority communities. Over the past three decades there have been important transformations in public policies concerned with this issue, and it is of some importance therefore to explore both the objectives and impact of policy initiatives. In the final parts of the chapter we take up some of the questions raised by new right commentators who have sought to question both the legitimacy and the utility of state intervention as a tool for tackling racial inequality. We then reflect upon some of the dilemmas and questions that are likely to confront us in the future in dealing with this question.

Racism and social relations

The question of what impact racism has on social relations has preoccupied many sociologists of race working within a variety of theoretical paradigms. The focus of much of the empirical research on contemporary racial relations has been on the analysis of specific aspects of inequality in areas such as housing or employment, or on the development and impact of anti-discrimination measures. Certainly the bulk of research in Britain, the United States and other advanced industrial societies has been on the changing face of racialised inequalities. In Britain, for example, there is by now a panoply of studies of virtually all aspects of racial inequality from both a national and a local perspective. These have been supplemented by other studies which explore the complex ways in which various migrant communities experience inequality and disadvantage in their daily lives.

However, what is interesting about this body of work is that there are a number of questions which need to be addressed in a fuller manner. For example: how does one account for the emergence and persistence of racialised inequalities in employment, housing, social welfare, education, as well as evident inequalities in other areas? What processes help to explain the structuring of inequalities along racial lines? What can liberal democratic societies do to ensure that racialised inequalities do not lead to the social and economic exclusion of minorities? These are some of the questions which have been raised in one way or another by researchers and politicians for at least the past three decades, and yet we do not seem to have moved much closer towards resolving them. Rather we have seen deeply politicised public debates about both the origins and remedies for racial inequality.

The highly politicised nature of debates about racial inequality is partly the result of the fact that the interrelationship between racism and social inequalities has been and remains a deeply controversial question. It has given rise to quite divergent theoretical and political perspectives over the years. Part of the problem is that there is in practice very little agreement about how to conceptualise the interrelationship between racism and specific sets of racialised social relations. While some writers have used the notion of racism in a very broad social and political sense to cover both sets of ideas and institutional practices, this is by no means a position which is universally accepted. Indeed, some writers have questioned the way in which the general category of *racism* or the more specific notion of *institutionalised racism* has been used to describe forms of social relations and types of inequalities. Yet others have argued that the concept of racism should be delimited in such a way as to define it essentially as an ideological phenomenon. Over the past decade the lack of a commonly accepted notion about what racism is has become even more apparent, particularly in the aftermath of the controversies about the development of Marxist and postmodernist perspectives to the study of race and racism.

This kind of debate and disagreement signals some of the real difficulties that exist with the ways in which the linkages between racist theories and practices have been conceptualised. There is a very real sense, for example, that terms such as *institutional racism* have become catch-all phrases which are used to describe quite diverse and complex patterns of exclusion. At the same time, such notions tend to be underpinned by instrumentalist notions of the relationship between racist ideas and specific types of inequality in a very undifferentiated sense. But such problems do not in them-selves mean that we should not explore and understand the role of racism in structuring social relations. Rather they point to the need to develop a more open and critical framework for analysing such processes.

Despite this it is also the case that there are divergent perspec-tives about the interrelationship between racism and processes of racial discrimination. For example, an influential approach to this issue is the argument that *racism* can best be perceived as particular sets of ideological values, which propound either biological or cultural explanations of racial difference. From this perspective *racial discrimination* is a practice which may or may not be the outcome of racist ideologies. Michael Banton articulates this ar-gument clearly when he argues against the tendency to see racism and racial discrimination as interchangeable notions. For Banton and other researchers there is a clear danger that the notion of racism can become a catch-all term that encompasses quite dis-parate forms of social, political and economic practices. Similar arguments have been made by Miles, who warns of the dangers of 'conceptual inflation' in relation to the usages of the category of racism in the social sciences (Miles, 1989).

Yet it is also clear that in much of contemporary political dis-course and research the concepts of *racism* and *racial discrimination* have become merged, so that they have little apparent difference. The concept of racism is used in practice to mean almost the same thing as racial discrimination. This is perhaps not surprising, in the sense that from a historical perspective the linkages between racist ideologies and social and economic relations have been an important feature of many societies over the past two centuries. But what is also clear is that the relationship between racist ideas and specific practices and institutional forms is by no means simple. From a historical perspective it is quite clear that racism as an exclusionary practice can take various forms. The very complexity of the relationship between racism and forms of social exclusion makes it important that a distinction be maintained between *racism* and *racial discrimination*. As David Goldberg has cogently argued:

> Racism excludes racially defined others, or promotes, or secures, or sustains such exclusion. Often racist exclusions will be undertaken or expressed for their own sakes, for the recognition of the putatively inherent value the expressions are claimed to represent. In the case where persons insist that they are acting for the sake of racist principles, it is conceivable that exploitative acts will be a means of sustaining racist principles. (Goldberg, 1993, p. 101)

It follows from this line of analysis that the relationship between racism and forms of exploitation has to be established and cannot be assumed *a priori*. In other words, the processes which structure the relationship between racism and social exclusions have to be seen in the context of specific historical circumstances. As we saw in Chapter 2, one of the key lessons we can learn from the analysis of the changing forms of racial ideas and practices over the past two centuries is that it is quite impossible to conceptualise racism as a monolithic phenomenon which is unchanged by historical and cultural circumstances. Indeed one can go further and say that the force of historical research points clearly in the opposite direction.

A wealth of historical research has helped to illustrate how racism has interacted with specific social and political processes to produce racialised forms of inequality in a wide variety of societies. In the British context, a wide range of empirical studies have attempted to examine how racist ideologies have helped to create the conditions for deeply entrenched racial inequalities in employment, housing, welfare provision and related areas. Many of the early classics of the field of race relations in Britain were concerned with the ways in which racial discrimination affected the social and economic position of immigrants in localities such as London and Birmingham. A classic example of this approach is Rex and Moore's *Race, Community and Conflict* which attempted to provide a sociological analysis of the social and housing conditions of immigrants in the Sparkbrook area of Birmingham. Rex and Moore's account was and remains an influential text for those interested in the analysis of the dynamics of racial discrimination and exclusion in urban environments. Their account provided a particularly sharp analysis of processes of exclusion in relation to housing, pointing to the existence of exclusive allocation practices within council housing provision. In addition, migrants were positioned in varying locations within this housing class system, that is 'Pakistani landlords' occupied a 'pariah position' in a different housing class from those who lodged with them and who were predominantly 'West Indian' (Rex and Moore, 1967, p. 165). Running alongside this process of housing discrimination was the development of 'immigrant colonies'. The development of such colonies was a response to the 'anomie' and 'personal demoralisation' which migrants were subjected to in urban environments such as Birmingham (ibid., p. 277). It is in this context that community and immigrant organisation took on political meanings. Rex and Moore refer in particular to the political work that took place in (i) organisations within 'immigrant colonies' and (ii) the development of organisations which acted for particular housing class interests.

In more recent years a number of other community studies and surveys have attempted to explore the changing contours of racialised discrimination and inequality in British society at both the local and national levels. Much of the research on race relations in British society since the 1960s has been concerned with aspects of racial discrimination against black migrants and their descendants in employment, housing and education. Such studies have looked at the ways in which particular economic, social, racial and political relations have helped to shape the development of black minority communities in cities such as London, Birmingham, Leicester, Bradford and other urban localities (Rex, 1991; Cohen, 1993; Keith, 1993; Small, 1994; Solomos and Back, 1995).

Certainly in the context of the mainstream of the sociology of race relations in Britain, as well as the United States, a key theme on the research agenda has been the issue of how to explain the emergence and persistence of racial inequalities in such fields as housing, employment and education. Whether in terms of theoretical debates about the sociology of racial relations or more policy oriented research on racial inequality, the main question remains the same – namely, how do we understand the role that race plays in shaping key facets of social relations in contemporary societies. In the British context a whole panoply of studies since the 1960s have explored one or other dimension of racial discrimination and disadvantage. Such studies have taken a variety of forms, ranging from quantitative overviews of racial inequality in British society to qualitative accounts of the changing experience of black minorities in British society or specific sections within these communities.

Similarly in the United States, the research of both historians and sociologists has also focused attention on the relationship between racial ideologies and forms of structured segregation and exclusion, particularly those aimed at African-Americans. Such studies have focused on both the general historical context of the socio-economic exclusion of African-Americans, but an increasing number of studies have looked at the role and impact of the Civil Rights Movement and anti-discrimination legislation in transforming their position within American society. Such studies have shown that questions about racial inequalities have become intrinsically politicised and are often likely to become even more so in the future. This is partly because in the period since the 1960s there has been a noticeable backlash against the affirmative action programmes and civil rights initiatives introduced during the mid-1960s, leading to heated debates between liberals and neo-conservatives about the utility of public policies in this field. We shall return to this issue later on in this chapter, but the importance of the above point is that it highlights the centrality of racial inequality as a key concern within the sociology of race relations.

At a broader level the development and persistence of racialised inequalities is a feature of the situation in many advanced industrial societies. There is growing recognition in a number of Western European societies, for example, that migrant workers and their communities suffer from a variety of exclusionary mechanisms in employment and housing. More broadly, processes of racial and ethnic discrimination are seen as playing an important role in bringing about a racialisation of poverty. It is not surprising, therefore, that much intellectual energy and political debate has been focused on this question in recent years.

Racialisation and exclusionary practices

This leads us to the question of the specific workings of exclusionary practices and how they impact on racialised inequalities.

In other words, how do we define and analyse the workings of specific types of racial inequality? How can the interrelationship between racism, social relations and politics be conceptualised? What are the processes which help to structure contemporary racial inequalities and patterns of discrimination? All of these questions raise important political dilemmas and it would be false to pretend that there is agreement both on what racial inequality is and how it can be explained and dealt with. In this sense the experience of the past three decades has shown that the very notion of racial inequality remains an essentially contested concept, both in the context of political and policy debate and academic research.

This makes it all the more important to remember that when we talk of racial inequality we are not referring to a static and unchanging phenomenon. In practice when we talk of racial discrimination there is a whole range of complex social, economic and political processes at work. Within this context patterns of direct and indirect racial discrimination are only part of the story. It is important, in addition, to recognise the role of class, gender and spatial processes in shaping the ways in which racialised inequalities are formed and reproduced over time. As we saw above in relation to the situation in the United States and Britain, class can interact with racial processes to produce entrenched forms of racial inequality which are not amenable to race-specific policies as such.

It is interesting to note in this regard that as well as providing statistical evidence of patterns of inequality, researchers have been able to provide insights through qualitative research on the detail and processes of hidden discrimination and the economic and political pressures which ultimately lie behind racist judgements and acts. Now, some commentators are realising the need for more of this type of investigation. As Banton argues, we need to understand forms of racial inequality at levels on which decisions are taken which, consciously or not, either increase or decrease such inequalities: 'It is necessary to understand the workings of social institutions, such as those which socialise children, which channel job seeking and employee selection so that particular sorts of people end up in particular jobs' (Banton, 1992, p. 84). Such detailed investigations have highlighted the complex processes which have helped to shape racialised inequalities in both an institutional and an everyday context.

An interesting example of the interactions between historical and contemporary forms of racial exclusion and segregation is provided by the ongoing debates in American society about the changing patterns of ghettoisation in the urban environment. A challenging account of these transformations can be found in the work of Loic Wacquant on the new forms of spatial segregation in American cities. Referring to what he calls the 'new urban colour line', he points out that after the gains made by the black middle class in the period from the 1960s onwards there is evidence that 'the economic, social and cultural distance between inner-city minorities and the rest of society has reached levels that are unprecedented in modern American history as well as unknown in other advanced societies' (Wacquant, 1994, p. 233). At the same time, however, he rejects the argument that the urban ghettos of today are merely a continuation of the 'same old story' of the exclusion of African-Americans from the mainstream of American society. He points to two substantive differences between the situation in the 1950s and the 1990s, namely:

- first, the inner city urban ghettos of the 1990s have become spatially split from the working class and middle class suburbs that surround them;
- second, these inner city areas are experiencing accelerating physical degradation, economic exclusion and increasing levels of physical violence. (Ibid., pp. 237–8)

This process of the collapse of social and economic institutions within the inner city localities and the increasing degree of separation between these areas and the rest of American society has been commented upon by other researchers who have studied the period since the reforms of the 1960s. But Wacquant's account of what he terms the 'hyperghettos' of the 1990s serves to highlight the complex web of economic, racial and political processes that have shaped the processes of marginalisation and exclusion that confront the poorest sections of American blacks, even at a time when political institutions are publicly committed to tackling the root causes of racial inequality and discrimination.

The situation in the United States is to some extent unique among advanced industrial societies. But this is not to say that some of the trends that have emerged so markedly in the United States in the period since the 1980s have not been replicated to some extent in other societies. Some of the features of these processes can be seen at work if we look at the changing patterns of jobs occupied by black workers in Britain in the period since the 1950s. Migrants to Britain of the 1950s and 1960s came to find work primarily in those sectors experiencing labour shortages. Workers from the Caribbean, India and Pakistan were recruited for employment in foundries in the Midlands, textile mills in the North, transport industries in major cities, and the health service. In common with migrant workers across Europe, these workers experienced a high degree of exploitation, discrimination and marginalisation in their economic and social lives. Despite the need for their labour, their presence aroused widespread hostility at all levels, from trade union branch to government level. Employers only reluctantly recruited immigrants where there were no white workers to fill the jobs; white workers, through their unions, often made arrangements with employers about the sorts of work immigrants could have access to (Duffield, 1988). At this time the preference for white workers was perceived to be quite natural and legitimate – immigrant workers were seen as 'an inferior but necessary labour supply' (Brown, 1992, p. 48).

Over time these workers remained in a relatively restricted spectrum of occupational areas, overrepresented in low-paid and insecure jobs, working anti-social hours in unhealthy or dangerous environments. Although by the 1970s African-Caribbean and Asian people worked in a broader range of occupations than before, these were still jobs that were 'deemed fit' for ethnic minority workers rather than white workers (Brown, 1992, p. 52). In 1984, the Policy Studies Institute published a major survey on the state of black people in Britain, covering housing, education and employment, showing that black people are still generally employed below their qualification and skill level, earn less than white workers in comparable job levels, and are still concentrated in the same industries as they were 25 years earlier (Brown, 1984).

On top of this, black people have a higher unemployment rate, which increases faster than that of the white population. Particularly badly hit are ethnic minority young people, or the second generation descendants of migrants. A 1986 review of the statistical evidence reported:

> While employment prospects are discouraging for all young
> people, the evidence ... shows that black youth unemploy-
> ment has reached astronomical proportions in some areas. The
> differential unemployment rates between blacks and whites are
> in fact generally greater for this age group than for any other.
> When account is taken of the fact that black people are far
> more likely to go into further education than whites, we can
> see that young black people in the 1980s are facing a desperate
> situation. (Newnham, 1986, p. 17)

In a context of rapid economic restructuring in those industrial
sectors in which black workers were particularly concentrated in
the period from the 1950s to the 1970s, these trends are in fact
likely to create further problems and pressures over the coming
period.

The picture emerging from research in both Britain and the
United States is that there has been a hardening of racial and
ethnic cleavages among lower class groups. This is borne out by
the evidence of racial disadvantage in the major urban conurba-
tions and by what some have defined as the 'racialisation of
poverty'. But at the same time we have seen a noticeable growth
of a black professional middle class and of ethnic minority small
businesses with an impact at all levels of society (Farley and Allen,
1989; Daye, 1994; Small, 1994). This has led to much greater
emphasis in recent studies on the role of economic and social
processes which have helped to transform the class position of
sections of minority communities.

This perhaps explains why one of the most important features
of recent policy debates about race in the USA, and to some
extent Britain and other European societies, has been the question of the *underclass*. References in public debate and the media
to the underclass have become so commonplace that 'the
concept, has virtually become a household term within the past
five years alone' (Heisler, 1991, p. 455). The concept, first used
by Myrdal (1962), has come to signify a segment of people at the
bottom of or beneath the class structure, permanently removed
from the labour market, with no power or stake in the economic
system. More specifically, in the USA the term has come to represent the black urban poor. It is also clear that there are rather
distinct usages of the notion, ranging from the attempts by

William Julius Wilson to give it a strong empirical basis to the efforts of neo-Conservatives such as Charles Murray to use it as a general catch-all term in their critique of the welfare state and affirmative action programmes.

While the debate on the underclass in the United States has a particular history which may not easily be reproduced in the European context, it is perhaps of some significance that such notions are also beginning to be used in the European context in order to describe the position of migrant communities. In particular this has been stimulated by recent economic and social developments in Europe: economic stagnation and recession, deindustrialisation, high unemployment, welfare state contraction and new ethnically and racially distinct migrant populations. Contemporary debates in Europe about changing patterns of social exclusion have highlighted the linkages between new forms of poverty and the position of migrant workers and their communities. Recent research about Germany has stressed the severe impact of deindustrialisation and labour market restructuring on the economic and social position of Turkish and other groups of migrant workers. It has also pointed to the relevance of the underclass thesis to the analysis of the class position of migrant workers more generally.

In Britain, there is also a growing interest in the question of the underclass, although it is clear that the concept is by no means as deeply racialised as in the United States (Rex, 1988; Smith, 1992). Some of this interest can be seen as the result of attempts to introduce the arguments of Charles Murray and other neo-Conservatives into the British situation, largely inspired by right-wing think tanks such as the Institute of Economic Affairs and the Centre for Policy Studies. But there has also been a much broader debate about the underclass within both academic and popular discourses. This has been stimulated partly by fears that the situation in Britain's 'inner cities' may be moving closer to the one that is prevalent in the United States. It is also the outcome of a concern that processes of racial exclusion are helping to create a situation where some sections of black communities feel socially and culturally excluded from the mainstream of British society.

It is of some interest to note, however, that this move towards more detailed accounts of social differentiation within minority communities has not resulted in more detailed accounts of the role of the position of black and minority women. We have seen, as we noted in Chapter 1, a noticeable growth in black feminist writings on questions about race and ethnicity, although this has not necessarily resulted in detailed empirical studies of the position of black women in the labour market or other important social arenas. What little research has been done has pointed to the fact that gender is an important factor in shaping forms of racial inequality, and some of the most innovative research in this field has focused specifically on the position of black and minority women in relation to employment, education welfare provision and related social policy issues. There is a clear need, however, for more empirically but theoretically informed research on the interplay between race and gender in structuring contemporary racial relations.

Some of the most important studies in this field have focused specifically on the position of black and minority women in the United States. In more recent years, however, we have seen the emergence of a rich and rapidly growing literature on the situation in other societies, including Britain, other European countries and South Africa. What is clear from this research is that gender is a crucial variable in determining the life chances of racialised minorities in relation to education, employment, income and related issues. It is also evident that there are quite marked differences within and between racial and ethnic groups in relation to the role that gender plays both in structuring social relations and in influencing forms of political and community mobilisation.

Racism, integration and the liberal agenda

The development of public policy responses to racial inequality has been another important area of analysis. Ever since the 1960s there has been an ongoing debate about both the form and substance of policy initiatives to tackle racial discrimination and inequalities which have been shaped by the effects of historical patterns of racism and domination. This debate has been particularly vibrant in the United States and Britain, which have witnessed successive waves of policy initiatives to deal with various aspects of racialised inequalities. Although there has been no clear outcome from this long-running debate, it has at least helped to make clear some of the dilemmas which have to be confronted in trying to formulate policies and programmes which aim to tackle the root causes of racial inequalities. It has also helped to foreground the intrinsically politically controversial nature of policies in this field and the fact that there is little likelihood that there will be universal agreement about what kinds of policies need to be developed. Such controversy is not surprising, given the politically sensitive nature of all policies concerned with racial issues. After all as one commentator has noted 'race is the most fundamental cleavage in American history' (Orfield, 1988, p. 313).

As argued above, a number of commentators have pointed to the limitations of race relations legislation and other initiatives. This raises a number of questions. First, what kind of policies could tackle discrimination more effectively? Second, what links could be made between policies on immigration and policies on social and economic issues? What kind of positive social policy agenda can be developed to deal with the position of both established communities and new migrants in the 1990s and beyond? There are no easy answers to these questions and the experience of the past two decades indicates that any set of policies will by no means achieve unanimous support in society as a whole. But perhaps a starting point for future policy agendas is the recognition that there is a need for a coordinated public policy to deal with various social, political and cultural aspects of the position of black and ethnic minorities in British society. In the past policy initiatives have been at best *ad hoc* and piecemeal. This is partly because although public policy has been committed for some time to the pursuit of equal opportunity and multiculturalism, there is no clear political and social consensus in British society about what this means, either ideologically or in practice. There is little agreement, for example, about what public policies need to be developed to deal with discrimination in such areas as education, social policy and employment. Additionally, as recent debates about anti-racism seem to indicate, there is also a denial that racial inequality is an integral feature of British society or that racism is an important issue.

Whatever the merits of such arguments it seems clear that there is still much confusion about the objectives of public policy.

Because of the *ad hoc* nature of policy development in this field it is difficult to talk of coherent strategies to deal with the changing economic and social dynamics which we face today. Perhaps more fundamentally, there is also confusion about the links between:

- anti-discrimination legislation and its role is creating greater opportunities and providing remedies for ethnic minorities and new migrants;
- multicultural and anti-racist initiatives which address the situation in areas such as employment, education, social services and housing;
- national policies and local initiatives developed by local authorities and community groups in response to specific issues.

This lack of coordination needs to be overcome if the oft-repeated call for more effective policies in this field is going to become reality. The process of change is not likely to be easy. The very plurality of categories used in current debates would seem to indicate that the objectives pursued are by no means clear and are in fact essentially contested notions. In particular, researchers and practitioners do not concur on what they mean by such terms as equality of opportunity and racial equality or what they consider as evidence of a move towards the stated goals of policies. Some argue that the development of equal opportunity policies is the outcome of a process of political negotiation, pressure group politics and bureaucratic policy-making. Others, however, emphasise the need to look beyond the stated objectives and public political negotiations and explore the ways in which deeply entrenched processes of discrimination may be resistant to legal and political interventions, while inegalitarian social relations structure society as a whole.

There has been much heated debate about these questions, and in the process a host of new conceptual issues have entered into the discussion. At the present time one can delineate at least four quite distinct themes in recent debates about this issue:

1. The first theme is to be found in the criticisms of researchers who have studied the workings of anti-discrimination policies and have found that there is a major gap between the stated

objectives of such policies and their achievements in practice (McCrudden *et al.*, 1991; Brown, 1992).

2. The second theme is to be found in the work of writers such as William Julius Wilson who argue that, particularly in the period since 1970, industrial and geographic changes in the economy have had a major impact on urban blacks in the United States, and that the anti-discrimination and affirmative action programmes of the 1960s are not able to deal with these changes, leading to the creation and reproduction of the social dislocations characteristic of the ghetto underclass (Wilson, 1987, 1991).

3. The third theme is to be found most clearly in the work of new right and neo-Conservative commentators who argue that what is wrong with blacks now is *not* the result of discrimination or segregation, past or present, but of excessive welfare programmes that have destroyed their incentive to be productive (Murray, 1984).

4. The final theme is to be found in the writings of liberal critics of affirmative action programmes, such as Nathan Glazer and Christopher Jencks, who argue that positive discrimination in favour of blacks can encourage a white backlash and also perpetuate racist attitudes of a kind (Glazer, 1988; Jencks, 1992).

These perspectives have helped to shape policy and political debates during the past two decades, particularly in the United States and Britain. They have also done much to question the usefulness of existing legislation in this field and to suggest that there is a need for a fundamental rethinking of the role of public policies concerned with racial inequality.

The work of Wilson is particularly important in this context because in one way or another it has helped to influence both the academic and the social policy agenda in this field, both in the United States and Europe. Wilson, among others, has highlighted the centrality of social class inequalities in shaping the life chances of African Americans (Wilson, 1987, 1991). But Wilson's work goes further than this theme, in the sense that he seeks to challenge a number of the certainties and assumptions which have guided both academic and political discourses about (i) the role of class in structuring the position of minority communities and (ii) the importance of race-specific policies aimed at tackling the causes and consequences of racial discrimination and inequality. Wilson's work is therefore of some importance in trying to think about the implications of recent socio-economic transformations on the position of African–American workers and other minority groups in American society (see also Boston, 1988; Wacquant, 1994).

Equally influential are the critiques of racial equality policies which have been articulated by new right and neo-Conservative writers. In the United States this is a perspective which has been around for some time, and is represented by neo-Conservative black commentators such as Thomas Sowell and Walter Williams and critics of welfare such as Charles Murray (Omi and Winant, 1994). Although it would be misleading to see all these writers as expressing one unified critique, it is also clear that they symbolise a much broader attempt by new right thinkers to question both the efficacy and the efficiency of using public policy as a tool for achieving equality for racialised minorities. At the heart of these criticisms of the role of public policy dealing with racial inequalities lies a pessimistic and negative evaluation of the role of state interventions which aim to use anti-discrimination initiatives as a means of ensuring greater equity and justice.

Despite this intense debate, however, there has been surprisingly little detailed analysis of the workings of public policy concerned with racial inequality, and we still know relatively little about the workings of the race relations legislation and related social policies. Such research as has been carried out has helped to shed some light on the workings of public policy in this field, particularly in relation to the labour market. But there is also a clear need for more detailed analysis of the everyday workings of specific policies and programmes in order to resolve some of the questions raised by the critical perspectives that we have outlined above.

Racial inequalities and social change

As we have tried to show in this chapter, racial inequalities are produced and reproduced by a variety of social, economic and political processes. They are also subject to constant change and are by no means fixed over time and place. Whether one looks at employment, housing or other specific institutional areas it is clear that racialised inequalities are reproduced and challenged at the same time. Within liberal democratic societies racialised inequalities are also the subject of political conflict and controversy. One clear outcome of these controversies is the development of anti-discrimination policies and initiatives in various national political contexts.

It is likely, whatever the limits of existing policies, that questions about racial inequality are likely to remain at the heart of the public policy agenda in a variety of countries. We have highlighted aspects of the situation in the United States and Britain in this chapter, but it is also clear that similar kinds of debates are likely to arise in many European countries in relation to the position of migrant workers and minority communities. Already there is much debate in Holland, France and the Scandinavian countries about the question of what measures are necessary to tackle the forms of discrimination suffered by racialised minority communities and migrant workers and refugees. Additionally there are ongoing discussions within the European Union about the need for common anti-discrimination initiatives and policies.

In practice, of course, as we have seen in recent years, there are quite different models of policy action in relation to racial inequality. Persistent public debate and controversy about the limits of affirmative action programmes in the United States provides evidence of the variety of policy agendas that are on offer. In recent years, aspects of these debates have begun to be reproduced in the British context, albeit in a different ideological and political climate. But what is beyond doubt is that we cannot take the boundaries of public policy debate about racial inequality as fixed and given. Rather they are the subject of constant debate and conflict over both what kind of legislation is necessary and how it should be implemented.

As a result we are faced with a situation where the institutionalisation of anti-discrimination policies and practices still has a long way to go. What is also clear, however, as we look towards the future is that the processes which help to structure racialised inequalities are by no means static. In the present economic and social climate racialised inequalities are being constantly transformed. A case in point is the relationship between the spatial restructuring of industries and jobs in both Europe and the United States and its impact on employment opportunities for minorities. As recent debates on the so-called underclass have suggested, such patterns of restructuring may end up having a major impact on those sections of racial and ethnic minorities which are most vulnerable and least likely to be able to benefit from equal opportunity policies. Yet we still know relatively little about the complex ways in which such processes have an impact on social and economic conditions within particular communities and localities.

Part of the problem with many existing accounts of this issue is that the analysis of racial inequalities has tended to start from either an overtly deterministic perspective or at the other extreme in isolation from other social relations. This has tended to produce rather static accounts of the interrelationship between racial inequalities and racism. Such accounts tend to say little that can help us to understand the transformation of social, cultural and political relations in contemporary Britain and other societies. What, for example, are the processes which have helped to produce a new politics of race and ethnicity? What impact have these political mobilisations, in turn, had on the articulation of new political discourses about race at both local and national levels? Questions such as these need to be addressed directly if we are to achieve a clearer understanding of the dynamics of racial inequality and social change in the present environment.

4 Racism, Class and Political Action

In many advanced industrial societies one aspect of contemporary race and ethnic relations has attracted an inordinate amount of attention in recent years, namely, the racialisation of political life that is evident in both national and local political environments. This in itself is not a surprising trend. It could be argued after all that the interface between political and social relations is perhaps the key area we have to address if we are to understand the underlying reasons for the resurgence of political racism and the possibilities of social and political mobilisations against racism. But what is surprising is the extent to which political institutions, including political parties and representative institutions, have recently become preoccupied with questions about race and immigration in quite diverse national political situations. In this chapter, therefore, we want to focus our attention on two key questions: first, why has political life become inextricably racialised of late? Second, what is the likely impact of this process on the morphology of race and racism in advanced industrial societies in the future?

Given the extent of ferment over questions of race and immigration in recent years, one may expect that a sizeable body of research would have addressed such important issues. As yet, however, very little research has addressed these issues in a direct manner, although it is widely recognised that political relations have played and continue to play a central role in the production and reproduction of racial relations in contemporary societies. There are few studies, for instance, on the dynamics of racialised politics. Despite widespread public debate about the politics of race and ethnicity a number of key questions remain to be answered; for example, how can we explain why people respond to the ideas and values of racist movements and political parties? What impact have ideas about race and racist movements had on political action and mobilisation? What kinds of political mobilisation have emerged from within black and minority communities? What kinds of political alliances are necessary in order to tackle racism as a political movement?

The experience of the past decade has tended to heighten interest in the study of how and why questions about race, ethnicity and immigration have become such a key concern of political institutions and activists in a wide variety of nation states. It is also clear that governments of all political hues have become aware of the potentially explosive nature of racialised politics within the context of liberal democratic societies. For these reasons alone the interrelationship between racism, political action and forms of participation in political parties and other institutions is an issue of intense political debate at the present time. In addition, the past decade has witnessed a number of other processes that have in one way or another helped to politicise questions about race and ethnicity on a scale which many societies have not witnessed before. This is partly the result of the emergence of new racist social movements, along with the resurgence of neo-fascist political parties in some societies. Over the past decade this has been most evident in various parts of Western Europe, especially since the major transformations of 1989 in Eastern Europe and the component parts of the ex-Soviet Union. Yet in other societies it is becoming an important issue because of new and strident forms of political mobilisation that have emerged within minority communities themselves. Such mobilisations have become more evident in recent years as these communities have begun to lay claim to more extensive social and political rights, and therefore to challenge the existing boundaries of their inclusion/exclusion from the dominant political institutions. It has also become clear recently that a wide variety of nationalist, religious and ethnically based movements have sought to mobilise minority communities in order to achieve political influence and support.

It is precisely to these trends and developments that we want to turn to in this chapter. First, we explore the conceptual dilemmas we face when we examine the interface between race, politics and social relations. Second, we look at the role of racist parties and movements in the racialisation of political life. Third, we take up the question between racialised politics and class-based forms of political mobilisation. Fourth, we analyse the development of forms of political mobilisation from within racialised minority communities. Finally, we take up the issue of the changing political discourses about race that have emerged in recent years within popular and official political cultures.

Race, politics and society

The use of racial and ethnic symbols in political debate and conflict is an inescapable aspect of the situation we face in many parts of the world today. Whether at the level of media representations or in the mainstream political institutions questions about the politics of race and ethnicity have come to the fore. In a number of European societies it can be said that questions about race and immigration are at the heart of contemporary political debates and conflicts. From a rather different historical background the same can be said of the United States, where the issue of race is perhaps the key social and political dilemma in a variety of policy arenas, including employment, housing and social welfare. Whatever the reasons for the politicisation of race, it is now clear that one cannot ignore the centrality of the political sphere in contemporary debates about racial issues.

In recent years, a key dimension of political debates about race has been the noticeable growth in the activities of organisations and movements which espouse racist political programmes and which therefore seek to use racialised symbols as a basis for political mobilisations. It is true that in most cases such movements remain relatively small and it is overstating their influence to compare them, as is sometimes done, to the Nazi Party in Germany during the early 1930s. But it remains the case that over the past decade we have seen a resurgence of support for racist movements in a variety of national contexts, accompanied in many cases by a noticeable rise in levels of racial violence and attacks against minorities. Moreover, it is also the case that despite their relatively small size most of the extreme racist movements have been able to attract a considerable level of media coverage and have become a familiar part of the political scene in countries across Europe and elsewhere.

What has also become increasingly clear is that minority communities are far from powerless in a political sense. Rather they have been very actively involved in mobilising themselves politically in order to improve their social and economic position and to defend their interests as a whole. Questions concerning whether and how ethnically and racially defined groups should be recognised in politics are among the most salient and vexing on the political agenda of many societies today. What Charles Taylor has called the 'politics of recognition' has become a key concern on the political agenda of countries as diverse as the United States, Canada, Australia and Britain. We have seen the emergence in recent years of a variety of social and political organisations within minority communities, along with growing involvement in more established political institutions. Such political mobilisations may take very different forms in practice, but they are all crucially concerned with the affirmation of the social and political rights of minorities.

Yet it is also the case that the racialisation of contemporary political discourses and institutions has proceeded at a number of levels, quite apart from the two mentioned above. Evidence for this can be seen at all levels of political systems. Thus in Britain there have been major transformations of late in the role that racial minorities play in the political system, and in the representation of minority politicians in Parliament, local government and other institutions. This has resulted from a number of intertwined processes over the past two decades, involving transformations in the main political parties as well as important changes in the forms of political involvement prevalent among minority communities. We have analysed key aspects of these processes in a recent study of the changing terms of racialised politics in contemporary British society at both a national and a local level (Solomos, 1993; Solomos and Back, 1995). There is no need to retrace all the arguments developed there. Suffice it to say that we emphasise the need to (i) develop a model of minority involvements in the political system that is not static but action oriented and (ii) that allows for the possibility of complex and often contradictory responses to minority mobilisations within the mainstream political institutions. In emphasising these two points we

have argued for the need to move away from idealised and abstract formulations of minority politics and develop grounded accounts of the everyday mobilisations and conflicts that shape the
meanings attached to race issues within political processes and
institutions.

At the same time, we have seen the articulation of new forms
of racialised discourses in both popular and official political language. These discourses have emerged partly as a response to the
new forms of mobilisation among minorities and the shifting
terrain of public debate about issues such as immigration, urban
unrest, the inner cities and related issues. They are also the
product of developments within elite discourses about race that
have emerged from the ways in which issues about race and immigration are conceptualised within and outside the political
system.

Part of the problem we face in exploring this issue is that the
question of how to conceptualise the interplay between race and
political action is not purely an academic matter. Theorisations of
race and politics are inextricably linked to wider social and political transformations. In the United States, for example, the up-
heavals of the 1960s resulted in a wealth of research about
minority politics and the changing face of electoral politics. In
the British context, it is perhaps not surprising that we have seen
a growing interest in this question in recent years, at the same
time as we have seen important changes in forms of political mobilisation among minorities.

It is within this broader environment that theorising about
questions of race, ethnicity and politics has become a key concern
of social theorists in recent years. Whereas critical theorists in the
early 1980s were bemoaning the lack of analytical clarity about
what constituted the *politics of race* or what was meant by the
notion of *racism* in contemporary societies, today there is a wealth
of theoretical and conceptual work going on in this field. This
has taken various forms. First, there have been attempts to construct theoretical models for explaining the increasing role of *race*
as a symbol for political mobilisation, the role of racial ideologies
in national and local agendas and the impact of ideas about race
on the development of government policies and programmes.
This has led to the emergence of various schools of thought and
there have been many valuable research studies produced in

recent years. We shall be exploring some of the key approaches in the course of this chapter. Second, there has recently been a growing interest in the role that race and ethnicity play in the affirmation of a *politics of identity* in advanced industrial societies. Stimulated to some extent by the growing literature on the *condition of postmodernity*, a number of writers have sought to go beyond the limits of existing theories in this field and explore the complex ways in which identities articulated in terms of race and ethnicity are expressed in contemporary social relations.

This has led to important interventions from researchers working in the fields of cultural studies, literary theory, and political theory exploring the multiple political and social identities which are characteristic of multicultural societies today. Such accounts have done much to highlight the need break away from narrow and fixed notions of what we mean by 'politics' in contemporary societies, where the boundaries between the political and civil society are often very flexible and in a constant state of flux. They have also pinpointed the complex forms of political identity which have become a feature of multicultural societies.

Racism and political action

While the question of racism and political action cannot by any means be reduced to the activities of racist parties and movements, it is also evident that these organisations are an important and influential part of the morphology of contemporary racism. The history of racist ideas and movements has to some extent been covered in Chapter 2, where we attempted to situate some of the key changes in the usages of notions of race in particular historical situations. The history of the rise of Nazism in Germany during the 1920s and 1930s is perhaps the most clear illustration of the complex ways in which racist ideas could be mobilised within a broader ideology and used as a basis for mobilising political support. Certainly there is well-documented evidence of the ways in which the Nazis were able to manipulate and use anti-Semitism as a core theme in their political mobilisations throughout the period leading up to their seizure of power.

Rather than focus our attention on these processes, however, what we want to explore in this chapter are some of the more recent forms of racist political mobilisation and their influence on the political agenda. By focusing on these more recent trends and developments we hope to show that racist ideas and political movements are by no means fixed and unchanging. Rather racist political parties and movements, with the notable exception of those which model themselves on the Nazis, are always seeking to adapt and refashion their politics to new conditions. It is undoubtedly true, for example, that anti-Semitism remained an important theme in racist discourses after the Second World War, particularly in those movements that use neo-fascist political language and symbols. But at the same time other movements and parties have sought to construct and manipulate new political symbols in order to make themselves more viable political organisations in the present social and political environment. It is clear, for instance, that alongside the rhetoric of anti-Semitism a key theme in the political language of racist movements over the past few decades has been the attempt to use popular concerns about immigration and race as a means of attracting political support. This has led to the fashioning of political programmes which place questions about immigration and race at the forefront of their national and local political agendas.

The complex mixture of racial and nationalist symbols that is used by contemporary racist movements is evidenced in the experience of a number of European societies in recent years. The varied forms of racist political mobilisation in Britain in the period since the 1970s, in France since the 1980s and in post 1989 Germany are cases in point. In all these countries we have seen a variety of movements which have sought in one way or another to use questions about race and immigration in order to mobilise support for openly racist and anti-immigrant political platforms. Such movements have met with a mixed response and it would be an exaggeration to say that they have managed to dominate the political agenda (Miles, 1994). But it is clear from accounts of the situation in a wide range of national and local situations that they have managed to fashion some degree of influence on political language and on the policies pursued by governments of various hues. It is also clear that the activities of such organisations are an important factor in the massive growth of racist violence that has taken place across Europe in recent years. And in the case of the Front National in France they have shown that it is possible in the right circumstances for such movements to achieve a degree of electoral success.

In the British context racist movements have never managed to gain a mass political base. But organisations such as the National Front in the 1970s and more recently the British National Party have succeeded in mobilising some support in specific localities. They are also widely seen as involved in one way or another in various kinds of racial violence in many localities. The small-scale nature of racist movements in Britain at the present time is no guarantee that such groups will not be able to exploit debates over immigration for their own objectives. The continuing high levels of racial violence and the beginnings of neo-Nazi youth mobilisation provide worrying signs for the future (O'Hara, 1992, 1993).

Part of the problem in many of the current debates about racism is that we know relatively little about the longings and hopes which it arouses. Little research has been done on the workings of racist movements and ideas in specific spatial and time contexts, and thus we end up with rather monolithic theories of racism which tell us little about why it is that racist ideas exercise such a strong appeal and force in some contexts but not in others. We also know little about the composition of racist movements and the values and attitudes of their members and supporters. Such research as has been done has not addressed this dimension of racist politics and is, in addition, rather dated. Somewhat more recent research has been carried out in France, where there has been more of a concern to understand the social contexts within which racist movements manage to mobilise political support (Wieviorka, 1992).

Given this paucity of grounded research on racist movements and their supporters it is not surprising that a number of serious gaps in our understanding of contemporary racist political mobilisations remain. One important question, for example, is the issue of what factors motivate people to become either active members or supporters of racist movements. There is also the issue of what role active members of racist movements play in mobilising around specific social and political issues. It is also interesting to note that what research has been done about the values of supporters of racist movements indicates that (i) they have little trust in existing social and political institutions, (ii) they tend to be pessimistic and fearful of the urban environment and (iii) see themselves as threatened by 'immigrants' and 'foreigners' even when they have little or no contact with them.

This opposition to existing social and political relations is evident in the attempts by racist movements to reinvent the past and the future through myths of origin and destiny. As George Mosse has pointed out in his magisterial analysis of the history of racism in contemporary societies, part of the power of racism is the way in which it helps to explain specific social relations in a simple manner. He argues with reference to racial ideologies over the past two centuries: 'Racist myths not only explained the past and brought hope for the future, but through their emphasis on stereotypes rendered the abstract concrete' (Mosse, 1985a, p. 233). This process of rendering the abstract concrete is, of course, part of the work of all ideologies up to a point. But what is important in relation to the morphology of racial ideas is that intrinsically they involve a visual ideology in which particular categories of people are classified on the basis of stereotypes, and are attributed specific social and cultural characteristics. From the very earliest stages of modern racial thinking men and women were clasified in terms of 'physical types'. The tendency to visualise the 'other' as both different and inferior depended on the visual images which lay at the heart of racial reasoning.

In a very real sense the upsurge in racist political mobilisation in the current conjuncture is not simply some return to the racist politics of the Nazis. Rather it is important to situate contemporary racism within our present day social, economic and cultural institutions. Michel Wieviorka, writing about the situation in France, sees the development of social movements which articulate openly xenophobic political arguments, and engage in direct action against migrants and refugees, as but one example of a much wider process that is evident in a number of societies. He argues that the growth of such movements is (i) partly explained by the decline of the traditional working–class movement, a key social actor, and (ii) the transformation of class relations more generally in advanced capitalist societies as a result of economic and social change (Wieviorka, 1993). How these changes are experienced is, of course, determined partly by economic and social relations in particular regions and localities. More importantly, from the perspective of writers such as Wieviorka the rise of new racist movements is influenced to a large extent by the decline of traditional working-class culture and the institutions that it helped to engender.

Studies of the situation in other European societies have highlighted similar trends. This is particularly the case in Germany, where the social and economic costs of reunification provide the immediate backdrop against which the resurgence of racist and nationalist movements is often seen. No doubt there are other factors which have led to the resurgence of racism as a political force in Germany, related both to local and national processes. But the German experience since 1989 has helped to show that even if one eschews an overtly deterministic analysis of racism, it is important to bear in mind the role of social and economic changes in shaping current debates about race and ethnicity. Certainly these changes have helped to shape some important aspects of political discourses about 'immigration' and 'racism' and have thus shaped both policy and popular responses to these issues. This is not to say that the conditions which have encouraged the growth of racist movements will somehow disappear once the socio-economic environment improves, but it does highlight the linkages between racist political mobilisation and processes of social and economic change.

Racism, class and exclusion

The above points take us back to one of the recurring themes in the sociology of race relations, namely the relationship between social class and forms of racialised political mobilisation. This issue has been much discussed, as we have seen already in previous chapters, in debates about the origins of both contemporary and historical forms of racism. It is clearly of some relevance in the context of attempts to make sense of the changing social context of political mobilisations around notions of race and ethnicity. This is why we want to return to some of the issues raised by this question in the rest of this chapter.

As we have argued in Chapter 1, this concern with the interface between race and class partly arises because the question of the class basis of political action is a frequently recurrent theme within political writing that can be referred to as falling broadly within Marxist and radical thinking. Though there are clear differences of approach about what is meant by 'class analysis', the relationship between class formation and racial formation has been an important concern of Marxist writers working on these issues. But it is also clear that this preoccupation with the relationship between race and class is also the outcome of the ways in which migrant and ethnic minority communities have been integrated into particular positions within the class relations characteristic of receiving societies.

We can exemplify some of the processes we have discussed above by looking more explicitly at an issue which has been at the heart of some recent debates, namely the role of what is called *working-class racism*. Miles and Phizacklea's classic study of this issue is indicative of a broader trend when they argue that although black and white workers share significant political commonalities within specific class locations, this does not mean that racism is not an important factor within working-class communities. On the contrary, they argue that it is specifically within the context of changing class and economic relationships that the growth of working-class racism can be understood. Within this framework the political usages of *race* as a mechanism for political mobilisation only make sense within an analysis of the class and ideological relations that shape the meaning of notions of *race* in specific societies. Thus working-class racism cannot be reduced to individuals or society. Racial views in the inner city are part of the daily pattern of everyday life.

It is also clear from the research of Michel Wieviorka among others that the emergence of the Front National as a significant political force over the past decade or so is also linked to the changing morphology of class-based politics in French society and the social dislocations in urban localities. Interestingly enough many of its supporters do not necessarily live among immigrant communities but near them and they generally have negative images of the social makeup of 'immigrant areas'.

Writing from a neo-Marxist perspective, writers such as Miles have sought in one way or another to contextualise the relationship between racism and class relations:

> By seeking to contextualise the impact of racism within class relations, one can begin to contextualise the specificity of the

experience of racism, not in order to deny it, but rather in order to highlight and generalise it by means of demonstrating its linkages with other means of exclusion. (Miles, 1989, p. 134)

Miles's work represents perhaps the most consistent attempt to develop a class analysis of racialised politics. For Miles the idea of *race* refers to a human construct, an ideology with regulatory power within society: 'The influence of racism and exclusionary practices is always a component of a wider structure of class disadvantage and exclusion' (ibid., p. 9) Within this framework race constitutes an idea that should be seen as having no autonomous social impact on its own. While Miles would agree that the struggle against racism is a vital political issue confronting contemporary societies, he argues that *race* in itself is not a scientifically valid medium for political action. Thus the forms of class consciousness which are legitimate for Miles must ultimately be seen in terms of wider social and class relations.

For Miles processes of racialisation are intertwined with the material conditions of migrant workers and other racialised groups. Its effects are the result of the contradiction between 'on the one hand the need of the capitalist world economy for the mobility of human beings, and on the other, the drawing of territorial boundaries and the construction of citizenship as a legal category which sets boundaries for human mobility' (Miles, 1988, p. 438). Within the British setting this ideological work is conducted primarily by the state and acts as a means of crisis management (Hall *et al.*, 1978; CCCS, 1982; Miles and Phizacklea, 1984). From this perspective Miles argues that the construction of political identities which utilise 'racial' consciousness play no part in development of a 'progressive politics'. In this sense he views black political movements as ultimately operating on false premises, and he disputes the analytic value of talking about the politics of race.

Miles's work has been a major influence in contemporary debates about race and racism, and the limits of political strategies based on *race*. But it says surprisingly little about the issue of how he can explain the development of political action and mobilisation within migrant communities which is based on ideas about racial and ethnic identity. A key argument that could be derived from his analysis is that black and minority politics are really dis-tillations of class conflict. If this is true any movement away from class-based political action (i.e. movements towards black com-munity politics) is doomed to failure (Miles, 1988; Miles, 1989). If one takes this argument further, class-based political action is ultimately in opposition to any sort of sustained political organisa-tion around a notion of *race*. This is largely because for Miles the *politics of race* is narrowly confined to the struggle against racism.

Another major influence in recent debates about the politics of race can be traced to the work of authors who have at one time or another been associated with the Birmingham Centre for Contemporary Cultural Studies (CCCS). This research was stimulated in many ways by the publication of Hall's program-matic essay on 'Race, Articulation and Societies Structured in Dominance' (1980). Hall's most important argument was that while racism cannot be reduced to other social relations, it cannot be explained autonomously from them. Thus racism commands a relative autonomy from economic, political and other social rela-tions. Taking as their theoretical starting point Hall's rather ab-stract and programmatic argument, a number of attempts were made by writers associated at one time or another with the CCCS to retheorise the significance or nature or racism within British society (CCCS, 1982; Gilroy, 1987; Solomos, 1993). The works of these writers explored the changing political dynamics of race in the environment of the 1980s, by focusing on the emergence and impact of new discourses and political agendas about race.

While Hall essentially initiated a reconceptualisation of race within Marxist theory at CCCS, this position achieved a more developed expression in the work of the Race and Politics Group, resulting in the publication of *The Empire Strikes Back* (CCCS, 1982). This volume initiated a fierce controversy when it was first published and it still occupies a controversial position in the history of studies of race in British society. It sought to use Hall's theoretical insights to analyse race and politics in British society, but it can be seen as differing from his work in two significant ways. First, it placed a greater emphasis on the role of authoritarian state racism, especially in managing a British social formation that was undergoing a period of crisis. Second, the degree of autonomy given race from class—social relations was reworked (Gilroy, 1982; Solomos *et al.*, 1982). It is this second development which is most significant with regard to the study of political action and social change. It is also the key area where the approach of these writers can be seen as differing from the analytic framework about the relationship between race and class proposed by Miles among others.

A key theme of *The Empire Strikes Back* is that the working class in Britain does not constitute a continuous historical subject; and that black communities can constitute themselves as a politically conscious, 'racially demarcated class fraction'. It is in this sense that class cannot always be assumed to be the primary political force in any specific conjuncture. Thus black communities can act as autonomous political forces in specific situations where their interests are threatened or attacked.

In recent years this kind of approach to the analysis of the role of racial politics has become more influential. Significant analytical frameworks which foreground a political analysis of race are to be found in the work of British writers such as Paul Gilroy and Michel Keith and American writers such as Michael Omi, Howard Winant and David Goldberg. Although all of these writers can be seen as starting out from within a neo–Marxist or post–Marxist analytic framework, their works also engage with other approaches emanating from post-structuralism and postmodernism. Without wanting to ignore the obvious differences between these writers, it can fairly be said that their work reflects (i) an uneasiness with the limits of the Marxist model represented by Miles and other researchers and (ii) a concern to investigate the mechanisms through which *race* is constructed through social, cultural and ideological processes.

Gilroy has developed this line of analysis further in *There Ain't No Black in the Union Jack*, where he moves more clearly towards a perspective which he calls *race formation* (Gilroy, 1987). Rejecting the various analytical arguments associated with a neo-Marxist analysis of race and class, Gilroy emphasises the need to conceive of race as the key aspect of the black experience in British society. In developing this argument he rejects any argument that prioritises class over race in the analysis of political change. He argues forcefully: 'The proletariat of yesterday, classically conceived or otherwise, now has rather more to lose than its chains. The real gains which it has made have been achieved at the cost of a deep-seated accommodation with capital and the political institutions of corporatism' (ibid., p. 246). Here there exists, perhaps surprisingly, a great deal of similarity between Gilroy's notion of the relationship between class and race and Rex's theoretical conclusions (Rex and Tomlinson, 1979; Rex, 1988). Both authors are arguing that the continuous historical project of working-class struggle has been fractured, leaving a number of classes or class/race fractions involved in specific struggles. Equally, Gilroy and Rex both emphasise that their formulations are models of social action. It is essential to both positions that the significance of race is located within the salience that this term of reference has developed in the world of political actors.

It is here that Gilroy utilises the concept of *race formation*, a notion he shares with the analysis of Omi and Winant (1994) in the United States. The notion of *race formation* emphasises above all that race is not simply a concept that can be dispensed with. Gilroy, for example, accepts that the meaning of race as a social construction is contested and fought over. In this sense he is suggesting something close to a Gramscian position on ideology whereby race is viewed as an open political construction where the political meaning of terms like 'black' are struggled over. He makes the case for the existence of an inclusive black community in which political identities are formulated that address numerous but linked everyday struggles against racism (Gilroy, 1987, p. 38). It is this political possession of race by actors that leads to a social movement located around notions of racial identity: 'Collective identities spoken through "race", community and locality are for all their spontaneity, powerful means to co-ordinate action and create solidarity' (ibid., p. 247). Gilroy, like a number of other authors working in this field, utilises the literature on social movements (Touraine, 1981; Castells, 1977, 1983; Melucci, 1989) to provide theoretical support for an interpretation of 'non class-motivated' political action. Gilroy argues that it is in this context that both black community politics in general and the black sections movement within the Labour Party take on a political meaning of their own outside specific class locations (Gilroy, 1993b).

Along with Gilroy a number of other researchers have sought to develop an analytical model to incorporate simultaneously a number of political engagements without necessarily having to

attempt to qualify these sites of struggle in terms of a class reductionism. Within this model of political action a multiplicity of
political identities can be held. For example, an inclusive notion
of black identity can prevail and at the same time allow heterogeneity of national and cultural origins within this constituency
(Hall, 1991a; Rattansi, 1992; Brah, 1993). Omi and Winant's
analysis of the United States provides a good example of this kind
of approach to the question of political mobilisation. Taking as
their starting point the changing politics of race in the period
since the 1960s, they argue for the need to see processes of *racial
formation* as the outcome of the unique social, cultural and political processes that have characterised the United States over the
past three decades (Omi and Winant, 1994). In this sense their
model of the United States experience ties up quite closely with a
key strand in the theoretical literature on the politics of racialised
mobilisation in Britain and other European societies.

Race, community and resistance

So far in this chapter we have mentioned political actions and
mobilisations by racialised social groups and communities but we
have not looked at them in any detail. Yet it is noticeable that
over the past four decades minority political mobilisations have
played an important role in both traditional and non-traditional
politics. Whether one looks at the situation in Britain, the United
States or other advanced industrial societies, there is clear evidence of the development of social movements and organisations
which take as their starting point the assertion of the rights of
racial minorities to equal treatment and justice, and make claims
for the empowerment of racially excluded groups.

   A key turning point in the formation of a politics of identity
around the question of race is the experience of mobilisations
around the Civil Rights Movement and later Black Power in the
United States (Van Deburg, 1992). The Civil Rights Movement
was a particularly powerful symbol of an attempt to create a political alliance of various groups in American society to challenge
the social and political marginalisation of African-Americans that
had become institutionalised in the period of the late nineteenth
and early twentieth centuries. Drawing together a variety of

political ideas and social and ethnic groups under the broad umbrella of a movement aimed at ensuring civil rights and equal access to political power, the Civil Rights Movement did much to shape debates about race and discrimination in American society during the period of the 1950s and 1960s.

In the period since the 1960s the historical legacy of the Civil Rights Movement and Black Power has cast a long shadow over the development of new forms of political mobilisation among minorities in advanced industrial societies. This is evident in the attempts to construct a new basis for an alliance such as the Civil Rights Movement and in the role that nationalist discourses have come to occupy within black communities over this time. The complex variety of political mobilisations emerging from within racialised minority communities has become even more evident in recent years. This is clear both in the context of mainstream political activity and at the level of community politics. In a wide variety of different national political environments there is evidence that new forms of minority political mobilisation have began to have at least some impact on electoral politics and on the structures of political parties. On the basis of our own recent research in Birmingham we have argued that increased levels of black political participation and representation within local and national politics have already done much to shape political discourses and to influence policy agendas (Solomos and Back, 1995).

It is also clear, however, that alongside this growing level of minority political involvement in mainstream politics there has been a noticeable growth in forms of black nationalism and ethnic absolutism within minority communities. There is a wealth of both historical and contemporary research which has shown that forms of nationalist political discourse have been an important and influential strand of thought within minority communities, certainly in the United States and South Africa (Gerhart, 1978; Moses, 1978). In this sense nationalist politics have been an important strand of black political opinion for most of this century (Martin, 1976, 1991; Hill, 1987). But in recent years nationalist political discourses within minority communities have taken on new forms. This is perhaps most evident in the United States, where there has recently been a noticeable flowering of nationalist politics and Afrocentric ideologies. It is also clear that the political impact of nationalist discourses goes way beyond the boundaries of Afrocentrism and Black Islam in the United States. Similar trends can also be seen at work among African–Caribbean and Asian communities in Britain, where there has of late been a noticeable growth of religious, nationalist and communalist movements which often have important transnational links (Bhatt, 1994a, 1994b). It has to be noted, of course, that such trends are not just limited to ethnic minorities. In recent years religion has also proved a key mobilising symbol for the neo-Conservative right in the United States and elsewhere.

Such contemporary political trends have a somewhat longer history in the context of black nationalist politics from the earlier part of this century. Marcus Garvey, for example, articulated a clear message about race consciousness and racial pride as a core theme of his movement to inspire people of African descent to think of themselves as a collective entity. Garvey's philosophy was based on the assumption that race and nation are the major forces moving world history and that ultimately a people need a state to express their racial identity.

The Black Power Movement in the United States during the 1960s did not simply follow the arguments of Garvey and earlier ideologues, it also articulated a racial notion of black identity. The political rhetoric of Black Power was concerned both with the powerlessness of African-Americans and with the condition of black people globally. In their classic statement of the ideology of *Black Power,* Stokely Carmichael and Charles Hamilton made it clear that they saw the first step in the development of a powerful political movement of African-Americans as the formation of a clear racial and political consciousness.

It is interesting to note here that some forms of black nationalist politics have been a vehicle not only for expressing ideas about black supremacy but have articulated quite traditional racist themes. The role of anti-Semitism within black nationalist and Muslim fundamentalist politics is a case in point. One of the political and analytical challenges of the present conjuncture is how to understand the processes whereby people who are the objects of racism in one setting can become the perpetrators in another. The similarities in the way Jewishness and blackness are constructed within racist cultures does not necessarily lead to mutual recognition or alliance. A good example of this can be found in the anti-Semitic sentiments expounded by British Muslims of the Hizb ut-Tahrir (Islamic Liberation Party) particularly in London and Manchester. Equally, in the United States the Ku-Klux-Klan has expressed support for the Nation of Islam leader Louis Farrakhan. In their journal *The Klansman* an editorial commented that unlike 'Jew controlled puppets like Martin Luther King' Farrakhan 'is well aware of the Jewish menace' (quoted in Institute of Jewish Affairs, 1994, p. 225).

Today, however, it has also become evident that two of the key areas around which sections of racialised minorities are likely to mobilise are culture and religion. To many this aspect of minority politics became an issue of public debate partly in the aftermath of the Rushdie Affair in the late 1980s, though it is clear that it was also the outcome of a complex set of social and cultural transformations that have been at work for some time. The debate about Rushdie was in practice concerned with a number of issues, of which religion was but one. But in the aftermath of Ayatollah Khomeini's *fatwa* it rapidly became apparent that the issue of political mobilisations by radical Islamic groups against Rushdie had become a key theme in political debates about race and ethnicity in countries as diverse as France, Britain and the Netherlands.

In the period since the Rushdie Affair the importance of religion and culture as a basis for political mobilisation among minority, and majority, communities has become even more evident.

Dynamics of racial formation

In many ways the account of race, class and political action in this chapter has hinged around the key argument that the relationship between racialisation and political agency is by no means static and unchanging. As we hope we have shown in the course of this account of various kinds of racialised mobilisations, political movements and ideologies, the dynamics of racial formation are contingent and shaped by the changing balance of political forces in specific historical conjunctures. Part of the dilemma we face, therefore, in thinking about the contemporary situation is how to make sense of the new forms of political mobilisation about and around the question of race and ethnicity. Since it is not possible to assume that political identities and struggles are determined in a simple way by social and economic processes (Castoriadis, 1991, 1993), it is vital that we develop adequate models for the analysis of those processes which produce specific understandings of race in terms of politics within a variety of social contexts. Such processes include a variety of social, cultural and psychological processes which help to give meaning to notions of race within particular societies.

The constantly changing nature of racist political mobilisations is evident in the emergence of new terms of political discourse about race. As we have noted already, the political language of racist movements and organisations cannot be reduced to the arguments associated with older forms of racist discourse. Contemporary racist political discourses are increasingly preoccupied with questions of culture and difference. Thus contemporary racisms are organised around the idea of asserting the right to cultural difference, and increasingly use code words and ethnic categories to describe racialised politics. In Germany, for example, the discourse of racism is closely tied up to the issue of immigration.

Indeed, perhaps the most important aspect of contemporary political discourses about race is that they have become increasingly ambivalent and complex. Whether one looks at local or national political discourses, it is quite clear that in recent years there has been a noticeable transformation of both political and policy debates about race and related issues within political institutions.

In the present environment of fundamental restructuring of economic, social and political relations racial symbols can take on specific forms within particular spatial and historical contexts. The wholesale reorganisation of regions, localities and nation states has, if anything, helped to strengthen mythological claims about the uniqueness of specific national cultures and the threats which they face from the other. It is not surprising in this overall environment that the quest for definite boundaries for 'race' and 'nation' coincides with fears about threats to national identity from within and without (Carter *et al.*, 1993; Keith and Pile, 1993). Such threats are part of the mythology of contemporary political discourse and serve to emphasise the power of imagined historical time in shaping racist political mobilisations.

It is also important to remember, however, that race and ethnicity are experienced and negotiated in specific spatial–historical contexts. It is difficult, therefore, to generalise that there is one common idea of race and ethnicity which characterises all societies or all localities and regions in a particular society. Rather, ideas about race and ethnicity have to be constructed and reconstructed in specific national political environments. David Goldberg encapsulates the importance of space and time in the formation of racial symbols when he argues:

> Race has fashioned and continues to mould personal and social identity, the bounds of who one is and can be, of where one chooses to be or is placed, what social and private spaces one can and dare not enter or penetrate. Race inscribes and circumscribes the experiences of space and time, of geography and history, just as race itself acquires its specificity in terms of space-time correlates. (Goldberg, 1993, p. 206)

From this perspective ideas about race and the meanings attached to it can enter particular social contexts in complex forms, and this makes it impossible to conceptualise discourses about race and identity as monolithic and unchangeable. Rather, we have to see such discourses as situated within particular social, cultural and political environments.

This line of analysis has also been pursued in his recent work by Paul Gilroy (1993a, 1993b). While the specific objects of Gilroy's analysis are somewhat different from our own concerns, ranging from the social history of the *Black Atlantic* to the changing morphologies of black cultures in contemporary Britain, his account of the dynamics of racialised ideas and languages has the merit of emphasising the flexible and constantly changing character of black political identities. Rather than assume that there are fixed and historically changing cultural and political meanings which can be derived from notions of race and ethnicity, he argues that we can only understand how meanings are actually constructed if we focus on specific socio-historical situations. Gilroy maintains forcefully that we have to see the modern history of race and racism as the product of the complex historical processes involving contact with and theorising about the 'other', which have been at work from the very beginning of modernity (Gilroy, 1993a, pp. 313–23).

What needs to be stressed even more emphatically, however, is that we have to be attentive to the spatial and contextual boundaries within which particular ideas about race and ethnicity develop and take on social meaning. When faced with the need to analyse how ideas about race are worked through in political discourses and in political mobilisation, it is clear that there are major analytical problems in applying such a conceptual framework to the analysis of racism as it appears within specific socio-historical situations. George Mosse's analysis of the history of European racism illustrates some of the problems in an instructive fashion. Mosse's work can be seen in its broadest terms as a historical narrative of the complex variety of processes of identity construction that have helped to shape racism over the past two centuries (Mosse, 1985a). Taking as his starting point the origins of racial thought from the eighteenth century onwards, he shows in a masterful survey of European societies that there has always been a linkage between racial ideas and politics with the wider social and economic transformations of modern industrial societies. For Mosse a key aspect of racist thought in the nineteenth and twentieth centuries was that it represented a reaction 'against social, economic, and political conditions' combined with a refusal 'to use these conditions to explain the world' (ibid., p. xxvii). Rather, racist thinkers sought to use ideas about race and nation to make sense of the changes and uncertainties brought about by socio-economic change, and to provide a basis for political mobilisation and action.

In a very real sense, therefore, the 'power' of racism as a mobilising force can best be understood in the context of social and economic transformation, and the political and ideological uncertainty about how to respond to the challenges posed by the formation of new patterns of social and economic organisation. If we take the example of racist social movements what seems clear from the experience of Western Europe in recent years is that they a have a variety of social and political bases. While they may share a certain common language and use similar cultural symbols, it does not seem to be the case that they cannot be seen as having the same kind of social base or to exercise the same degree of political influence. Given this broader framework it is not plausible to argue that their dynamics have not been influenced in one way or another by questions of space, time and place.

If anything it seems clear that the politics of racialised identity are likely to take ever more complex forms in the coming period. This is true for both majority and minority communities, depending on the wider social and political context. Perhaps the most vibrant forms of contemporary racial politics at the present time are those which articulate arguments which can be described under the broad heading of racial nationalism. But we should be aware that new forms of racialised politics are likely to arise in the future, and that we need to have a basis for understanding both how they come about and what their likely impact on social and political change is likely to be.

5 Racism and Anti-Racism

In previous chapters we have concentrated on the interface between racism and specific forms of social and political relations in contemporary societies. In doing so we have touched upon the issue of what is popularly called anti-racism, and the role of both public policies and popular mobilisations against racism. Additionally, we have discussed some aspects of public policies aimed at tackling various aspects of racial discrimination and racism within areas such as employment and housing. We have not, however, explored the issue of anti-racism in terms of what it is taken to mean and how it has helped to shape and structure contemporary debates about racism. Yet it is clear that this is a much discussed issue in contemporary debates in many societies. Partly because the term anti-racism is used in a variety of ways it is by no means clear what it means, either conceptually or at the level of practice. Nevertheless, it has come to occupy an important role in both theoretical debates and in public policy debates. In one way or another the question of what can be done to counter the influence of racist ideologies and political movements remains at the heart of contemporary concerns. Indeed it could be argued that one of the main features of the changing politics of race over the past two decades has been the rise of ideas and movements which project themselves as anti-racist (Gilroy, 1990b; Anthias and Yuval-Davis, 1992; Goldberg, 1993). Certainly for the political left and right the issue of anti-racism, as both an ideology and a specific set of policies, has proved to be an important point of reference in articulating their views about race and racism in the contemporary environment. Writers from both the left and right have sought to engage with the conceptual and policy dilemmas raised by the articulation of anti-racist strategies and programmes (Palmer, 1986; Cambridge and Feuchtwang,

1990). It is interesting to note that in the present political environment many of the most trenchant critiques of the political
rhetoric associated with anti-racism have come from the left
(Cohen, 1992; Rattansi, 1992).

In this situation there are a number of key questions that
remain to be addressed more fully. What is meant by the notion
of *anti-racism* in the present political environment? What strategies
are necessary in order to tackle the growth of racism from both
an ideological and political perspective? Are there competing understandings of anti-racism in different societies? These questions
are in a sense at the heart of all attempts to develop practical
policy initiatives and intellectual arguments against racism. But it
is evident from recent experience that responses to them take on
somewhat different forms in particular political contexts. It is also
clear that this is an issue on which there is little research, either
on historical trends or contemporary processes. It is largely as a
result of the lack of research that much of the public discussion
about anti-racism remains at the level of rhetoric and abstract
generalisations. Without a detailed analysis of the role of anti-
racism in contemporary societies, however, we shall not be able
to understand the changing dynamics of racial ideologies and
political mobilisations or the possibilities for defeating racist
movements (Cambridge and Feuchtwang, 1990).

It is to these sets of issues that we want to turn to in the course
of this chapter, by focusing on the relationship between racism
and anti-racism in contemporary societies. We shall begin by
looking at the changing terminology and political debates about
anti-racism. We then move on to look at the role of anti-racist
policies and movements in the context of the emergence of new
forms of racist political mobilisation in contemporary European
societies. Finally, we return to the thorny problem of what kinds
of strategies are necessary in order to tackle the types of racist
ideas and movements that have emerged in recent years.

Conceptualising anti-racism

The first and perhaps obvious point to make is that there is by
now a wealth of evidence from a number of countries that the
politics of anti-racism is both complex and constantly changing

(Cohen, 1992; Bhatt, 1994a; Rattansi and Westwood, 1994). At the same time, it is also evident that there is no shared notion of what is meant by notions such as 'multiculturalism' or 'multicultural society', either at the level of ideology or political practice (Ålund and Schierup, 1991; Goldberg, 1994). Indeed of all the issues in public debates about race and racism at the present time one of the most controversial is the question of what strategies are necessary in order to counter the influence of racism.

After all it seems self-evident that contemporary discourses about anti-racism and multiculturalism have helped to structure the terms of both official and popular views about race and racism in contemporary societies. Indeed, at the present time, it has become clear that the racialisation of social and political relations is shaped both by *racism* and by *anti-racism*. Within the political discourses of contemporary liberal democratic societies anti-racist discourses are perhaps a more important component of contemporary debates. In terms of official government policies at least there is a public commitment in most societies to the promotion of anti-racism and multiculturalism at all levels of political and social institutions. But what exactly is meant by general commitments of this kind in an environment where racist movements and ideas are increasingly part of public political debate and an important component of the political culture? What are the possibilities and limits of anti-racism as a political ideology and as a set of policy objectives? What kind of social change do anti-racists envisage and what kinds of discourses do they employ?

The controversial nature of anti-racism is quite clear at the present time, particularly since in both Britain and the United States it has become tied to broader controversies about 'political correctness' and multiculturalism. But this has not always been the case. As we pointed out earlier there is a long historical tradition of ideas and movements opposed to racism, colonialism and imperialism. The legacy of such movements can be seen at work today in the form of the rhetoric of anti-colonialism which is still commonly used in contemporary debates about race and ethnicity in various national contexts. But the high point of these movements was the period of the 1950s and 1960s, which was in many ways the high point of anti-colonial movements in many third world countries (Howe, 1993). It was also the period when opposition to imperialism and a rhetorical commitment to the 'national liberation' struggles of countries such as Vietnam became a key concern of the political left in many advanced industrial societies. The experience of this period has done much, both directly and indirectly, to shape contemporary perspectives and debates about racism, particularly in countries with a legacy of colonial domination and exploitation (Bhabha, 1994).

At a broader societal level the experience of Nazism and the holocaust provided an important point of reference for the articulation of anti-racist perspectives in the period after the Second World War (Montagu, 1964; Arendt, 1973). This can be seen clearly, for example, in the context of Germany where contemporary debates about racism are overshadowed by the historical reality of the Nazi period. It is noticeable that in the period since reunification the renewed activities of extreme nationalist and racist movements have given rise to an ongoing public debate about the dangers of a resurgence of racism and fascism in German society (Enzensberger, 1994; Miles, 1994). This has proved to be an important mobilising symbol for the anti-racist organisations which have sprang up to counter the activities of the extreme right, both at a rhetorical and a symbolic level.

What is interesting, however, is that despite this historical background anti-racist movements and ideas have tended to attract less attention than racism, but they cannot easily be ignored in the current socio-political environment. Part of the reason for this may be the result of a political preoccupation with the history of racism and the role of racist ideas and movements in contemporary societies. It is also the case that in much of the recent social science and popular literature on this issue there is what Miles has called 'a one-sided emphasis on racism and associated practices of exclusion in the absence of an analysis of resistance' (1994, p. 561). Whatever the reason for this relative absence of an analysis of the role and limits of anti-racism, it is clearly the case that any rounded account of the role of racism in contemporary societies needs to examine in some detail the complex web of issues that underlie contemporary debates about anti-racism.

Given the paucity of research on anti-racism it is perhaps not surprising that there is a noticeable lack of rigour in both academic and popular usages of the term. With a few notable exceptions there have been few attempts to untangle the rather

divergent meanings which the notion of anti-racism has come to
encompass in recent years, or to provide a clear analytic framework for analysing ideas and practices that are associated with it.
Moreover, in popular discourses the notion of anti-racism has
become entangled in wider political and academic controversies
that go far beyond the narrow issue of what can be done to coun-
teract the influence of racism in contemporary societies. This en-
tanglement has become all the more evident in the past decade,
particularly as a result of the media attention that has been given
to anti-racist policies and initiatives.

It has to be remembered, however, that the question of how to
confront racism, in both an intellectual and an organisational
sense, has been a concern for a much longer period. Despite the
ahistorical nature of much of the literature on racism it is important to remember that the question of how to oppose racism and
mobilise counter-movements and ideologies is not new. To take
just one example of many, the rise of Nazism in Germany during
the 1920s and 1930s was not a linear and uniform process.
Throughout the period leading up to the establishment of the
Nazi regime there was definite political opposition to fascism and
the racial and anti-Semitic ideas which it espoused (Mosse, 1966;
Adorno and Horkheimer, 1986; Pulzer, 1988; Sluga, 1993). The
rise of the Nazis in Germany and of fascism in other societies
during the 1920s and 1930s led to intense and heated debates
within and outside academia about how to deal with the racial
ideas and practices of these movements (Arendt, 1973;
Weindling, 1989; Burleigh and Wippermann, 1991; Sluga, 1993).

In the aftermath of the Second World War and the evidence of
the genocidal impact of the policies of the Nazis towards Jews,
Gypsies and other groups, international bodies such as the United
Nations attempted to develop common policies against racism
and to encourage a better understanding of the conditions which
helped or encouraged its growth. Such initiatives were modelled
on the principle that the 'lessons' of the Nazi period had to be
learnt by all nation-states in order to provide a basis for countering racist movements and ideologies in the future.

A more recent example is the response to the racial theories associated with the apartheid regime in South Africa in the period
before the recent reforms. Throughout the time from the 1950s
to the 1990s the attempt by the South African state to impose the

apartheid system and to institutionalise the 'separate development of racial groups' led to renewed international discussion about how to tackle both the ideological foundations and political practices of racism in the modern world. At one level the situation in South Africa was seen as a powerful symbol of the virulence of racism in the contemporary world, while at the same time it was conceptualised as a throwback to older forms of racist thinking and values.

The importance of situating anti-racism within the wider social and political climate is evident from the experience of a number of societies over the past two decades. In the British context, for example, the question of anti-racism came to the fore in the late 1970s and early 1980s, largely as a response to the growth of political support for the National Front and other extreme neo-fascist movements (Miles and Phizacklea, 1979; Cohen and Bains, 1988; Solomos, 1993). The emergence of the Anti-Nazi League, Rock Against Racism and other anti-racist organisations during the late 1970s was seen at the time as signalling a conscious attempt by sections of the left to (i) respond to the danger of a resurgence of neo-fascist ideas in political life, and (ii) as an attempt to use popular opposition to neo-fascist groups as a means of political mobilisation. These mobilisations took place at a time when political debates about race and immigration had reached a volatile stage in British political life generally and there was a shift in both official and popular debates about how to respond to the 'race problem'. In this sense the rise of anti-racist mobilisations can be seen as very much a product of a particular political climate which characterised the period of the late 1970s and early 1980s. The revival of the Anti-Nazi League in the early 1990s, and the formation of a competitor in the form of the Anti Racist Alliance, was similarly the product of (i) evidence of attempts by neo-fascist groups such as the British National Party to renew their activities, and (ii) the outbreak of racial attacks and violence against black minorities in many urban localities during this period.

In the wider context of the growth of racism in other European societies the question of anti-racism has been conceptualised from a somewhat broader perspective, focusing particularly on the role of anti-racist social movements and organisations as well as on the ideologies they articulate (Wrench and Solomos, 1993). But even this somewhat broader conceptualisation of anti-racism has led to widespread controversy, especially in France and Germany, about the relative failure of these movements to mobilise mass support and to ensure widespread controversy, especially in France and Germany, about the relative failure of these movements to mobilise mass support and to ensure the development of effective public policies against racism and discrimination.

In some contexts, however, it is clear that anti-racist ideas have played an important role in the development of policy agendas. Certainly in the British context, during the late 1980s, the notion of anti-racism became a symbol of wider debates about the role of policies initiated by radical left local authorities, trade unions and other organisations to promote the idea that they were committed to a positive programme to tackle racialised inequalities (Ball and Solomos, 1990). This meant that throughout this period a widespread campaign against 'anti-racist' policies and initiatives was evident in the popular press, which highlighted what they saw as the 'loony left' rhetoric associated with them. At the same time, elements of the new right chose to provide more academic critiques of the key arguments associated with what they constructed as the 'anti-racist lobby' in areas such as education and social welfare (Palmer, 1986). For a time the question of anti-racism became perhaps one of the key concerns of public debates about the politics of race and led to numerous local and national controversies (Mercer, 1994; Smith, 1994).

In the somewhat different intellectual and political climate of the United States, the issue of what measures can be taken against racism has become intimately linked with wider disputes about the politics of affirmative action and what Studs Terkel calls the 'American obsession' with race (Terkel, 1992). The wide-ranging controversy about the issue of who exactly has benefited from the past three decades of affirmative action programmes has led to quite divergent perspectives about the role of government policies in this field (Boston, 1988; Blauner, 1989; Brooks, 1990; Hacker, 1992; Omi and Winant, 1994; Roediger, 1994). At the same time, it is also clear that the issue of anti-racist politics has become entangled with the debates about *political correctness* and *multiculturalism*. A clear example of this can be found in the area of higher education where the role of measures to promote affirmative action and transform the curriculum to reflect the multicultural nature of American society has become deeply controversial over the past decade. The 'multicultural wars' raging throughout American higher education, and making some impact in Britain as well, reflect widely divergent views about the position of universities in contemporary societies and the impact of social programmes imposed by the state on the autonomy of academic institutions and on the kind of education that they can provide (Bloom, 1987; Graff, 1992; Hughes, 1993; Jacoby, 1987, 1994). In this environment commentators from both left and right have sought to use academic scholarship to inform historical debates about the legacy of slavery and colonialism as well as more contemporary debates about race and poverty and the role of affirmative action programmes.

What these disputes and controversies have made clear is that anti-racist arguments and policies are by no means popular or universally accepted. There are in practice quite divergent, and indeed deeply entrenched, schools of thought about such policies and their value in dealing with racism and racial discrimination. The existence of different schools of thought on such a controversial issue may come as no surprise. But it helps to highlight the degree of controversy and downright confusion that has shaped contemporary debates about anti-racism. This diversity of understandings of what is meant by the notion of anti-racism symbolises the absence of a common theoretical language and the paucity of historical studies about the role of anti-racist ideologies and movements. As we argued in Chapter 2 from a historical perspective, the anti-slavery and anti-colonial movements have played a crucial role during the past two centuries in shaping our social understandings of race and racism. This historical legacy has not always received appropriate recognition. It is clear that apart from a few notable exceptions we have seen few studies of either the ideological foundations of anti-racism or of movements and organisations that espouse an avowedly anti-racist political strategy. This is a major lacuna in the mainstream of research in this field. For this reason we want to concentrate on this issue in the rest of this chapter in order to place the question of anti-racism within the changing social and political debates about racism. In particular we shall argue that we need to develop a clearer understanding of the politics of anti-racism if we are to comprehend the possibilities of developing strategies which can both challenge racist ideas and movements and undermine the appeal of racism.

The politics of anti-racism

Thus far we have tried to establish the degree of confusion that surrounds the very definition of what is meant by anti-racism and the policies and programmes associated with it in different national contexts. But what of the political agendas which are articulated in one way or another around the label of anti-racism? Is there such a thing as an anti-racist politics? These are questions which need to be addressed directly if we are to get to grips with the ethical and political dilemmas which have been raised in recent debates about what needs to be done to promote arguments, policies and movements which counter the influence of racism in contemporary societies. Yet there is, as a number of writers have noted, surprisingly little discussion of the politics of anti-racism and its limits (Cambridge and Feuchtwang, 1990).

In the period since the 1960s, however, the question of how to develop strategies against racism has taken on new forms. This is partly because of the changing nature of racism itself. But it is also because it is during this period that we have seen a flowering of political discourses which proclaim anti-racism as one of their key objectives. Within both academic and popular political debates the issue of anti-racism has come to occupy centre stage in much of the discussion in this field. But there is by no means agreement on how to develop a politics of anti-racism in the present environment. The conceptual and ideological confusion we have highlighted above has seeped through into the debate about how to develop practical political strategies against racism. Above all the very notion of anti-racism has become an essentially contested one and there are divergent accounts of what is meant by it.

Stephan Feuchtwang (1990), for example, has criticised the lack of clarity as to what a politics of anti-racism may mean in practice. He has suggested that the starting point of anti-racism needs to be contextualised in terms of a politics of civil liberty and universal rights. Arguing against the tendency to use terms such as anti-racism as catch-all terms, he attempts to show that measures against racism and discrimination need to be seen in terms of what practical initiatives are necessary to challenge racist practices. From this perspective anti-racism needs to be seen in essentially practical political terms:

> The attacks [on racism] would be specific, targets would neither be whole societies nor mere individuals. It can be seen that anti-racism must have implications in the discourse of civil rights. But that is where it begins. It begins in the discourse in which the ambivalence of human population, sovereign individuals and things of government, gives rise to disavowals of humanity and their justification. It begins, in other words, with the reassertion of humanity, citizenship, and social being. But from there it must go on to new ways of recognising cultural difference, without assigning individuals to categories of essential and differentiated social being in communities of cultural identity. (Ibid., 23–4)

Within the terms of this account there are two constituent elements of an anti-racist politics: (i) opposition to racist arguments and policies and (ii) the articulation of new ways of recognising and living with cultural difference. Such a strategy remains very limited and confined to achieving strategic objectives, but it does highlight the need for political debates about racism to come to terms with wider debates about 'difference' and the consequences of developing conceptions of justice and equality which allow for the expression of cultural and religious identities (Young, 1990; Connolly, 1991).

While this account is by no means complete it has the merit of situating perhaps the key dilemma which an anti-racist politics has to confront; namely, how to go beyond an essentially oppositional political stance to the articulation of an alternative view of racial and cultural difference to those to be found in racist discourses.

Anti-racist movements

Movements against racism have a long and complex history. Whether one looks at attempts to organise against racism through formal organisations or the emergence of ideas which sought to counter racist ideas and values by other means, it is important to remember that racism has never been left unchallenged either intellectually or at the level of practical politics. In the context of France, for example, such organisations have a history going back to the Second World War. Whatever the history of anti-racist movements in each society, it is important to emphasise that part of the political context within which racist movements and ideas have developed has involved both formal and informal oppositional trends. As we shall see in Chapter 7 such opposition may have not always been 'political' in any traditional sense, but it has been present in one form or another in a wide variety of societies.

Within the British context there have been two key phases in the history of anti-racist movements in the period since the 1970s. The first coincided with the rise of the National Front in the period after the mid 1970s and the key organisation was the Anti Nazi League. The second dates from the early 1990s and can be seen partly as a result of the growing concern about the growth of racist violence and fears about the resurgence of neo-fascist movements in Western Europe more generally. During this period we have seen attempts by two competing organisations, a revived Anti Nazi League and the Anti Racist Alliance, to establish themselves as the main representatives of the struggle against both neo-fascism and racism. Both of these phases have been characterised by attempts to build broadly based anti-racist movements aimed, on the one hand, at countering the growth of support for extreme racist organisations and, on the other, at popularising anti-racist ideas to audiences that may in one way or another be attracted to racist ideas.

The performance of anti-racist movements in the period since the 1970s has been the subject of much discussion and speculation, but we still know relatively little about their efficacy with regard to countering racism. The Anti Nazi League was certainly quite successful in the late 1970s in mobilising support among some groups and in channelling opposition to the National Front through public demonstrations and other related events. But it is far from clear that it was the most important factor in the demise of the National Front during the early 1980s. During the 1990s it seems that the ANL and the ARA have been more concerned with fighting each other than at developing a coherent strategy for mobilising against the racist movements either on a local or national basis. This has meant that in many cases it has been left to local campaigns to organise some of the most effective responses on issues such as racial violence and the activities of groups such as the British National Party.

In other countries the response to racist organisations has been in some ways more successful. In Germany, for example, the resurgence of racist attacks on foreigners in the period after 1991 led to protest marches and mobilisations against racism. Throughout 1991 and 1992 numerous 'candlelit processions' took place. This was particularly the case in the aftermath of well-publicised attacks on refugee hostels in Rostock during August 1992 and the death of three Turks as a result of an arson attack in Mölln in November 1992. These attacks were followed by mass demonstrations against racism across the major cities of Germany and widespread publicity against racism. At a more public level many German sports personalities and other public figures joined the campaign against the racist attacks and urged support for foreigners and tolerance of others. Teams in the Bundesliga wore the statement 'I am a foreigner' on their shirts.

Whatever the eventual impact of such mobilisations it remains the case that in many societies anti-racist movements have not always provided a coherent and mass basis of political mobilisation against racism. Given the growth of support for racist movements and parties it is certainly disappointing that anti-racist movements have not been able to develop a mass basis of support. This makes it all the more important to develop a clearer understanding of what factors encourage the development of anti-racist alliances in specific national and local political environments.

Multiculturalism and anti-racism

From the above account it should be evident that at the core of recent debates about anti-racism there is an underlying concern with two key issues: (i) first, the question of how to undermine the logics of racism and create the possibility for the development of anti-racist policies and movements; (ii) second, how to use anti-racist mobilisations and policies to bring about the development and maintenance of truly multicultural societies. Both of

these issues are intrinsically complex and have led to the emergence of a variety of political perspectives about what kind of
ideas and policies are necessary to tackle the growth of racism.

In the British context, in the period since the 1980s, the term
anti-racism has been used in a very expansive way to refer both
to public policies aimed at dealing with racial inequality and to
the development of ideologies such as 'race awareness training'
(Sivanandan, 1990b). Such an expansive usage of the notion of
anti-racism was encouraged by political developments in local
politics, which became the main site of public debate about anti-
racism once it had shifted to the local political arena (Ball and
Solomos, 1990; Solomos and Back, 1995). There was widespread
debate and controversy about the anti-racist initiatives pursued by
radical left local authorities and professional bodies in areas such
as education, welfare provision and training. Commentators from
the right and the left produced critical studies of both the ideological foundations of these initiatives and of their practical
consequences.

Part of the confusion has arisen because it has not always been
clear what the term anti-racism actually means and how it is used
in specific socio-political situations. This is partly because of
(i) the confused nature of the way this notion has been used
in public discourse, and (ii) the adoption by some proponents
of anti-racism of simplistic and fixed notions of 'culture' and 'difference' to legitimise some of their policy objectives. This has
led to intense debate about the limits of anti-racism, and a
number of critical accounts from both the left and the right.

One of the key themes in the critiques of anti-racism emanating from the right is the very notion of racism, which it is argued
has been expanded into a general ideological notion that is used
too crudely by the left and by the race relations experts. The basis
of this critique is that in a sense it is not racism that is the
problem but the race relations experts, who are seen as having a
self-interest in promoting the idea that racism exists in order to
justify their own existence. While the existence of forms of
prejudice is not necessarily denied by new right commentators,
they argue against any notion that racism is endemic in societies
such as Britain and the United States. For new right commentators anti-racism is not only another form of racism but it is
represented a threat to traditional social and political values.

Some of the critical accounts of anti-racism emanating from the left are equally sharp. A case in point is Gilroy's conceptual critique of the terms of anti-racist discourses in Britain. Pointing to what he calls the 'ethnic and cultural absolutism' characteristic of the discourses of anti-racists, Gilroy suggests that both racists and anti-racists, tend to work with somewhat similar notions of cultural exclusivity:

> Black Britain's specific condition – what might be called the peculiarity of the black English, requires attention to a variety of distinct cultural forms, political and intellectual traditions which converge and, in their coming together, overdetermine the process of our social and historical formation. This confrontation is misunderstood if it is conceived in simple ethnic terms, but right and left, racist and anti-racist, black and white share a view of it as little more than a collision between mutually exclusive cultural communities. (Gilroy, 1992, p. 188)

Pointing to some of the policies pursued by local authorities in Britain and by other institutions, as well as the views of community activists, Gilroy suggests that by using fixed notions of cultural difference anti-racists are in danger of simply reversing the terms of racist discourses under the label of anti-racism (Gilroy, 1990b). Gilroy's critique of the discourses used in anti-racist political discourses has served to highlight some of the limitations of anti-racist policies during the 1980s. This kind of critique has been articulated by other writers who have sought to go beyond the simplistic certainties of local government anti-racist strategies (P. Cohen, 1991, 1993; Bonnett, 1993; Bhatt, 1994b).

It is interesting to note in this context that critiques of anti-racism have been a feature of the debate in France for some time. Colette Guillaumin, for example, has argued that in certain respects the modern anti-racist argument in favour of 'the right to be different' involves an inversion of racist argument (Guillaumin, 1991, 1995). Writers such as Taguieff also argue that one of the features of anti-racist discourses is that in many ways they are a kind of mirror image of racist discourses (Taguieff, 1988, 1990).

At the same time, it is also of some importance to note that the debate about anti-racism has become entangled with wider concerns about the politics of multiculturalism and of 'political correctness'. One of the most clear examples of this process is to be found in the so-called 'PC Wars' and 'Multicultural Wars' that have had such an important impact on both academic and intellectual discourses in the United States, and to a lesser extent in other societies. Although such debates have often focused on higher education and not on wider institutions, it is clear that at root they are also concerned with some of the same issues. It is noticeable, for example, that within the context of the public debates about 'PC' there are underlying concerns about the role that anti-racist ideologies play in shaping both popular and public policy debates about racial inequality.

Such critical assessments have done much to ensure that there is a broader debate about the limitations of anti-racism. But interestingly enough they have done little to show what kind of alternative to existing anti-racist strategies is possible in the present political environment. It is to this issue that we now turn.

Anti-racist policies and practices

Whatever the conceptual debates about what anti-racism means or could mean the main controversies in recent years have centred around the attempts to develop and implement anti-racist policies and practices. This is partly because during the 1980s and 1990s the question of anti-racism has become a key area of dispute between the left and the new right, in the context of disputes about the proper role of public policy in this field.

One of the most controversial political debates has centred on attempts to institutionalise anti-racism through racism awareness training. Racism awareness courses have been used in particular by local authorities and other public bodies as a way of countering both racial ideologies and institutionalised racism within organisations. Such courses aim both to educate public officials about racism and to deter them from engaging in discriminatory actions in areas where they exercise power and influence. But they have proved to be very controversial in the way they are formulated and the manner in which they are implemented. One clear example of the controversy caused by such courses was the, public furore in the mid to late 1980s about the role that local authorities played in introducing them. In Birmingham, for example, a furious debate took place about the Council's attempt to ensure that its employees attended 'racism awareness' courses. A local Conservative MP, Dame Jill Knight, criticised the courses, arguing that they amounted to indoctrination and referring to allegations that Council staff needed psychiatric help after taking part in them. She was supported in her criticisms by Councillor Blumenthal, among others, who spoke of the courses in terms of 'Orwellian' techniques of brainwashing (*Birmingham Evening Mail*, 25 August 1987). Although the courses were initially supported by the Labour Party, the leader of the Council responded to these criticisms by distancing himself and the party from what he saw as the radical 'anti-racist' ethos of such courses.

The content of such initiatives has often become blurred and inflated in the theatre of political debate. But there are clearly issues which have highlighted some of the most obvious limitations of anti-racist rhetoric. A case in point is transracial adoption which has consistently attracted the attention of the popular media, particularly in the aftermath of the adoption of a 'same race' policy by most of the agencies concerned with this problem (Rhodes, 1992; Gaber and Aldridge, 1994; Tizard and Phoenix, 1989, 1993). It is also an issue which has produced sharp criticisms from both the left and right about the way in which a supposedly anti-racist practice, namely 'same race' adoption, has been justified using very fixed notions of racial and cultural difference.

Interestingly enough, critiques of the ideology of anti-racism are no longer the preserve of either the traditional or the new right. Increasingly such critiques have been constructed from both left and new right perspectives, and indeed it can be said that there is an overlap in the kinds of arguments which are used by both sides in the debate about anti-racism (Gilroy, 1990b).

What kind of anti-racism?

From the perspective of contemporary political debates the attempt to develop political strategies around the notion of *anti-racism* has proved problematic. At a conceptual level there has been a notable lack of clear conceptualisations of the political and social objectives of anti-racist movements or their limitations. At the level of policy and practice there has been both confusion and hostility to the attempt to institutionalise a bureaucratic

framework for the implementation of anti-racist policies, in relation to such areas as education, social welfare, adoption and
training.

In the present political environment it is also clear that there is
no guarantee that those discourses that are defined as *racist* or *anti-
racist* are as distinct as the terminology suggests. Part of the complexity of the current situation is captured in the following
argument put forward by Hans Magnus Enzensberger when he
comments on the similarity between slogans such as 'Germany
for the Germans' and those more commonly associated with third
world nationalist movements:

> A recent argument against immigration derives, interestingly,
> from the arsenal of anti-colonialism. Algeria for the Algerians,
> Cuba for the Cubans, Tibet for the Tibetans, Africa for the
> Africans – such slogans which helped many liberation move-
> ments to victory are now also taken up by Europeans, and not
> without a certain insidious logic. (Enzensberger, 1992, p. 44)

The usage of slogans which derive from the rhetoric of anti-
colonialism by proponents of nationalist and racist politics does
not of course mean that there is necessarily a symmetry between
the language of racism and anti-racism. But it is surely of some
importance to understand that political slogans and claims made
in the name of some amorphous 'anti-racism' can share notions
about 'culture' and 'difference' with those movements that they
are ostensibly opposed to. Certainly Enzensberger has at least
highlighted one of the ambiguities in the seemingly unproblematic acceptance of nationalist rhetoric in the name of liberation.

While it may be objected that Enzensberger somewhat over-
states his argument, it is clear from recent debates about the politics of anti-racism in Britain and France that there are obvious
dangers in the kinds of arguments which have become part of the
established rhetoric of anti-racist activists. Talking about the situation in France, for example, Guillaumin has noted that many
contemporary anti-racists often work with fixed notions of race,
ethnicity and difference that share some conceptual ground with
the arguments articulated by racist movements. More forcefully
she sees arguments about the 'right to be different' as quite often
involving nothing more than the assertion of a fixed cultural
essence. Thus 'in certain respects this antiracialist trend is only a

continuation of the old traditionalist racialist attitude' (Guillaumin, 1980, p. 64). Indeed she also points to the complex ways in which the French right use notions of 'difference' to support their arguments (Guillaumin, 1991, p. 12; see also Guillaumin, 1995)

As we saw above, a number of left critics of the rhetoric of anti-racism in contemporary Britain, most notably writers such as Phil Cohen and Stephan Feuchtwang, share some of the criticisms of the 'cultural essentialism' commonly associated with anti-racist politics. There are clearly many unresolved issues in contemporary debates about what kinds of strategies are necessary to tackle the growth of racism. More importantly, there are no clear guidelines about what an 'anti-racist' or 'non-racist' alternative is and what it means in terms of practical policies and politics.

Amy Gutmann encapsulates perhaps the key theme in contemporary debates about multiculturalism when she poses the question as to how we can establish mechanisms for treating citizens in societies, which are increasingly multicultural, as equals:

> What does it mean for citizens with different cultural identities often based on ethnicity, race, gender, or religion, to recognise ourselves as equals in the way we are treated in politics? In the way our children are educated in public schools? In the curricula and social policy of liberal arts colleges and universities? (Gutmann, 1992, p. 3)

Gutman's question was formulated with the recent debates in the United States about the politics of multiculturalism very much in mind. It is also part of a much more complex and ongoing dialogue about the future of multiculturalism in liberal democratic societies (Connolly, 1991; LaCapra, 1991; Taylor 1992a, 1992b; Calhoun, 1994).

Such arguments notwithstanding, however, there is still the question of what can be done to deal with such issues as the waves of racist attacks and violence that have spread across Europe and the emergent forms of racist political mobilisation that have spread across numerous advanced industrial societies. Such issues require urgent action and there is therefore a need for greater clarity about what the basis of such action should be. The limits of anti-racist rhetoric may have been cruelly exposed in recent years but this does not mean that the dilemma about how to offer an alternative vision to that articulated by the racists has been resolved. If anything events over the past decade have pinpointed how far we have to go in developing a vision that does not simply reverse the imagery of racism.

6 Identity, Hybridity and New Ethnicities

In the present changing global environment there seem to be two seemingly contradictory trends. On the one hand, there is a wealth of evidence that points towards greater globalisation of economic, social and cultural relations. Increasingly the contemporary world is becoming, to use Marshall McLuhan's phrase, a 'global village' (McLuhan, 1964, p. 12). A consequence of this is the transportation of symbols, styles, music and other cultural materials across national boundaries, integrating and connecting communities in new time–space combinations. Some commentators have gone as far as to argue that the tendency towards global integration or globalisation has produced a fascination with the marketing of ethnicity and cultural difference (Robins, 1991). On the other hand, there is also substantive evidence that the increasing integration of networks of communication and cultural contact has not resulted in a weakening of nationalism, racism or narrowly defined ethnic identities. Indeed it could be argued that ethnic and national conflicts promise to be as destructive in the twenty-first century as in previous periods. There are signs that places as diverse as Bosnia, Rwanda, Britain and Germany may experience ethnic and racial confrontation at an unparalleled level over the next few decades.

The coexistence of these seemingly contradictory trends has proved difficult to deal with, both politically and conceptually. This is why we want to focus in this chapter on contemporary debates over how to conceptualise ethnicity and cultural change. In particular we shall review the new cultural theories which have attempted to develop a conceptual language which embraces the transnational and hybrid nature of contemporary formulations of identity (Appiah and Gates, 1992). This discussion is divided into three broad sections. First, we look at the ways ethnically plural situations contexts have been analysed within anthropology and in particular evaluate the situational model of ethnicity. Second, we review the new cultural theories that have attempted to understand how new forms of identity are formed through difference and the complex relationships between ethnicity, class and gender. Third, we evaluate some of the limits and contradictions of concepts like cultural hydridity and syncretism by applying them to the analysis of fascist culture and iconography.

Throughout this account we shall concentrate on the following key questions. How are contemporary forms of ethnic identification formed? Are new ethnicities emerging? If so, what conceptual tools do we need to understand them? These are complex questions and they have, in one sense or another (see Chapters 1 and 2), been at the heart of the analysis of this volume as a whole. But in this chapter we want to shift gear somewhat and go beyond the account we have provided so far by exploring the specifics of debates about ethnicity and culture.

Anthropology in the metropolis: ethnic identity and models of ethnicity

Before moving on to these questions, we want to situate some of the more recent debates about ethnicity and identity against the background of the anthropological models that have been used to understand ethnicity within complex societies and the ways in which such accounts have dealt with questions about race and racism. Early anthropological studies of ethnicity in metropolitan settings were the result of a variety of influences. Certainly the complex social alignments occurring within late-colonial and newly independent post-colonial states meant that anthropologists had to grapple with ethnically plural contexts and multiethnic conflict and competition (Epstein, 1958; Gluckman, 1961). Perhaps more practically, anthropologists working in the 1960s and 1970s were faced with the dual problem that newly independent states were less welcoming than the former colonial administrations, and grants for extended periods of fieldwork abroad were less available. In this sense anthropology 'at home' and 'in cities' solved a number of problems, although it created many others, as we shall see later. In the United States this meant that ethnicity and poverty became the focus of anthropological activity, while in Europe international labour migrations were changing the cultural character of many of the major European cities. Ulf Hannerz comments: 'There was a search for new understandings, and anthropologists felt they could play a part in it. They had specialised in "other cultures" but had looked for them far away. Now they found them across the tracks' (Hannerz, 1980, p. 1). Others like Robin Fox have stated less charitably that this meant an undignified scramble to find 'substitute savages' in the ghettos and inner cities (Fox, 1973, p. 20).

In Britain anthropologists have not, with a number of notable exceptions, attempted to apply their perspectives to the study of ethnic identity and cultural processes (Khan, 1976, 1979; Wallman, 1979; Wallman *et al.*, 1982; A. Cohen, 1980, 1982, 1993; Bhachu, 1985; Hewitt, 1986). Anthropological activity has confined its interest to discovering pockets of difference and examining social boundaries. Little anthropological attention, for example, has been paid to the nature of 'majority culture' and identity. While there is an interesting literature on 'Celtic difference' (Condry, 1976; Chapman, 1978, 1982; McDonald, 1986), practically no attention has been paid to understanding the way English culture is constructed. While interesting discussions of the national culture of countries in mainland Europe are emerging (Forsythe, 1989), in Britain this area has been left to anthropological humorists (Barley, 1989) and historians and social commentators (Rowe, 1991; Porter, 1993). Serious anthropological investigation has focused on *ethnic groups* (Dahya, 1974; Anwar, 1979; Foner, 1979) or *remote communities* (Frankenberg, 1957; A. P. Cohen, 1982, 1985) where subsocieties are discovered within mainstream Britain. Anthropology in Britain has in general looked for corporate groups or social systems to which traditional anthropological techniques can be applied. Indeed some writers such as Richard Jenkins (1986, pp. 172–8) have argued that there is a direct continuity between the methodological and theoretical approach applied to tribal societies and their 'modern' equivalent – *ethnic groups*.

More generally, however, there has been a growth of interest in the study of ethnic identity and social change in a variety of advanced industrial and developing societies. Such studies of ethnicity in multiethnic contexts have been highly influenced by the work of Frederik Barth (1959, 1969). Prior to the 1960s anthropologists had not given much attention to the nature of cultural boundaries and the focus of enquiry had been on examining the differences between cultures identified as discrete entities (Barth, 1969, p. 9). Barth observed that social boundaries were enduring in ethnically plural contexts and that cultural contact does not result in the lessening of cultural diversity. In short, social actors who move across boundaries retain their cultural identity. For Barth the nature of interaction between social systems cannot be explained by simply describing the internal workings of each cultural system, rather what needs to be discussed is the social activity at the boundary. Barth's major contribution was the insistence that ethnic groups are essentially social constructs. His starting point was that ethnic groups are categories of ascription and identification. As a result, ethnic categories constitute 'organisational vessels' into which a range of symbols and markers can be poured. These may be significant for all social behaviour or they may be confined to specific situations (ibid., p. 14).

Barth's formulations shifted the attention away from identifying integrated socio-cultural systems towards developing a theoretical appreciation of poly-ethnic settings. However, his model has several shortcomings. First, the possibility of ethnic conflict is not fully appreciated in his work. In particular he states that ethnic groups must be acknowledged as legitimate within the ethnic group and by those outside it. This does not allow for the possibility of the labelling of relatively powerless groups by powerful ones. The simple point here is that self-ascribed identities may not be recognised within the wider society. John Rex has pointed out that this perspective does not allow for the internal structuring of ethnic groups according to social class, status and estate (Rex, 1986a, p. 89). Second, Barth's conception of ethnic categories as 'organisational vessels' is ultimately a fixed and static notion. As Abner Cohen points out, Barth's 'Separation between "vessel" and "contents" makes it difficult to appreciate the dynamic nature of ethnicity. It also assumes an inflexible structure of the human psyche and implicitly denies that personality is an open system given to modifications through continual socialisation under changing socio-cultural conditions' (A. Cohen, 1974,

p. xv). Cohen points out that the logic of Barth's framework is essentially circular, that is people act as members of ethnic categories because they identify themselves, and are identified by others, as belonging to those categories. It is this tendency within Barth's work to reify social collectivities which haunts many of the anthropologists who have been influenced by his work.

Barth's model of ethnicity has been most clearly incorporated by Michael Banton (1983) and Sandra Wallman (1979). It is in Wallman's theory of ethnicity that we find perhaps the most sustained attempt to apply anthropological perspectives to urban settings. Sandra Wallman's work shows clearly how her own thinking is rooted in Barth's framework:

> Ethnicity is the process by which 'their' difference is used to enhance the sense of 'us' for purposes of organisation or identification... Because it takes two, ethnicity can only happen at the boundary of 'us', in contact or confrontation or by contrast with 'them'. And as the sense of 'us' changes, so the boundary between 'us' and 'them' shifts. Not only does the boundary shift, but the criteria which mark it changes. (Wallman, 1979, p. 3)

Like Barth, Wallman emphasises that ethnic identities are ascribed and they are always articulated in particular situational contexts. The crucial element in understanding this dynamic is the appreciation that ethnicity can only happen where two or more cultural groupings come into contact. She states: 'Ethnicity is about the organisation of society *and* the organisation of experience (ibid.). From this perspective ethnicity is a product of subjective differentiation and not objective difference. This is a point that has been developed by a range of anthropologists and historians who have argued that ethnicity and nationalism constitute 'imagined communities' (Anderson, 1991) in which tradition is the product of 'invention' (Hobsbawm and Ranger, 1983). Some have stressed the contrived nature of these identities by foregrounding the operation of ethnogenesis which 'creates ethnicity' (Roosens, 1989).

Wallman emphasises that the structural feature of social boundaries is that it marks the edge of a social system. This interface defines the beginning of a contiguous social system (Wallman, 1979, p. 6). Here a criticism levelled at Barth is applicable, namely the tendency to rigidify the nature of social systems either side of the boundary. The result is that the model starts off arguing that ethnicity is dynamic and situational, but ends up allowing a relatively static conceptualisation of the social system, or subsystem. The boundary itself can generate cultural forms and operate as a kind of social system. To put it simply, the boundary does not constitute a 'thin line', but rather a *cultural zone* where 'traditional' ethnicities are destabilised (Hewitt, 1991) and new cultures emerge.

Wallman's model states that ethnicities cannot exist without an ethnically, or racially defined, opposite number. Here the sense of 'us' and 'them' is locked into a functional relationship. Simply put, the definition of others is the product of the classifier's 'ethnicity'. This point is enormously important in view of what we will argue in the following pages because it shows that ethnic identities are not simply the product of 'traditional mores', but the result of an unequal conversation between dominant and minority groupings.

Wallman also argues that race is a social construct (Wallman, 1978b, p. 306) and that, '[We] cannot know which relations involving people of different origins or different general appearance are "ethnic" or "race" relations unless and until we know in which situations these particular differences are relevant, and in what way they are relevant' (ibid., p. 201). From her perspective the starting point is to question the ontological status of ethnic or other group constructions (ibid., 202–3). Central to her theoretical work is a critique of the writing of Michael Lyon (1972–3, 1973). Lyon had suggested that West Indian migrants should be classified as a racial minority, while Asian migrants should be viewed in terms of ethnicity. The reason for this argument was simply that Asian migrants were seen by Lyon to possess a strong culture which threatens Englishness, while West Indians were distinct from the English primarily in terms of colour or phenotype. In hindsight these formulations seem quite overstated. Lyon, for example, on the basis of little evidence, suggests that ethnic Asians are less exposed to discrimination (Lyon, 1973, p. 6). These papers were significant, however, because they led Wallman to reply: 'It seems to me useful to set the racial/ethnic quibble to one side and to consider simply how social boundaries are marked, how they are maintained and how they shift' (Wallman, 1978a, p. 205). Her critics have been quick to seize on this statement as evidence of a political naiveté in Wallman's work (Jenkins, 1986, p. 175; Rex, 1986, p. 97). However, on closer scrutiny there are elements within her thinking that go unnoticed. First of all, the focus on the criteria of boundary definition allows for a more complex model of contemporary racism(s).

Returning to a point raised earlier, Wallman suggests that boundaries and social definitions are always the result of an encounter between at least two sets of social actors. She states with regard to racism: 'I am putting the focus on the ethnic majority, not on the minority populations. I do so to draw attention to the fact that it is English ethnicity which determines the boundary of "them" and determines its significance' (Wallman, 1978b, p. 308). Wallman uses the concept of social refraction to show how dominant groups within society identify and distort the way minorities are socially constructed: racism is, in effect, a function of 'our' ethnicity, not of 'their' race (ibid., p. 309). The point which is important to grasp is that the boundary between 'them' and 'us' is policed by contemporary racism. Within this model of race–ethnic relations there is a flexibility that can cope with the development of new racisms. In particular this model can accommodate the shift from 'pigment' to 'culture' within contemporary racisms mentioned in previous chapters.

Perhaps the major strengths of the perspective developed by Barth and Wallman is that it allows for the importance of social context in the expression of ethnicity. The boundary system approach shows clearly that all actors, both classifiers and classified, are involved in the production of racial and ethnic definitions. In this regard there is a similarity between anthropological approaches and those developed within cultural studies and by the post-colonial writers reviewed in the next section.

This is not to say that the situational model of ethnicity is without its problems. As a number of critics have pointed out there are a number of major weaknesses in this approach. First, there is a tendency to define the markers of ethnicity in a stable or static way. Ethnicity remains something which is either active or inactive. The result is that there is not enough room to explore the ways in which the cultural expression of ethnicity changes through time because in the final analysis, and counter to the spirit of this model, it is characterised as primordial. Second, the situational ethnicity approach does not articulate the micro structure of the boundary system with the macro context of class and gender-divided metro-politan situations. Rather ethnicity becomes a reified notion that transcends relations of class, gender and sexuality. As we will show later, this omission hides the complex articulation that exists between the formations of ethnicity and other social relations. Third, the situational model reproduces a particular model of the sociological subject over which there is currently some controversy. We shall return to some of these issues later on, but first we want to explore some of the wider debates about ethnicity and identity that have emerged in recent years.

Ethnicity and identity

Whatever the conceptual problems with the approach outlined by Wallman and others it does have the potential to help develop a fuller understanding of contemporary racisms. But this has not necessarily been realised by writers working within this frame-work. Over the past decade, however, other influential work in this field has worked with similar ideas. Stuart Hall, for example, has shown the importance of viewing the formation of Englishness as a particular expression of cultural identity or eth-nicity which is situated in relation to a history of global expansion and imperialism. Like Wallman, he argues that the formation of Englishness is constituted through the representation of the colonised Other (Hall, 1991a). English ethnicity, coded 'white', masks its own existence by being equated with the universal and normal (see Chapter 1). Hall comments that considerable anxiety results when this neo-imperial formation of identity is forced to acknowledge its own limited particularity:

> [We have] to try and convince the English that they are just another ethnic group. I mean a very interesting ethnic group, just hovering off the edge of Europe, with their own language, their own particular customs, their rituals, their myths. Like any other native peoples they have something which can be said in their favour, and of their long history. But ethnicity, in the sense that this is that which speaks itself as if it encompasses everything within its range is, after all, a very specific and peculiar form of ethnic identity. (Ibid., p. 21)

While not wishing to grudge Stuart Hall this rhetorical flourish, it must also be remembered that ethnicity, in this case Englishness, may also be contested and alternative reformulations posited. But the important point to emphasise at this stage is that recent theorisations of race and ethnicity by writers such as Hall, writing from the perspective of cultural theory and post-colonial theory, overlap substantively with the concerns of writers such as Barth and Wallman. This is a relatively recent development in theoretical debates about race and racism, but it is one with immense consequences.

As Hall observes, what is at stake in contemporary debates about ethnicity and cultural identity more generally is the development of a model for how we understand individual human beings as social entities. This intellectual process is in itself a profoundly historical and social enterprise. From Hall's perspective there are three types of conception of identity (Hall, 1992). The first he calls the *enlightenment subject*. With its origins in Western philosophy this approach is:

> Based on a conception of the human person as a fully centred, unified individual, endowed with the capacities of reason, consciousness and action, whose 'centre' consisted of an inner core which first emerged when the subject was born, and unfolded with it ... The essential centre of the self was personal identity. (Ibid, p. 275)

The second conception of the human subject he calls the *sociological subject*. The growing complexity of the modern world was understood by sociologists and anthropologists through an awareness that the inner core of the subject was not autonomous from the culture and symbols present in the social domain. He suggests the important thing here is: 'The fact that we project "ourselves" into these cultural identities, at the same time internalising their meaning and values making them "part of us"' (ibid, p. 276). Hall cites the work of G. H. Mead and C. H. Cooley and the symbolic interactionists as key figures in the development of an interactionist conception of identity, which bridges the gap between the psychic inside and social outside. The last of Hall's conceptions of identity he calls the *postmodern subject*, and we will come on to this in the next section.

The point that we want to emphasise here is that the situational model of ethnicity can be seen as operating within what Hall calls the sociological conception of the subject. However, in practice there are some important similarities between this and earlier conceptions of identity. The most important of these is the preoccupation with associating ethnicity with sovereign or prime expressions of identity. In the case of ethnicity the sociological subject has one option. S/he either chooses ethnicity or some other expression of identity depending on the social context.

Yet a key problem with this approach is that it sets oppositions and classifications which are constructed as mutually exclusive categories. This was particularly the case within discussions of the position of the British born children of Caribbean and south Asian migrants during the 1970s and 1980s (Cashmore, 1979; Garrison, 1979; Pryce, 1979; Troyna, 1977a, 1977b, 1979). Within these accounts young black people were presented as in one way or another 'caught between two cultures'. Common to these analyses was the way in which they constructed the assertion of ethnicity with the rejection of Britishness. This treatment of ethnic and cultural processes was most convincingly challenged in the early 1980s by the authors of *The Empire Strikes Back* (CCCS, 1982). Lawrence, in particular, criticised race relations research during the 1970s for focusing on 'cultural deficiencies' like the instability of the family, and generational conflict (Lawrence, 1981, 1982). More specifically, he also took issue with the narrow subculturalist approach to Rastafari offered by authors such as Troyna, Cashmore, and Garrison and argued that these analysts failed to grasp the mass character of the movement. In particular the authors of *The Empire Strikes Back* pointed to the dangers of a static, reductionist view of culture which could result in an emphasis on black youth as a problem in its own right.

Yet others argued that a preoccupation with 'ethnicity' could lead to a failure to articulate the position of black minorities with an integrated understanding of the racial inequalities endemic within British society (Bourne, 1980; Fisher and Joshua, 1982). From this perspective the subcultural approach accentuated this process by placing emphasis on the inner workings of a cultural logic, and thus did not give sufficient weight to the role of racism and social and economic processes in shaping the position of racialised minorities in British society.

This issue led to intense debate during the 1980s both among academics and community activists. One of the consequences of this debate, in hindsight at least, is that it served to create a deep suspicion among both academics and non-academics about the dangers of a preoccupation with ethnicity in the study of race and ethnic relations. It is during this period that researchers in this field drew away from research which concentrated on cultural and ethnic variables. Such work was perceived as problematising the cultures of ethnic groups themselves and shifting attention away from racism and social structures.

Whatever the limits of this rejection of research on ethnicity it is important to draw attention to some of the dangerous assumptions which are made about the nature of racial–ethnic identity. First, it is important to emphasise that much of the discussion on this issue works with a sociological model of the human subject which assumes that individuals should utilise their ethnic identity in a unitary, constant and strategic manner. During the House of Commons debate on the 1981 Nationality Bill, for example, one of the major arguments used against dual nationality for the children of migrants born in Britain was that this status would promote a 'crisis in interests'. There are alarming parallels between political discourses of this kind and the accounts which characterised Afro-Caribbean and Asian youth as being locked in a crisis of identity. Common to both is the assumption that the unitary, rational self is the normal and required mode of identification. While this may be a powerful ideological construct, it does not reflect the multiple and varied ways in which people construct themselves (Wallman, 1983). The 'sociological subject' is compatible with, and may even reinforce and give legitimacy to, this version of identity. The result is that sociological models of ethnicity can come dangerously close to legitimising the sovereign identity enshrined within pernicious colour-coded state legislation. However, as we shall see in the following section this model of identity also provided the means by which black communities mobilised politically.

Second, ethnic identity is almost uniformly viewed as only relevant to minority populations who have to resolve 'their' contradictory position within British society. With some notable exceptions (P. Cohen, 1972; A. Cohen, 1974; Husband, 1977; Hebdige, 1981; Gorer, 1982) there are very few discussions of the nature of majority identities. Consequently, the question of 'majority identity' is left unexplored because it is assumed to be somehow less problematic and by implication homogeneous (Back, 1991). The unwritten assumption is that minority populations and their children constitute a group which exhibit interesting, problematic and varied identities, while the identities of the majority are viewed as unproblematic.

Third, it is important to counter the idea that socio-cultural groups – including nations – are essentially unchanging and atavistic entities. This phenomenon, which Gilroy (1987, p. 59) calls 'ethnic absolutism' ossifies the complex and changing nature of social and cultural life in Britain. He writes: 'The absolutist view of black and white cultures, as fixed, mutually impermeable expressions of racial and national identity, is a ubiquitous theme in racial "common sense", but it is far from secure' (ibid., p. 61). In addition to Gilroy's work there is emerging a small but significant literature that documents the cultural creativity of young people who reside in multiracial areas (Hewitt, 1986; Jones, 1988; Rampton, 1989). The detail of this process promises to transform the way we understand the politics of race and the paradigms that have been utilised to analyse multiracial contexts within British cities. Consequently, it is important, on the one hand, to view cultural meanings as in a constant state of negotiation and evolution, and on the other, to be sensitive to the political, historical and ideological context in which this process takes place.

Identification, hybridity and the new ethnicities

If the intellectual climate of the 1980s did not encourage research on issues about ethnicity it is clear that in the past few years the situation has changed quite markedly. Whatever the critiques of writings on ethnicity articulated by books such as *The Empire Strikes Back* there has been a noticeable renewal of interest in questions on the subject. One of the most important features of debates about race and ethnicity in the past few years has been the rediscovery of ethnicity, particularly by writers influenced by debates about postmodernism and post-colonial cultural theory. The main idea that these writers have in common is that human identity does not possess a fixed, permanent or essential quality.

According to Hall, the *postmodern subject* is produced as part of the wider predicament of contemporary societies in late modernity. Here he draws on the work of a range of authors who have argued that contemporary societies are experiencing a far-reaching crisis which is destabilising or 'de-centering' established models of identity, knowledge, reason and science (Lyotard, 1984; Harvey, 1989). The details of this highly contested hypothesis are not vital to the issues discussed here, but it is important to appreciate their repercussions for conceptualising identity in general and ethnicity in particular. One of the most important of these, on the basis of Hall's reading at least, is the rejection of the notion of a unified identity that can be justified in terms of a biological or cultural essence. Rather, Hall suggests a model of the human subject which allows for the occupation of a range of a identities at different times, while often harbouring contradictory allegiances within a social context that is relentlessly mutating. Hall concludes:

> If we feel we have a unified identity...it is only because we construct a comforting story or 'narrative of the self' about ourselves... The fully unified, completed, secure and coherent identity is a fantasy. Instead, as the systems of meaning and cultural representation multiply, we are confronted by a bewildering, fleeting multiplicity of possible identities, any one of which we could identity with – at least temporarily. (S. Hall, 1992, p. 277)

For writers like Hall this uncertainty not only questions the Eurocentred and male inflected enlightenment and sociological models of the human subject, but it also challenges the very mode of communal mobilisation that has been developed within black communities in Britain, the United States and elsewhere.

In particular post-colonial writers have attempted to face this challenge by talking about what Cornel West referred to as a 'new cultural politics of difference' (West, 1992). The literature associated with this turn in contemporary debates has no simple homogeneity and signifies a range of critical discourses that have been developed by intellectuals who work inside but not confined to Western modernity. Following Ruth Frankenberg and Lata Mani we explore the work of post-colonial writers in 'the context of a rigorous politics of location, of a rigorous

conjuncturalism' (Frankenberg and Mani, 1993, p. 307). This discussion is organised around two main themes which include a
discussion of gendered processes and ethnic and racial formations,
and the use of the concepts of diaspora, syncretism and cultural
hybridity. However, we want to look first at the way debates on
the notion of black identity are framed and contested in
contemporary Britain.

Blackness and the end of innocence

A unique dimension of the British experience during the 1970s
and 1980s was the formation of an inclusive notion of blackness
configured as the political colour of opposition to racism. This
was closely connected to black socialist movements which in one
way or another opposed a preoccupation with ethnicity and
ethnic politics (Bourne, 1980; Mullard, 1982). In this respect the
rejection of ethnicity was closely tied to a political refusal of the
sociological subject as elaborated in the sociology of race and
ethnic relations. However, by the mid 1980s the hegemony of
this version of political identity came under pressure from a
variety of sources. Perhaps the most significant of these pressures
was the controversy that followed from the publication of Salman
Rushdie's book *The Satanic Verses* and the subsequent political
debates about this and related issues. The whole debate about
fundamentalism and religious absolutism within minority communities challenged the utility of the political category 'black' in
the changed social and political environment of the 1990s. In particular the emergence of religious and communal movements
within minority communities suggested that a new political align-
ment was taking shape.

Two very different stands of thought and writing emerged
from these transformations. The first argued for the importance of
identifying social, economic and political divisions between distinctly African–Caribbean and Asian interests in British society
(Cross, 1989). The most sustained exposition of this line of argument can be found in the work of Tariq Modood (1988, 1990,
1992). Modood dismisses the notion of and inclusive 'black identity' as a 'meaningless chimera' (Modood, 1988, p. 399) and
argues that the political culture which had produced this mode of

organisation had sidelined issues which affect Asian communities most deeply. He concludes: 'The choice, then, is not between a separatist Asian ethnicity and unity of the racially oppressed; the choice is between a political realism which accords dignity to ethnic groups on their own terms and a coercive ideological fantasy' (ibid, p. 403). Modood's key argument is that the emphasis on a 'black' political identity gave too much weight to the ability of racism to frame the subjectivity of minority communities. He argues forcefully that 'everybody is somebody, not just a victim' (Modood, 1990, p. 95). He has also suggested that there is a need to incorporate a model of ethnicity that was not reducible either to class analysis or race and which allows room for religious factors to take a central place in the formation of cultural identities. From this starting point Modood develops a trenchant critique of race relations sociology and radical anti-racism, arguing that both in effect deny the possibility of the emergence of ethnicity as an autonomous and important social identity within minority communities.

There is no doubt that Modood's writing has helped to highlight a deeply felt sentiment within some sections of south Asian communities in British society. There are, however, a number of problems with his account of identity politics and Asian self-affirmation. First, there is a tendency within his work to reify social definitions. In the context of his early work he presented the notion of Asian identity which suppressed the cultural diversity found within this category. There is also a tendency in some of his work to subsume people from Bangladesh, Pakistan and India who are also of the Muslim, Hindu and Sikh faiths under the notion of Asian as a racial appellation. In this respect writers such as Modood could be seen as being as guilty of suppressing difference in a similar way to 'black perspectivists' and the race relations sociologists whom he criticises so passionately. Second, Modood operates within a model of human subjectivity which is squarely in the tradition of the enlightenment and the sociological subject. His work constantly espouses the need to recognise Asian or Muslim particularity as a paramount or sovereign identity. In this sense his work is confined within an either/or model of identity which fails to recognise that social identity can be multi-inflected.

This brings us to the second strand of thinking that emerged during this period. This strand is represented in the work of

Stuart Hall since the late 1980s, which can be seen as an attempt to summarise the state of black cultural politics in Britain (Hall, 1987, 1988). His writings define many of the themes taken up by other writers in this tradition and signify an important shift in the way the cultural politics of race have been conceptualised in recent years. Although Hall's work is difficult to summarise the following seem to be the key arguments he advances. First, Hall offers a periodisation of black cultural politics. Referring to the points made above, he argues that the coining of the term 'black' during the 1970s was a means to reference a common experience of racism and marginalisation. He suggests that this moment was a product of a political challenge within the 'dominant regimes of representation', which included the media discourses and anthropological and sociological frameworks mentioned in the previous section. He also argues that this definitional politics is best understood in terms of a struggle that took place over the relations of representation in which a counter-position of positive black imagery was offered to unsettle the reified images of black culture (Hall, 1988, p. 27). Hall characterised this counter-position as the first phase in the development of black cultural politics: 'In that moment, the enemy was ethnicity' (Hall, 1991b, p. 55). He accepts that an unintended consequence of this politics was a tendency to homogenise cultural, class and sexual difference within blackness.

The second phase in the development of black cultural politics was marked, he argues, by the end of an innocent notion of the essential black subject:

> Once you enter the politics of the end of the essential black subject you are plunged headlong into the maelstrom of a continuously contingent, unguaranteed, political argument and debate...You can no longer conduct black politics through the strategy of a simple set of reversals, putting in the place of the bad old essential white subject, the new essentially good black subject. (Hall, 1988, p. 28)

Hall argues that this new politics had to work through multiple inflections. The black subject needed always to be crossed with references to class, gender, sexuality and ethnicity. This can be summarised as a plural blackness which holds on to a likelihood of identity. Hall does not want to give up on the possibility of some kind of black identity and we will return to this in a moment. He sees racial identity as a fiction, but one which is necessary in order to make 'both politics and identity possible' (Hall, 1987, p. 45). Hall thus asserted a politics which is composed of unities within difference.

Hall has suggested that this second phase involved reinscribing ethnicity outside the discourses of the sociology of race and ethnic relations and the rhetoric of nationalism. He argues that ethnicity needs to be decoupled from its former associations, and has found evidence of this shift in the expressive cultures of Britain's black arts movement:

> It seems to me that, in the various practices and discourses of black cultural production, we are beginning to see constructions of just such a new conception of ethnicity: new cultural politics which engages rather than suppresses *difference* and which depends, in part, on the cultural construction of new ethnic identities. (Hall, 1988, p. 29)

In his later work Hall has expanded this conception of 'identity through difference' (Hall, 1990, 1991a, 1991b) and stressed the importance of placing black cultural production in the context of global networks (Hall, 1992). Thus 'new ethnicities' are produced in part through a productive tension between global and local influences. This way of framing ethnicity can be seen as radically different from the situational model reviewed in the previous section, for it avoids the tendency to define ethnicity in primordial ways and acknowledges the simultaneously local and translocal nature of these identities. 'New ethnicities' not only challenge what it means to be 'black' but they also call into question the dominant coding of what it means to be British. This opens a range of issues that are related to the way notions of authenticity and belonging are defined within racist and absolutist conceptions of culture.

Third, drawing on feminism, psychoanalysis and in particular the work of Frantz Fanon, Hall has shifted the emphasis away from focusing on unitary forms of identity to plural processes of identification:

> Identities are never completed, never finished; that they are always as subjectivity is, in process...I want to open that process

up considerably. Identity is always in the process of formation...Identity means, or connotes, the process of identification,
of saying that this here is the same as that, or we are the same together, in this respect. But something we have learnt from the
whole discussion of identification, in feminism and psychoanalysis, is the degree to which that structure of identification is
always constructed through ambivalence. Always constructed
through splitting. Splitting between that which one is, and that
which is the other. (Hall, 1991b, pp. 47–8)

This point is similar to the one made within interactionalist sociology, namely that the external world structures the internal and
vice versa. The result is that identifications operate through bina-
ries of fear/desire and love/loathing. Hall's analysis has been
influenced partly by Fanon's classic study *Black Skin, White Masks*,
in which he argued that colonial societies produce a racial masquerade in which colonial subjects mimic their masters (Fanon,
1986). In this sense blackness and whiteness do not operate as
sealed and separate elements in the formation of subjectivity,
rather they are forms of personhood to be performed on the
colonial stage.

Whatever the intentions of Hall's interventions in these debates
a key question remains to be addressed: how far does the 'new
ethnicities' approach 'decouple' previous conceptions of ethnicity? Hall, and other writers on 'new ethnicities', can be seen as attempting to navigate between essentialist notions of identity and
the 'anything goes' pluralism of postmodern ideology by arguing
that fictional forms of closure are required to make possible a politics where ethnicity provides a 'grounding' for the self in particular collective identities. This is close to what Gayatri Spivak has
referred to as 'strategic forms of essentialism' (Spivak, 1987). But
it can be argued that this 'necessary' protocol comes dangerously
close to the very models of subjectivity it aims to transcend. In
this sense, it is important to continue to be suspicious of reified
notions of 'the community', 'homogenous ethnic identities' and
fetishised 'traditionalism'. Lastly, and perhaps most importantly,
the pervasiveness of the trends identified by Hall and others
writing in the same vein need to be evaluated carefully. This type
of cultural theory takes its empirical clues from the black arts
movement and the work of film-makers, photographers and

musicians. Little empirical evidence is available to demonstrate the relevance of these issues outside the black arts movement. In this sense we must view these works, and the ideas that have been formulated around them, as heuristic and informed meditations on the state of the politics of race in Britain.

One of the most significant things that has emerged from current debates is the importance of articulating the discussion of race and ethnicity with an understanding of gender relations and sexuality. bell hooks, for example, reflects on the need for feminist criticism and gender dialogue within US black politics in the following manner:

> Until black women and men begin to seriously confront sexism in black communities, as well as within black individuals who live in predominantly white settings, we will continue to witness mounting tensions and ongoing divisiveness...We need to hear from black men who are interrogating sexism, who are striving to create different and oppositional visions of masculinity. Progressive black liberation struggle must take seriously the feminist movement to end sexism and sexist oppression if we are to restore to ourselves, to future generations of black people, the sweet solidarity in struggle that has historically been a redemptive subversive challenge to white supremacist capitalist patriarchy. (hooks, 1991, p. 77)

Addressing a different but related set of issues Gilroy has examined the relationship between race, identity and masculinism. Commenting on the controversy over the obscenity trial of Florida-based rap act 2 Live Crew, he reflected:

> An amplified and exaggerated masculinity has become a boastful centrepiece of a culture of compensation that self-consciously salves the misery of the disempowered and subordinated. This masculinity and its relational feminine counterpart become special symbols of the difference that race makes. They are lived and naturalised in the distinct patterns of family life on which the reproduction of their racial identities supposedly lies. These gender identities come to exemplify the immutable cultural differences that apparently arise from absolute ethnic difference. (Gilroy, 1993b, p. 85)

Elsewhere he has argued that the reduction of black culture to the maintenance of a pure racialised body produces a politics that has become 'subject-centred to the point of solipsism' (Gilroy, 1994a, p. 26). The intertwining of race and gender provides a key starting point for understanding how old and new versions of blackness are realised.

Notions of whiteness and nationhood are generated through comparable and no less complex composites. Vron Ware's study of the articulation between whiteness and womanhood argues that attention to such a conceptual reciprocity is vital if feminism is to oppose one form of domination without being complicit in another (Ware, 1992). Ruth Frankenberg examines related issues in her work on the way race has shaped the lives of white and black women in America (Frankenberg, 1993). Whiteness is predicated on particular versions of femininity and masculinity. Marcia Pointon exemplifies this point in her fascinating essay on the media representation of the white English sportsman, Ian Botham (Pointon, 1994). She argues that within the public spectacle that surrounds these images there lingers an ideal form of racialised heterosexual masculinity.

While stressing the importance of the interconnection between different forms of social division it is equally important to avoid conflating their relationship. Avtar Brah makes this point succinctly when she argues: 'The search for grand theories specifying the interconnections between racism, gender and class has been less than productive. They are best construed as historically contingent and context specific relationships' (Brah, 1993, p. 208). She goes on to argue that it is important to understand the specific context of any articulation between race and gender if we are to appreciate how the multiple modalities of power interconnect (Brah, 1994, p. 812).

Recent studies of the position of minority women within Britain point to the urgency of developing such a rigorous contextual analysis. Parminder Bhachu, for example, has argued that white feminist representations of Asian women have indulged models of multiple subordination which completely ignore their complex social and economic locations. Stressing the self-determinative qualities of Punjabi Sikh women in 1990s Britain, Bhachu has argued powerfully that these women are 'active agents [who], interpret and reinterpret, construct and reconstruct their identities and cultural locations in [the] process of continuous economic change' (Bhachu, 1991, p. 410). Similarly, Heidi Mirza has argued that African–Caribbean women in Britain are falsely viewed as multiply subordinated underachievers. She argues that the economic success of young black women has played an important role in redefining black womanhood (Mirza, 1992). There are two important points which follow from these studies. First, it is vitally important to understand that the interplay of ethnicity and gender does not produce mechanistic outcomes that can be easily predicted. Second, they foreground the importance of developing detailed accounts of the precise nature of this articulation.

Diaspora, hybridity and belonging

How do groups which share a common culture, language or symbolism maintain connections while separated geographically? This issue has been largely ignored in the anthropological accounts of ethnicity. But in recent years this is perhaps the one question which has attracted the most attention in discussions of how dispersed or migrant communities develop new forms of identification and feelings of belonging. A whole body of work has emerged which in one way or another addresses facets of the diasporic experience of various communities. A key concept in this discussion is diaspora, which literally means dispersal. The notion of diaspora has been used to describe the complex modes of belonging where dispersed communities are in but not of particular social formations (Safran, 1991; Boyarin and Boyarin, 1993). James Clifford, in his wide-ranging review of the use of diaspora within cultural theory, has argued that what is at stake in the notion is the creation of 'resources for a fraught coexistence' (Clifford, 1994). Other writers have used the notion as a way of talking about the changing cultural dynamics of minority identity and cultural change. This approach is most evident in the work of writers such as Gilroy and Bhabha on the changing forms of black culture in Britain and America. They conceptualise black cultural forms as in a constant state of creation and reformulation. The forms of identification produced within this culture invoke the legacy of a diverse range of social movements including the civil rights movement in America, anti-colonial struggles in Africa, the Caribbean and South America.

Writing more specifically about black vernacular culture in Britain, Gilroy argues that it can be seen in part as a response to British racism but it could not be simply reduced to it. Rather, he outlines a more complex and contingent set of identifications within cultural politics:

> Black expressive cultures affirm while they protest. The assimi-
> lation of blacks is not a process of acculturation but of cultural
> syncretism...Accordingly, their self-definition and cultural ex-
> pressions draw on a plurality of black histories and politics. In
> the context of modern Britain this has produced a diaspora
> dimension to black life. (Gilroy, 1987, pp. 155–6)

Such a framework challenges the idea that national culture and ethnicity can exist as entirely separate entities. The negotiated cultures of black Britain developed within an 'alternative public sphere' incorporate and carnivalise linguistic and regional elements of 'British culture'. Consequently, Gilroy argues, 'It is impossible to theorise black culture in Britain without developing a new perspective on British culture as a whole' (ibid., p. 156).

The work of Gilroy and others writing about diaspora culture has not only challenged the orthodoxies of anthropology and sociology. It has also raised fundamental questions about the position of slavery within modernity and the echoes this relationship had in subsequent forms of black cultural politics. The abject dispossession of slavery produced a situation where the need to recover and reincarnate a sense of being assumed a central axis around which these syncretic cultures formed. Within the cultural matrix of the diaspora *multiaccented* forms of belonging can and are produced that stay simultaneously inside and beyond the prime organisational vessel of modernity, namely the nation state (Apter, 1991).

These themes are further articulated in Gilroy's influential *The Black Atlantic*, where he examines the affect that travel and European encounters had on successive generations of black intellectuals who criss-crossed the Atlantic. Gilroy argues that black intellectual engagements with Europe have produced a counter-culture of modernity viewed through the 'second sight' or 'double consciousness' attributed famously to new world blacks by W. E. B. Du Bois (1989). Gilroy emphasises that diaspora identification is produced through cycles of call and response – referred to as antiphony – whereby identity can be lost, found again and renewed with new vitality (Gilroy, 1993a, p. 138). Using Leroi Jones famous phrase, he has suggested that the social and cultural lives of black people within the diaspora can be characterised as a 'changing same': 'A determinedly non-traditional tradition, for this is not tradition as close or simple repetition. Invariably promiscuous and unsystematically profane, diaspora challenges us to apprehend mutable itinerant culture. It suggests a complex, dynamic potency of living memory: more embodied than inscribed' (Gilroy, 1994b, p. 212). This process not only involves the transmission of cultural resources from siblings elsewhere, but also their recombination within particular local circumstances. The result is a complex composite of local and diasporic elements.

Such a perspective offers a way to transcend the tired debates between racial essentialism and anti-essentialism by arguing that racial subjectivity is embodied in acts. The deeds provide the defining moments, and from this follows the argument that there is no essence in skin or nature from which these acts are derived. The relativism of anti-essentialism is avoided by maintaining that something enduring is preserved within these mutable syncretic cultures. Equally, this 'non-traditional tradition' cannot be viewed as a conversation between a fixed racial self and a stable racial community. The result is a critique of 'anti-essentialism' that does not resort to ideas of racial particularity, but embraces the realisation that the inner secrets of black culture can be taught and learned:

> Apart from anything else, the globalisation of vernacular forms means that our understanding of antiphony will have to change. The call and response no longer converge in tidy secret, ethnically coded dialogue. The original call is becoming harder to locate. If we privilege it over the subsequent sounds that compete with one another to make the most appropriate reply, we will have to remember that these communicative gestures are not expressive of an essence that exists outside the acts which perform them and thereby transmit structures of racial feeling to wider, as yet uncharted, worlds. (Gilroy, 1993a, p. 110)

From this perspective the structures of feeling which black culture invokes can be preserved in a manner which avoids their ossification and offers the possibility that it may flourish beyond the narrow confines of racial ontology with possibly unforeseen consequences.

Homi Bhabha (1994) has also stressed the importance of translation and negotiation in the process of cultural change. He utilises the notion of hybridity to describe the composite qualities of cultural forms in the colonial setting. Commenting on the transformation of Christianity in India through native demands for an Indianised Gospel, Bhabha comments: 'When making these inter cultural, hybrid demands, the natives are both challenging the boundaries of discourse and subtly changing its terms by setting up another specifically colonial space of the negotiation of cultural authority' (Bhabha, 1994, p. 119). This is reminiscent of the cultural politics found within diaspora communities. Like Gilroy's preoccupation with the affect of travel and passage, Bhabha's work stresses the ambivalence found in the heterogeneous 'in-between'. Hybrid identifications combine elements that are incommensurable but this space also constitutes an arena in which boundaries can be reconfigured and cultural authority contested. From this angle the social relations of race and identity are never fixed or pre-given, since they are the product of complex processes of cultural hybridisation and social change.

In the work of Gilroy and Bhabha we thus find a sustained attempt to examine the formations of identity without producing singular or essentialist modes of human subjectivity. They argue for complex combinations of continuity and change in the performance or embodiment of culture. This type of analysis is, of course, not limited to the study of race and ethnicity, since it is also evident in broader trends in social theory. But it is interesting to note that in recent years the study of race has become a site of important debates about the changing forms of identity and subjectivity in contemporary societies. However, notions of diaspora, hybridity and syncretism may presuppose, as Manthia Diawara has pointed out, 'that there are such things as pure Black culture and pure White culture that are transformed by mixing them' (Diawara, 1991, p. 82). Curiously, then, the very attempt to transcend the essential subject may be prefigured on a spurious notion of cultural purity. Both Gilroy and Bhabha provide complex answers to this dilemma by insisting that cultural syncretism is constantly *in process*, mutating, retaining familiar features while incorporating new elements. The result is a compelling and complex model of identity that is expressed through relentless movement, creation and performance.

The literature we have reviewed has in general stressed the expressive and redemptive dimensions of the syncretic cultures of diaspora communities. This approach offers the means whereby a cultural politics that does not slip into ethnic absolutism can be constructed. But what is also clear is that within contemporary societies there is a strong trend towards the creation of new essentialisms on the basis of religion, ethnicity or race. Yet this trend has not been fully analysed in the accounts we have explored so far in this chapter, since they concentrate on the liberating characteristics of new ethnicities and identity politics (Gregory, 1993). Some researchers have begun to question such optimism. Bhatt (1994a, 1994b) has argued forcefully that contemporary forms of fundamentalism and neo-traditionalism within minority communities are themselves the product of the diversity and difference which is sometimes celebrated as liberating and progressive. He views the search for pure religious and cultural identities by minority communities in Britain and elsewhere as very much the end result of hybridity and cultural syncretism, rather than as a return to some earlier or 'primitive' forms of belonging. Such a perspective presents a real challenge to some of the key themes of the literature we have reviewed above but there is surprisingly little research on what Bhatt has called 'reactionary ethnic formations' (Bhatt, 1994b, p. 146).

Syncretic fascism? Transnationality and racist culture

This silence is not surprising, given that the emphasis on a decentred model of 'identity through difference' is seen by some as providing an alternative to fixed notions of human subjectivity. The assertion of cultural hybridity is also seen as undermining the conceptual tenets that prefigure racism and ethnic absolutism. The historical accuracy of this idea has been questioned by some writers, who have pointed out that contemporary debates lack a reference to the varied usages of notions of hybridity in earlier times (Young, 1995). It is interesting to note, however, that the hybrid elements of *racist ethnicities* have received little attention in contemporary cultural theory. Most theorists have focused their attention on the development of complex and hybrid identities within minority communities. But if we look at both classical and contemporary racist and fascist movements it is also clear that cultures may have hybrid transnational and multicultural elements without necessarily engendering a transgressive politics. The most repugnant and genocidal movements have been, and continue to be, for want of a better word – hybrids. This should stand as a salutary reminder to those of us who want to embrace with cautious optimism, what Salman Rushdie has termed the project of 'change by fusion' (Rushdie, 1991, p. 394).

The association of fascism with ideas of cultural purity and racial purity can be established easily enough. At one level fascist racial theories can be seen in terms of cultural purity and the rejection of difference. Certainly the loathing of mixture, both racial and cultural, was at the heart of the racial ideology of the Nazis. In *Mein Kampf*, originally published in two volumes in 1924, Adolf Hitler wrote:

> The result of all racial crossing is therefore in brief always the following:
> (a) Lowering of the level of the higher race;
> (b) Physical and intellectual regression and hence the beginning of a slowly but surely progressing sickness.
> To bring about this such a development is, then, nothing else but to sin against the will of the eternal creator. (Hitler, 1992, p. 260)

Such arguments were used by the Nazis to legitimise their policies of racial purity and finally the genocidal extermination of whole ethnic and racial groups. They also became part of the racial mythology of the Nazi racial state in its project of protecting the 'purity' of the Volk.

Nazism as an ideology and a movement, however, did not represent a simple return to a mythic past of racial purity and cultural coherence. It combined modern technologies alongside ancient and premodern emblems. If one takes perhaps the key symbol of Nazi iconography, namely the swastika, as a case in point, it is clear that its appropriation by the Nazis was no simple matter but the result of a long process of cultural and political struggle in which different meanings were attached to it. Roger Griffin comments: 'However barbaric the connotations of the Swastika for the untold millions of victims of Nazi violence, for those mesmerised by its mythic power it symbolised not death but rebirth, not herd-like somnambulism but national reawakening' (Griffin, 1991, p. 105). In fact the use of the swastika by both Austrian and German ultra-nationalistic movements can be dated back to the nineteenth century, when writers and orators set about the task of 'rediscovering' a racial heritage for the German Volk. Malcolm Quinn in his recent study points out that the nineteenth-century fixation with mapping the distribution of the swastika provided a 'symbolic vehicle or focusing device' for the defining or reinventing of a concept of race coupled with territory (Quinn, 1994, p. 10). As Mosse has shown, Vienna was a particular centre for the German Volkish movement in the late nineteenth century, including such figures as Guido von List whose ideas combined occultist racism with pseudo scientific speculations on the Nordic origins of the Aryan race (Mosse, 1966). List's ideas filtered into Germany through the poet Alfred Schuler, who was based in the artist quarter in Munich where he gave public lectures extolling national reawakening and anti-Semitism. It was Schuler who was credited with establishing the swastika as the sign of the imminent national rebirth. It made its first appearance as an instrument of genocide in Schuler's poem *Epilogus Jahwe-Moloch* (Pulzer, 1988). Here the swastika was defined as a Teutonic sun symbol which expressed the eternal quality of the German Volk. This astral emblem stood for the external manifestation of an invisible spiritual power (Mosse, 1987). The symbol was also alleged to have Aryan origins in ancient India. Ultra-nationalist organisations such as the *Germanen-und Walsungsorden* (Order of Teutons and Volsungs) founded in 1912 used the swastika on the cover of their journal. This secret lodge was dedicated to combating the alleged conspiracy of secret Jewish organisations. In 1907, Lanz von Liebenfels hoisted a swastika flag over his Austrian castle in Burg Werfenstein (Pulzer, 1988).

But it is also clear that despite the claims of Nazi ideologues the swastika is, and has been, present in an incredible variety of human cultures. The origin of the name symbol is from Sanskrit where the term means 'of good fortune'. Also this form is known in other contexts as the 'Greek gamma or fyflot cross'. While it is true that swastikas were present in India and among Germanic peoples, Volkish thinkers overlooked the fact that this emblem is one of the most common of all ancient symbols. It is found almost universally in the cultures of Eurasia, and it may have had an independent origin among African and native American peoples (Catholic University of America, 1967). Quinn rightly warns against a 'banal travelogue' approach to the swastika, since such an approach he argues does little to historicise the uses to which the swastika has been put and 'does nothing to draw the sting out of Nazism' (Quinn, 1994, p. 2). However, it is important to appreciate that the swastika had been associated with contexts before its Occidental Aryanisation.

Prior to its Nazi appropriation the swastika was associated with a range of meanings. It was a symbol of good omen, a bringer of luck, prosperity, fertility, protection and long life. The swastika was also used as a symbol of fire, lightning and planetary bodies. It has a prominent place in various forms of Buddhism and in Hinduism and Jainism. Within Greek art and Roman floor mosaics the swastika was used as an ornamental figure for decoration. The symbol was also utilised privately in the worship of early Christians and by the reign of Constantine the cross was displayed publicly as an accepted symbol of Christian faith, although the swastika never became a favoured emblem within Christianity (Child and Colles, 1971).

The Hindu use of the swastika had two forms. The right-handed swastika, like the ones used by the Nazis, is associated with the sun and provides an emblem of 'the Verdic solar Visnu and the symbol of the world-wheel, indicating cosmic procession and evolution around a fixed centre' (Stutley, 1973, p. 139). This form also signifies the male principle. The left-handed form, or *sauvastika,* is associated with the sun during the autumn and winter and this is regarded as an inauspicious symbol for men. This variant is gendered female but it is not taken to be unlucky for women. The two symbols taken together represent balance within the Hindu cosmos. In vernacular usage the right-handed swastika is used as a mark of good fortune and is found on temple doors, houses and cattle sheds often to protect families and live stock from the 'evil eye'. In addition, the swastika is associated with a range of cultural/religious practices. A *mundra,* or symbolic hand poses, is referred to by this name in which the fingers cross each other. In yoga there is a sitting posture called the *svastikasana* where the toes are placed in the hollows behind the knees (Varenne, 1973). The swastika has also been found in the Indus Valley, Mesopotamia and in Palestine. Wilhelm Reich pointed out, in his important study of the *Mass Psychology of Fascism*, that swastikas were also deployed by Jews, quoting examples found in the synagogue ruins of Edd-Dikke in East Jordania on the lake of Gennesaret (Reich, 1970). Reich concluded that the power of the swastika can be found in its appeal to unconscious emotionality and he regards it as a sexual symbol. While the truth or falsehood of this claim is not our concern here, it is clear that the swastika has transcultural resonance: it is in this sense a hybrid.

The swastika was thus a complex cultural symbol long before it became an emblem of Volkish nationalism or the key symbol of Nazism. But in the aftermath of the First World War the penetration of Volkish ideology was manifest in the popularity of the swastika amongst students of all ages. The swastika became associated with anti-Semitic youth groups and the level of its use reached such a degree that the Prussian ministry of education took steps to prohibit it in 1919. The young Adolf Hitler is likely to have heard Schuler's lectures in Munich around this time (Mosse, 1966). The swastika was introduced to the Nazi Party, in August 1919, by the dentist Friedrich Krohn who owned a large private library much used by Hitler. Later in the aftermath of the unsuccessful Beer Hall Putsch the imprisoned Hitler wrote unambiguously about its meaning:

> As National Socialists, we see our programme in our flag. In red we see the social ideal of the movement, in white the nationalistic idea, in the swastika the mission of the struggle for the victory of the Aryan man, and, by the same token, the victory of the idea of creative work, which as such always has been and always will be anti-semitic. (Hitler, 1992, p. 452)

The connection between the swastika and the racial theories of the Nazis is made clear in this passage, and when they achieved power in 1933 the swastika held a central position in the elaborate political aesthetics of the Nazi state. Viewed as a radiant sun symbol, it was closely related to a whole range of iconic representations. For example, the ideal Nazi body was presented in the art of the Third Reich as translucent before a blazing sun. Equally, the swastika was commonly represented enclosed by a wreath incorporating Roman references. The central monument of Zeppelin Fields Stadium in Nuremberg, the site of the infamous mass rallies, provided a good example of this combination. The swastika was also presented held in the talons of an eagle. The eagle within fascist iconography assumed heroic qualities and became the animal equivalent of the Aryan naked hero. The proud eagle and the stormtrooper's gaze became synonymous within Nazi art and painters like Michael Kiefer presented images of these birds soaring on high that provided power symbols of conquest and ruling (Adam, 1992). The combination of these signs provided the means by which Nazi ideology was visualised.

In a very real sense, therefore, fascist cultures themselves have a syncretic quality. They assimilate difference without contradiction while asserting racial purity and terror. The historical traces of diversity and difference within Nazism are deracinated in the service of creating an Aryan tradition. This is very important in view of the contemporary theoretical discussions about the politics of cultural hybridity. Nazi culture processed difference in the production of racial rhetoric. Take this quotation from the SS Training Manual:

> The high cultures of the Indians, Persians, Greeks, and Romans were Indo-Germanic creations. They unmistakably show Nordic creativity... Even today we feel an affinity with those cultures of the same racial origin. People of other races also created cultures, but when we approach the culture of Ancient China, of Babylon, of the Aztecs and the Incas, we feel something different. They too are high cultures but they are alien to us. They are not of our race; they transmit a different spirit. They have never reached the same heights as those created by the Nordic Spirit. (ibid., p. 22)

Clearly, Nazism could embrace difference as long as it could be located within some sense of racial commonality.

The point we are making through this example is that we cannot neatly divide the debate on ethnicity and identity into 'repressive essentialism' on one side and 'liberating hybridity' on the other. Racist and extreme nationalist movements are not necessarily preoccupied with asserting a narrow and xenophobic co-incidence between race and nation: historically speaking they have also embraced transnationalism. In the 1930s the Icelandic Nationalist Party sported a swastika while extolling racial purity (Griffin, 1991) and currently South Africa's Afrikaner Resistance Movement or AWB has adopted the emblem of three sevens joined at the bottom which is strikingly reminiscent of the Nazi swastika.

These patterns of transnational dialogue were also established during fascism's generic period. For example in 1938, Madhav Golwalkar, Supreme Leader of the Hindu rightist organisation *Rashtriya Swayamsevak Sangh* (RSS), a forerunner of The *Bharaiya Janata Party* (BJP), commented:

German national pride has now become the topic of the day. To keep the purity of the nation and its culture, Germany shocked the world by her purging of the country's Semitic race – the Jews. National pride at its highest has been manifested here. Germany has also shown how well-nigh impossible it is for races and cultures, having differences going to the root, to be assimilated into one united whole, a good lesson for us in Hindustan to learn and profit by. (Quoted in Bhatt, 1994a, p. 212)

The contemporary use of new information technologies by neo-fascist organisations has intensified the syncretic processes we have discussed so far. New technologies such as electronic mail, bulletin boards and computer games have all been incorporated within current forms of ultra-right-wing politics and racist culture. An important feature of this digitally assisted *virtual racism* is the degree to which various ultra-nationalisms have become commensurably equivalent with each other. Specific symbols and emblems are substituted without altering the ideological foundations of this fascist culture. This was neatly summed up by Aleksei Venediktov when commenting on the Russian fascist Vladimir Zhirinovsky's book *The Last Bid for The South*. He suggests: 'One could, of course, argue that Zhirinovsky's book is medicine for internal use only. Substitute the word "Englishman" every time you see the word "Russian" and read it through again. What do you say? Tempting is it not?' (Venediktov, 1994, p. 62). The use of computer simulation and transnational information networks provides a key context in which the theoretical and political tension between the ethnocentric and Eurocentric elements of contemporary racism can be worked through. In this sense such an examination would not merely be confined to addressing issues of technological changes, but it would also involve a reconceptualisation of how racism works within and beyond the boundaries of particular nation states. The nature of these patterns of substitution and commensurability disrupt received understandings of globalisation and localisation. On the one hand, the internationalisation of communication networks facilitates a global exchange of signs, symbols and structures of expression, but on the other, they serve to reinforce rather than threaten the intense forms of localisation at the heart of ultra-right nationalist ideologies.

Evidence first appeared in the early 1990s that electronic mail and computer bulletin boards were being used by neo-fascists. These technologies are virtually inaccessible to law enforcement agencies and provided neo-fascist groups with an international communication without surveillance. In March 1993, neo-Nazi organisations in Germany used E-mail in the planning of a memorial march for Rudolf Hess. The march, which had been banned in two states, was rerouted by using electronic communication, thus foiling the police and anti-fascist demonstrators. These systems work through the use of passwords including 'Germania' and 'Endsieg' (final victory) which enable activists to access information about forthcoming events and lists of far-right contacts. Equally, these networks are used to record names of anti-fascists, hostile judges and journalists. Additionally, long documents can be placed on bulletin boards via the Internet computer network. In Sweden there are estimated to be at least 15 to 20 active neo-Nazi computer bulletin boards. In recent times, these have included detailed instructions for making explosive devices and such texts as the *Leuchter Report* which denies that the Holocaust took place (Institute of Jewish Affairs, 1994, p. 39). Fascist materials can be circulated through these means regardless of the laws which prohibit them – for example, in Germany the use of Nazi symbols – including the swastika – are banned. However, these international networks allow fascist pop music, printed matter and information to be imported from the United Kingdom, Switzerland and the United States.

Donna J. Haraway (1991, 1992) has argued that transcendent political possibilities lie within the virtual reality of computer simulation, especially with regard to development of new modes of postmodern subjectivity. What is also clear is that these technologies may be used to reproduce and enhance the most odious aspects of the modern experience. We will examine in detail the relationship between popular culture and racism in the next chapter and return to the racial semiotics of the swastika with reference to youth styles.

Cultural politics and difference

In this chapter we have reviewed a range of models that have been used to conceptualise ethnicity and its role in shaping notions of identity and belonging. In particular we have shown how these different approaches are related to particular conceptions of human subjectivity and difference. We have stressed the dangers of reifying ideas about primordial difference which in one way or another haunt the anthropological and sociological literatures. In many ways the new cultural theory produced by post-colonial critics marks an attempt to break from this tradition. For post-colonial writers after all identity is conceptualised as operating through difference which produces 'new ethnicities' that celebrate rather than suppress internal diversity. This produces a framework for understanding ethnicity that incorporates an understanding of race, gender, class and sexuality. Beyond this these new ethnicities are seen as the product of interlocking histories. In this sense they have to be mapped within the coordinates of the local (national–regional) and global (diaspora). These are as Hall comments 'cultures of hybridity which have renounced the dream or ambition of rediscovering any kind of "lost" cultural purity, or ethnic absolutism. They are irrevocably translated' (Hall, 1992, p. 310).

What seems clear, however, is that the issue of translation has yet to be resolved. The controversy over the publication of *The Satanic Verses*, and the frequent attempts to reconstruct purified identities from locations as diverse as the Nation of Islam and British National Party, provide a healthy reminder of the importance of not being lured into a banal optimism. The tension

between 'tradition' and 'translation' promises to remain with us
well into the next century and indeed it may be irreconcilable
(Hall, 1992). And it is also clear that cultural hybridity – in itself –
need not be at all transgressive. Through looking at Nazi culture
and other racist ethnicities we have shown that some of the most
odious political movements have been cultural hybrids.
Contemporary neo-fascist groups are embracing digital technology and transnationalism to forge a global and virtual racist
culture. These examples point to the need to curb some of the
utopian excesses of the advocates of cultural hybridity.

Writers such as Cornel West in America have suggested that a
'new cultural politics of difference' is emerging out of the wreck-
age of late modernity. This he characterises as:

> A new energetic breed of new world *bricoleurs* with improvisa-
> tional and flexible sensibilities that side-step mere opportunism
> and mindless eclecticism; persons from all countries, cultures,
> genders, sexual orientations, ages and regions with protean
> identities who avoid ethnic chauvinism and faceless universal-
> ism; intellectual and political freedoms-fighters with partisan
> passions, international perspectives, and thank God, a sense of
> humour that combats the ever-present absurdity that forever
> threatens our democratic and libertarian projects and dampens
> the fire that fuels our will to struggle. (West, 1992, p. 36)

There is little doubt that the trends outlined by West and others
are an important feature of our time. But the efficacy of this new
prudence remains to be determined and there are commentators
who view the emphasis on intercultural processes with suspicion.
From Afrocentrist positions the multiply inflected new cultural
politics of difference is characterised as little more than a Euro-
assimilationist illusion that erodes the particularity and power of
cultural inheritance of Africa (Ekwe-Ekwe, 1994a). Others have
suggested that emphasising plurality and dialogue is tantamount to
cultural insanity and racial extirpation (Asante, 1994) that should
be more accurately described as promoting halfbreedity (Ekwe-
Ekwe, 1994a, 1994b). There is some irony in the fact that
Afrocentric responses to the new cultural theory should rely on a
unitary model of identity that provided the organisational vessel
through which numerous – often invidious – European nationalisms continue to be expressed. The point we are stressing here

is that a significant struggle is taking place over the way in which the politics of difference is conceptualised.

This debate can be summarised as a choice between either embracing the complex multiple formations of itinerant culture produced through movement and passage; or the assertion of arborescent traditions that in one way or another rely upon the simplicity of racial or cultural essences. We have stressed throughout this chapter that it is important to remain sceptical of group identities that rely upon invoking primordial definitions. However, that should not deflect us from appreciating the power and persuasion of the range of political movements that stress essentialist models of culture and identity. One enduring lesson that the history of Nazism and other forms of racism demonstrates is the potential currency of simple conceptions of race and belonging in situations when human beings are faced with political uncertainty.

The late twentieth century is the 'era of ethnic cleansing'. Establishing mutual coexistence within multicultural contexts has proved to be increasingly precious and volatile. Places ranging from Bosnia to London's East End have experienced growing forms of xenophobia, violence and conflict. What these diverse and contrasting settings have in common is that they provide examples where authoritarian claims to territory and space have been used to justify cultural incompatibility and exclusion (Carter *et al.*, 1993). The intellectual struggle against such contemporary political fundamentalisms has produced new and complex ways of theorising identity and belonging. The new cultural theory we have reviewed in this chapter points to the importance of being vigilantly against racism, while remaining equally suspicious of the artificial simplicities of cultural essentialism.

7 Races, Racism and Popular Culture

The currency of contemporary racisms cannot be fully comprehended without understanding their relationship to the various cultural mechanisms that enable their expression. Yet there is surprisingly little analysis of how race and cultural difference are represented in popular culture. Although some research has been done on the role of the media in shaping our images of race, there has been relatively little discussion of the other complex forms in which popular culture has helped to produce much of the racial imagery with which we are familiar today. This is why in this chapter we want to shift focus somewhat and explore the following two issues: how is racism made popular? What kind of technical infrastructure exists which transmits racist ideas and what are its origins? With these key questions in mind we want to look at how conceptions of race have been shaped by popular cultural forms. The key aim is to examine the ways in which racism intersects with the meanings, images and texts that furnish the banal aspects of everyday life.

A good example of how the new visual media began to have a major impact on questions about race can be seen in the development of the cinema. The power of film in the representation of racial issues became evident from a very early stage. The controversy surrounding D. W. Griffith's film *The Birth of a Nation*, which was first screened in 1915, is a case in point (Simmons, 1993). The film portrayed southern blacks after the end of slavery as ignorant, uncouth and driven by sexual lust. It represented the Ku-Klux-Klan as the saviours of southern whites, and in particular as the protectors of white women from the desires of black men. What is important to note, however, is that *The Birth of a*

Nation also constituted a major development in the art of film-making. Edward de Grazia and Roger Newman (1982) argue that no other single motion picture has had as important an impact on the history of the cinema. It was Griffith who mastered what others developed in terms of building scenes and creating imagery. While *Birth of a Nation* celebrated and romanticised southern racism it brought new techniques of film-making including fade-outs, close ups and long shots that were all assembled to constitute a powerful and elaborate narrative.

Griffith's film demonstrated vividly the power of the new form of cultural expression, yet it was banned more often than any other in the history of motion pictures and remains controversial to this day. The dissension surrounding this film shows that from their very inception the twentieth century's new electronic media became a crucial context in which racism could be both expressed and contested (Kisch and Mapp, 1992). A central theme of this chapter is the degree to which the elaboration of racist ideas has gone hand in hand with technological advancement. In this sense racism is not viewed as an ideological hiatus within the history of European societies, since it constitutes a key element in the history of modernity (Bauman, 1989). Through the case studies that follow we want to exemplify this process and show how popular racism has shifted through time and place while pointing to key continuities in its form and effect.

Throughout the chapter we have deliberately adopted a broad definition of popular culture, to include printed, audio, film and televisual media and other forms of commercial culture. This somewhat broad definition of popular culture allows us to explore the complex mechanisms in which everyday cultural practices are at the heart of racialised discourses and racist imagery. It would be misleading, however, to portray popular culture as uniform and fixed in its role in popularising racial imagery. Rather, it seems evident that popular culture possesses a dual tendency with regard to the politics of race, whereby it is simultaneously the locus for the expression of racism and a site where the efficacy of racist images can be challenged. We want to illustrate these points through a series of case studies, as to the way racist sentiments are registered within popular culture in a variety of contexts and at different historical moments. Our aim here is not to give an exhaustive overview but to provide some detailed insight into specific cases while remaining sensitive to identifying broad trends.

The core sections of this chapter focus on four examples that show how historically situated racisms were expressed through the mass media. We start with an examination of the ways in which iconic representations of nationhood were produced within printed and commercial cultures in Britain during the eighteenth and nineteenth centuries. This leads into an examination of the relationship between racism, popular culture and propaganda in Germany during the Third Reich. The aim of these two sections is to demonstrate the significance of commercial cultures and the media in maintaining the cultural hegemony of imperialism and Nazism. This is followed by a discussion of the ways in which black minorities have been represented in the media in the post 1945 period. The final example looks at the complex and shifting nature of contemporary media representations of race, culture and difference. Here the ambivalent nature of racial imagery in popular culture is examined with particular reference to the sophisticated coding of current racisms.

Icons of nationhood: John Bull, Britannia and empire

As we have seen earlier in this volume the history of European expansion and colonialism is replete with attempts to produce visual images and cultural representations of the 'other'. Such attempts were an integral component of the history by which European societies came to conceptualise the 'people without history' (Wolf, 1982). A number of historical studies have highlighted the ways in which from the earliest stages of European exploration and settlement images of the 'body' and 'soul' of the 'native' became part of popular culture (Jordan, 1968). However, it was in the late nineteenth and early twentieth centuries that the 'mechanical reproduction of culture', to use Walter Benjamin's (1968) famous phrase, took on an unprecedented complexity. It was also during this period that the powerful role of visual culture in reproducing images of race became most evident. This has been illustrated in a number of recent studies of the changing images of Africa and Africans and how these were represented through popular culture (Appiah, 1992; Pieterse, 1992; Coombes, 1994; Mudimbe, 1994).

Within the context of British society an interesting example of the role of popular culture in shaping images of race and otherness can be found in the ways in which imperial propaganda helped to situate images of British society and of colonial peoples. John MacKenzie has demonstrated that imperialist propaganda was produced in Britain by a large number of imperial agencies in the late nineteenth century. The notion of propaganda here is defined as the transmission of ideas and values from dominant groups who control the means of communication, with the intention of influencing the receivers' attitudes and thus enhancing and maintaining their position and interests. According to MacKenzie, the influence of imperial propaganda extended 'deeply into the educational system, the armed forces, uniformed youth movements, the Churches and missionary societies, and forms of public entertainment like the music hall and exhibitions' (MacKenzie, 1984, p. 23). Imperial propaganda was disseminated in two distinct forms via the institutions of church and state and the new and popular forms of culture and communication. The extraordinary explosion of advertising was coupled with the growth of commercial ephemera targeted particularly at young men (Richards, 1990). These took the form of cigarette cards that were collected and swapped, picture postcards and a wealth of juvenile journals. These texts became 'the prime source of news, information, and patriotic and militaristic propaganda' (MacKenzie, 1984, p. 17).

The technical revolution that took place in printing during the nineteenth century made this possible and turned the printed word and the visual image into a mass medium. The seemingly banal character of the 'cigarette card' hides the extraordinary impact that these texts had on the dreams and aspirations of their male consumers, for it was through images of exploration and conquest found there that they discovered not only the idea of Empire but also their place in the world (Roberts, 1973; Said, 1993). These printed media forms were as important in the context of the reproduction of racism as the electronic counterparts that were to come later. John Julius Norwich has written that in the period up until the First World War the British Empire was celebrated 'on our biscuit tins, chronicled on our cigarette cards, [and became] part of the fabric of our lives. We were all imperialists then' (quoted in MacKenzie, 1985, p. 24).

Through these means the colonial subject was represented through a restricted grammar of images that included a range of archetypes from the tamed servant, the obliging bearer to the dangerous and primitive savage (Pieterse, 1992). As Stuart Hall has noted this restricted grammar was to provide the 'base images' of twentieth-century British racism (Hall, 1981).

Advertising represented the excitement of an expansionist age where colonial campaigns, exploration of remote territories and missionary endeavour dominated the public imagination. An important feature of this process was the way these representations articulated race and nation with images of gender. The explorer was always presented as a white man suffering adversity for the national interest. The advertisers sometimes coupled figures from the pantheon of English heroes with incongruous and unlikely commodities, as in the case of 'Stanley Boot Laces' and 'Kitchener Stove Polish'. Commercial images of exploration in the colonies rarely included references to white womanhood. This omission was underscored by the connection between colonial contexts, white womanhood and danger (Ware, 1992). This was symptomatic of a wider moral and political preoccupation with defending the national character and the purity of the race.

One exception to this was the iconic representation of Britannia. While the image of Britannia as a warrior queen equipped with trident and shield is a pervasive emblem of nineteenth-century advertising, the origins of this representation of nationhood lay in the Georgian era. The patriotic anthem 'Rule, Britannia' made its first appearance in 1745 alongside 'God Save the King' that was also written during this time. Britannia is represented in the prints of the time as a personification of the nation, which is being threatened by the French. The paranoid intensity of the gallophobia that was rife during this time is extraordinary even in comparison to modern racisms. The French are presented in the prints of Hogarth and Gillray as 'tonnish apes', lesser breeds with unspeakable intentions. Gerald Newman, commenting on a particular cartoon, describes one common racist stereotype of the French: 'In scenes truly nightmarish to behold, [the French] dismember the fair Britannia, administer emetics to her and force her to vomit English possessions into basins held by apish Frenchmen' (Newman, 1987, p. 79). Here the image of the 'French apemen' also doubles as a symbol of the devil. What is interesting, however, is the degree to which these images invoke moral outrage through deploying the image of Britannia and thus coding the nation feminine. In his study of the graphic prints of the era, Atherton suggests that Britannia is an image of 'Virtue, especially those virtues relevant to national and public life: love of country, dedication, honesty, selflessness, discipline, simplicity' (Atherton, 1974, p. 266). The violation of Britannia thus becomes a violation of those virtues. This form of ideography works to produce powerful and stirring emotions precisely because it crosses attributes associated with the feminine and national vulnerability.

Beyond this the nation from the mid 1750s onwards was modelled on the family, or more correctly an extension of it. The British character was constructed through invoking ties of shared blood that claimed that they were 'immutably the same'. As Stella Cottrell suggests, 'The King was the loving father. The country, as Britannia, was the mother' (Cottrell, 1989, p. 264). The traces of this gendered nationalism are found quite clearly in the popular culture of the nineteenth century, where references to Britannia are invariably presented in connection with 'domestic imagery'. An obeying lion is also commonly paired with Britannia as both her protector and an emblem of the violent potency of the nation (Colley, 1992). More often Britannia is portrayed sitting on a green landscape modelled in the shape of the British Isles looking out to sea, sometimes with white cliffs or a gun boat within her regal view. Manufacturers of cleaning products took these links a stage further by presenting Britannia 'polishing' her shield or even the globe (Opie, 1985).

The advertisement for Vinolia Toothpaste, dated 1915, provides a good example of the semantic interplay of femininity and nationhood (Figure 7.1). Here Britannia is inviting the viewer into a domestic scene, beneath the flags draped over her arms are pastoral images of rural England complete with a country house, church, oak trees and a river. The viewer is asked to buy goods that are 'British made' and 'British owned' but what is striking is that this advertisement is dominated by the cultural aesthetic of Englishness. This is also true of many of the representations of Britishness of this time and since. Britannia invites the viewers to identify with Britain through expressing their spending power. The elision between Britishness and Englishness is not accidental.

Figure 7.1   Britannia and the domestic: Vinolia toothpaste advert, 1915

This invitation is not about belonging to Britain but the assertion of the cultural hegemony of England. It is not surprising that there are few references to the Celtic fringe or regional cultures in this or other advertisements of its time. Beyond this, through the figure of Britannia, the representations of Englishness/Britishness are made incarnate and personified. This iconic figure embodied the nation in a racialised skin with phenotypic features and national attributes. It is with some irony then that this commodity that is being sold through invoking primal allegiances should claim that it 'Cleans and whitens without scratching'.

The masculine counterpart to Britannia in late nineteenth-century advertising was John Bull. This national icon has a fascinating cultural history. John Bull was created as a political caricature to stand as an allegory for the English character. It is fitting that his creator was not, in fact, an Englishman. John Bull was invented by the Scottish mathematician and physician John Arbuthnot for a series of pamphlets in 1712. Arbuthnot's essays were published subsequently under the title *The History of John Bull*. Bull was portrayed as of a sound although irascible nature:

> The reader ought to know, that *Bull,* in the main, was an honest plain-dealing fellow, Cholerick, Bold and of a very unconstant Temper ... he was very apt to quarrel with his Friends especially if they pretended to govern him ... his Spirits rose and fell with the Weather-glass. *John* was quick, and understood his business very well, but no Man alive was more careless, in looking into his Accounts, or more cheated by Partners, Apprentices, and Servants ... Loving his Bottle and his Diversion; for to say Truth, no Man kept a better house than *John,* nor spent his Money more generously. (Arbuthnot, 1976, p. 9)

This characterisation of the Englishman as honest and spirited, with sharp business acumen and beleaguered by opportunists and excessive indulgence proved a complementary male image to Britannia's high virtue. What is equally present in Arbuthnots original is the vicious animalistic representation of the French. Louis XIV is dubbed 'Louis Baboon' and the text provides in many ways a defining moment of British gallophobia. John Bull is a clothier and linen-draper who, along with his Dutch ally, acts against French interference. The popularity of the satire established John Bull as a national emblem but over subsequent decades his social character was to change.

During the period between the French Revolution and the Napoleonic Wars John Bull became a caricature of the nation manipulated through the pen of satirists such as James Gillray and Thomas Rowlandson. Cartoon portraits brought the politicians and rulers of the period to life and John Bull stood for the plight of the nations people either beleaguered by domestic taxation or threatened by revolutions abroad (Colley, 1992). By the beginning of the nineteenth century John Bull's social status had been raised from a simple clothier to portly prosperous landowner. His iconic status reached its high point by the 1850s in the work of the cartoonists John Leech and Sir John Tenniel who illustrated the satirical journal *Punch*. John Bull was transformed into a foursquare but jovial country gentleman, brandishing a riding crop and wearing a top hat, Union Jack waistcoat and riding boots with a bulldog at heel. This transformation shows the clear connection between images of the land, countryside and nationalism.

By the late nineteenth century John Bull was an omnipresent feature of mass advertising. Products were even named after him, the most notable examples being the *John Bull Printing Outfit* and the *John Bull Cycle Repair Outfit* which were essential for every child. The seeming banality of these commodities hides their importance as symbolic conductors of national identity. Buying these commodities could also involve the purchase of an image of the nation and its status in the world. The representations of John Bull during this time provided a male counterpart to the nebulous attributes identified with Britannia. In contrast to Britannia's image as an introspective, warrior queen sovereign over the domestic, John Bull was always presented as a proactive champion of Britains interests abroad. This manifested in images of his portly figure striding over a map of the world, carrying a packet of Coleman's Mustard or shouldering Cadbury's Cocoa Essence, bringing imperial goods to every table.

The *England's Glory Matches* advertisement presented here (Figure 7.2) and dated 1905 stands in sharp contrast to the previous image of Britannia. Here John Bull the pugilist is knocking out his foreign rival Kaiser Bill and through this blow he fights off metaphorically competitors for trade. The audience is invited

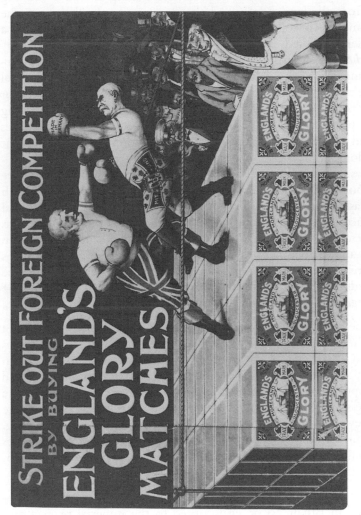

Figure 7.2 John Bull as an English champion: England's Glory Matches tin sign, 1905

to 'strike out at foreign competition' by 'buying English'. The matches themselves form the platform or stage for this battle of nationalisms. In addition to this there is an elision between the figure of John Bull – who is presented boxing as well as looking on from the ring side – and the commodity. In this sense the commodity is collapsed into a representation of John Bull as a gendered, classed and racialised subject. Buying *England's Glory Matches* is thus striking out at England's enemies as well as purchasing an identity. The industrialists who produced this material were above all concerned with capturing the domestic market for their produce. This led them to harness nationalism by associating their products with imperial imagery but in so doing these images added to the reproduction of English nationalism as a popular ideology.

In summary, imperial propaganda established some of the core symbols of British racism. It was also integrally connected with the fashioning of a national subject that possessed a distinct racial character, an imperial destiny and a standing in the world. It was these characteristics that were embodied in the images of John Bull and Britannia. Popular culture also provided the means whereby racial stereotypes could be conveyed to a wide audience regardless of class or social status. John MacKenzie sums up the implications of this image-making process:

> The working class in Britain could participate in the rule of others ... They were constantly reminded by the missionaries and other agencies of their own good fortune, and their own lot was contrasted by teachers and clerics, school texts and popular literature, with that of people in the Empire. The same message was proclaimed by the containers of every beverage they drank, and in a host of advertisements and packaging. Thus through the colonial connection domestic underclasses could become imperial 'overclasses'. (MacKenzie, 1985, p. 254)

Thus it became possible for even the most economically impoverished in Britain to be conscripted to the imperial project and gain advantage from white supremacy. The allure of this message was connected integrally with a national project: 'It was an enterprise tinged with a sense of moral crusade, aided by periodic war, led by charismatic figures, both alive and dead. In its ancestor worship, its ritual, its emphasis on authority, it linked tribal atavism with cultural self-satisfaction and technical advance' (ibid., p. 255).

John Bull with his bulldog at heel and Britannia protected by her lion were established by the early twentieth century as the key totems of Englishness. The point that we want to stress here is that these images are produced through a complex interplay between notions of race, gender and nation. Imperialism produced its own ideology through its visual culture of postcards, comics, newspapers and popular fiction. It was, however, in the fascist regimes of the twentieth century that the deadly impact of electronic technologies, national symbolism and popular culture became fully clear. Propaganda and popular culture under fascism provided the key weapon for establishing and maintaining its appeal and acceptance.

Nazism, propaganda and visual culture

A key and enduring part of the power of racism is the way in which it helps to account for specific social relations in a simple manner. This process of rendering the abstract concrete is a function of all ideologies. What is important in relation to the morphology of racist ideas is that they intrinsically involve the production of a visual culture. George Mosse, the eminent historian of Nazism, comments: 'Racism was a visual ideology based upon stereotypes. That was one of its main strengths. Racism classified men and women: this gave it the clarity and simplicity essential to its success' (Mosse, 1985a, p. xii). The transformation of German culture that began in 1933 was crucially implicated in what was to end with the concentration camps and the Holocaust. It is for this reason that Peter Adam (1992) has commented that Nazi popular culture needs always to be viewed through the lens of Auschwitz. Within the vernacular culture of Nazism we find the beginnings of an understanding of the cultural framework of feeling and emotion that produced this most modern form of genocide.

This process of rendering human beings via a repertoire of visual of stereotypes was perhaps most clearly exemplified in the representations of Jews within Nazi posters and cartoons.

However, the popular culture of the Nazis was also preoccupied with the reinvention of the Aryan character within art, film, sculpture and architecture. It was through this revolution that the Nazism reshaped the cultural landscape of Germany. This was not achieved through the invention of Nazi aesthetics, rather the 'Nazification of art' (Taylor and van der Will, 1990) involved the rewriting of history and combining Nordic and Germanic references. While Nazism did little more than assemble elements of German romanticism and mysticism this popular art was disseminated through new electronic media such as the newsreel and photograph. Thus Nazism could invoke a premodern Aryan inheritance while embracing the technological fruits of modernity. The artifice of Nazism was its ability to use this combination to ensure that politics was collapsed into popular aesthetics (Benjamin, 1968; see also Buck-Morss, 1991; McCole, 1993).

The art of the Third Reich attempted to present an image of Aryan Germans into which the individual could project him or herself. It espoused an eternal racial character through images of idyllic rural Germany and simple peasant family life. Through these images of heroic endeavour on the land an imaginary Germany was visualised. Nazi painting presented the peasantry as frozen stereotypes of undisturbed racial perfection in harmony with nature and eternally rooted in the land and soil. This connection was invariably achieved by using the plough, seed and scythe as key symbols of honest toil within the context of fashioning a sense of racial identity (Adam, 1992). It is striking that few references were made to Nazism's 'others' within their popular art, this representational space was given over to images of everything that was good and wholesome in the newly found Aryan culture. For most Germans who were living in conditions of urban poverty the consumption of these images meant their individual misfortune could be lost in the alluring racial fantasies of 'heimat' and the promise of a better future. This media-generated 'virtual home' provided Nazism with the antidote to the excesses of modernity often expressed through references to the decadent Jewish metropolis. The Nazis took their art to the German masses, they sent theatre groups to every village, orchestras played concerts of Wagner, Brahms and Beethoven in factories, and it was through the new technologies of the newsreel and the radio that their message was broadcast to every German home. Josef Goebbels, the Minister for People's Enlightenment and Propaganda, and second most powerful man in the Third Reich, was entrusted with the task of creating a popular culture in which Germans could simultaneously find a sense of racial destiny and abandon their responsibility to the highly assimilated Jews who lived as their neighbours.

It is revealing in this sense that Adolf Hitler enjoyed playing to an image of himself as theatrical political performer and later as an 'artist statesman'. He boasted responsibility for every novel aspect of the new regime, from the structure of the Reich's architecture to the design of the Volkswagen Beetle. Goebbels too stressed the connection between art and politics:

> Politics too is an art, perhaps the highest and most comprehensive there is, and we who shape modern German policy feel ourselves in this to be artists who have been given the responsible task of forming, out of the raw materials of the mass, the firm concrete structure of the people. (Quoted in Taylor and van der Will, 1990, p. 1)

The 'structure of the people' that Goebbels set about to form needed to purge all corrupting and impure elements (Sontag, 1990). In May 1933, Goebbels orchestrated an orgy of book burning where Jewish and leftist texts were publicly burned. This was more than merely erasing literature that was repugnant to the Nazis, it was also the assertion of a 'German spirit' that had expunged the intellectualism of urban European Jewry: a triumph of the racially pure body over the Jewish mind. The preoccupation of the Nazis with the body is at the centre of their popular art, where the lithe Aryan figure stood healthy and clean as a monument to their eternal racial character (Adam, 1992).

Nazism produced an image of the German 'Volk' into which individuality could be dissolved and where human conscience could be drowned by the deafening sound of the mass rally. Physical exercise along with dance and marching took on a kind of messianic fervour. Nazi dance organised its participants within a geometric discipline: 'It place[d] a grid over the mass of bodies, which both arranged individuals and separate[d] them from one another. Clear lines confine[d] them to their places and prevented them from escaping' (Servos, 1990, p. 64). The spectacular rituals of mass dancing recorded during the Olympic Games in 1936 and the display of Stormtroopers marching in perfect cohorts through the Brandenburg Gate anchored Nazism in the rhythm of the body. These public demonstrations were Hitler's rejoinder and stood as an answer to the very different rhythms that occupied the metropolitan night-clubs where his Volkish reverie was less secure.

During the Nazi period jazz was embraced by German young people much to the chagrin of the white supremacists. Nazi musicologists attacked jazz and justified their opposition to it by arguing that its rhythm was unsuitable. They complained that unlike Germans 'Negro tribes do not march' [sic] (Kater 1992, p. 31). This was also coupled with an attempt to show that jazz was the product of an abominable collaboration between 'Negroes' and 'Jews' with racially corrosive implications for Aryan Germans. While characterising jazz as another form of 'degenerate culture' the Nazis also attempted to develop their own saccharine form of jazz. These moves did not stop the development of a vibrant subculture of *jazz defiants*, known as 'Swing youth' after the jazz dance genre. Jazz was particularly popular in the city of Hamburg. The Swings utilised English rather than German with their prestige vernacular and would greet each other with the phrase 'swing high!' Swing style for men took the form of a caricature of the 'English spiv' and included sports jackets, crepe sole shoes, extravagant scarves, 'Anthony Eden' hats, an umbrella on the arm regardless of the weather, a dress-shirt button worn in the buttonhole often with a jewelled stone. Women styled their hair long shaved their eyebrows and pencilled them, dressing in flowing luxurious gowns, wore lipstick and lacquered nails.

The Swings were scrutinised by the Hitler Youth who compiled reports on their 'un-Aryan behaviour' and sexual degeneracy. One such account on a swing festival in Hamburg in February 1940 attended by 500–600 young people reveals the considerations of these youth spies:

> The dance music was all English and American. Only swing dancing and jitterbugging took place ... The dancers were an appalling sight. None of the couples danced normally; there was only swing of the worst sort. Sometimes two boys danced with one girl; sometimes several couples formed a circle,

linking arms and jumping, slapping hands, even rubbing the backs of their heads together; and then, bent double, with the top half of the body hanging down loosely, long hair flopping into the face... when the band played the rumba, the dancers went into wild ecstasy. They all leaped around and joined in the chorus of broken English. The band played wilder and wilder items; none of the players were sitting down any longer, they all 'jitterbugged' on stage like wild creatures. (Quoted in Peukert, 1987, p. 166)

The dance-hall provided a context in which to explore alternative forms of femininity and masculinity and offered opportunities for gaining sexual experiences. The import of American styles of feminine beauty was viewed as particularly abhorrent by the Nazis and the incorporation of Anglo-American styles by 'swing girls' posed a serious challenge to the femininities associated with Nazi ideology and the state youth organisations. Equally for young men their urban style challenged the dominant uniform of Nazi masculinity that combined the Aryan warrior hero with images of the responsible peasant patriarch. The Swing subculture was not a self-consciously radical movement, despite the vicious suppression meted out to them by the Gestapo and the Hitler Youth. It was estimated that from 1942 to 1944 75 Swing youths were sent to concentration camps by the SS who classified them as political prisoners. Within the context of the metropolitan night-clubs themselves Jazz dancing allowed for counter-hegemonic forms of bodily expression and individuality that was so emphatically repressed within Nazi popular culture, music and dance.

Nazi representations of the racial 'other' were principally confined to propaganda posters and cartoons (Rhodes, 1976). This included predictable portrayals of 'money grabbing' Jewish businessmen, alongside representations of the modernist decadence of Jewish Bolsheviks. During the war years Nazi propaganda combined anti-Semitic images with references to the 'black Allied soldier'. The propagandists deployed images of black soldiers to stand as a measure of Allied racial decay and a symptom of the mongrelisation of American society. The presence of the black soldier was thus turned into a corrosive threat to European civilisation. The black soldier as a moral threat has a particular history within the wartime German psyche. In the aftermath of

Germany's defeat in 1918 the Belgian and French armies used black colonial troops in their occupation of the Rhineland territories. This produced a moral panic within Germany and a sense of outrage that this was the ultimate insult to the vanquished nation's pride. The presence of black soldiers was stereotyped through the image of 'Jumbo', a monstrous sexual predator who threatened the moral chastity of white German women. The preoccupation with miscegenation was taken to considerable lengths and Afro-German children and their mothers were subject to ostracism and attack. The Society for Racial Hygiene that was founded in 1905 began conducting sterilisations of Afro-Germans in 1919. Eugenics provided the rationale for these barbaric acts that were explained as necessary for the protection of the Volk and the elimination of 'racial diseases'. After 1937 Hitler inherited this mission and hundreds of sterilisations were conducted (Opitz, Oguntoye and Schultz, 1992).

Late in the Second World War Nazi propagandists, again facing the possibility of defeat, invoked the Rhineland episode through cartoon portrayals of black Allied soldiers as primitive and devoid of culture. The cartoon presented in Figure 7.3 provides a good example of the genre. This is an image of barefooted savagery aimed to entertain the German audience. One soldier is presented twirling his finger to a non-Aryan rhythm while a smashed bottle of beer or alcohol signals their intoxication. The figure in the foreground announces in the caption 'We're fighting for culture, Jimmy'. His comrade replies, 'But what is culture?'. These cartoons enabled Germans to find humour in their racism, often published during periods when Allied planes were bombing German cities. In 1944 with the German army facing an impending Allied invasion, Nazi propagandists again turned to images of black Allied soldiers. This strategy was particularly tailored to the occupied countries of western Europe. Here the use of images of the black soldier's masculinity and cultural barbarism was aimed to arouse fear about the cultural consequences of the presence of black men in France and Holland.

A pamphlet circulated in Holland, in 1944, provides an example of this strategy. This document was produced by Goebbels' Ministry for People's Enlightenment and Propaganda. It was entitled 'Greetings From England – The Coming Invasion' and it was written in Dutch as if it were an Allied address to the

Figure 7.3 Nazi cartoon representations of the black Allied soldier. Underneath a caption read: 'We're fighting for culture Jimmy'. His comrade replies, 'But what is culture?'

occupied citizens of Holland. The pamphlet announces the arrival of the Allies latest 'secret weapon' – black soldiers. On one side of the pamphlet was the head of a grinning and wide-eyed black soldier wearing a helmet and on the other a picture of paratroopers falling from the sky. In the text it suggests that the Germans are wrongly expecting a sea invasion. The following is a translation of the main body of the text that outlines 'the real plan' (Figure 7.4):

'The Dark Cloud'

The British General Staff has now granted permission to divulge some further details about this.

From the beginning of the year, more than half a million Negroes have been brought from America to Scotland, where they get a special training in parachute jumping. An interesting detail is that their parachutes are made from dark-grey silk. As the clouded skies above Holland are usually dark grey as well, this handy camouflage makes it pretty much impossible for the Germans to shoot the parachute legion.

It will be an enormous humiliation for Hitler, the prophet of racial theories, when his warriors will be driven from western Europe by the black race. Dutchmen, your cooperation will be counted upon when the black legion is coming. Make your old jazz-records ready, because at the celebration of liberation your daughters and wives will be dancing in the arms of real Negroes.

Weird shaped ruins will form a fantastic background for the liberation orgy, where black and white will mingle so deeply, that it will remain a pleasant memory for the people of Holland to the invasion of the black cloud.

Dutch girls and women. A beautiful and pleasant task lies ahead of you, to which you will have to give yourself completely and without any restraint, in order to contradict the racial nonsense of Hitler.

This is quite clearly an attempt to invoke racial anxiety in the Dutch who also possessed colonial territories. The interesting thing about this piece of Nazi propaganda is the way in which it feigns parody of its own dogma, with references to Hitler being

Figure 7.4 'Greetings from England: The Coming Invasion'. Nazi pamphlet circulated in Holland, 1944

embraced by being driven back by the 'black race'. This is a reference to the Rhineland occupations. The Dutch are invited to fly in the face of the 'prophet of racial theories' by embracing the possibility of social and sexual intimacy with the soldiers of the 'dark cloud'. The allusions to black soldiers' visibility and invisibility are also interesting in this text. On the one hand, the soldiers are presented as a phantom force who will be invulnerable to the Germans because of their invisibility when backed by the grey Dutch sky. However, this extract ends by referring to the indelible racial imprint that will be left on the Dutch by the 'liberation orgies'.

The key mechanism being used to invoke Dutch fears in this text is the partially veiled references to miscegenation. This works through a highly gendered set of references. Dutch men are called upon by the Allies to advocate 'black and white intermingling', to make ready their jazz-records and to offer their daughters and wives to the 'black legion'. Dutch women are then charged to give of themselves 'without restraint'. This propaganda facade works at a sophisticated level through testing its male Dutch readers consent to the Allied alternative to Nazism. The question that underscores this text can be outlined in the following terms: the Allies are in favour of miscegenation and the Nazis want to maintain racial purity. In this sense the propaganda aims to work by invoking a common resistance to miscegenation and a shared sense of European–Aryan racial identity. Nazi propaganda not only concentrated on miscegenation it also used images of black soldiers as representing a threat to European culture.

The poster entitled 'Liberators' reproduced here was also displayed in Holland prior to the Allied invasion (Figure 7.5). In one image it registered all that Nazi popular culture despised and attempted to expunge. This figure of cultural invasion stands for everything that is decadent in American life. Somewhere between Frankenstein and King Kong the invader brings together the antithesis of the Nazi ideals of racial purity and their attendant versions of manhood and womanliness. The 'Statue of Liberty' and the New York skyline can be seen in the distance (bottom left-hand corner) which gives this monster a distinctly urban origin and reinforces the connection between the city and race: New York of all the great metropolises is the most strongly associated with Jewishness. There are other references that reinforce the association between the deviant city life and the Jew. Behind

Figure 7.5 Monstrous Regiment: Nazi poster portraying the GI as a jitterbugging marauder. Poster in Holland, 1944

the boxer's glove on the right-hand side of the image hides a Jewish businessman peering over a bag full of dollars and a Star of David hangs between the monster's legs. These images are coupled with other representations of urban delinquency, the set of white arms represents on one side criminality through the manacle and the striped prison uniform and on the other brandishes a stick bomb. These are accompanied by series of confused images relating to US racial politics.

The torso of the monster constitutes a cage that holds an apeman and apewoman associated with black music and dance – the caption reads 'Jitterbug – Triumph of Civilisation'. References to black masculinity are coded via the monster's top set of arms which are black and muscular. In one hand is a record that signifies the decadent music of jazz while on the other is a boxing glove, a symbol of brute strength. These images, which draw on relatively common racist themes, are then combined with a reference to domestic American racism. The head of the monster is hidden by the mask of the Ku-Klux-Klan and a hangman's noose is wound around one of the black arms as a reference to the practice of lynching black Americans in the South. The tragic irony is that this piece of propaganda was authored by a regime that exterminated a million Jews by this point in the war. The implication seems to be that the culture of the European mainland would be threatened by an Allied invasion because it would bring American racism to the continent.

Also signalled within this image is the potential import of immoral forms of femininity that revealed the sexual depravity of the Americans. The representations of the two white beauty queens on either arm of the monster register this abhorrence of the artificial femininity of white American women and the fetish for such beauty. This is also supported by the female coded right leg of the monster that has a tape measure around its calf and thigh and the ribbon that is tied above its knee announces it as the 'world's most beautiful leg'. We cannot read the significance of this image without a prior knowledge of the ideal models of Aryan femininity. Nazi art and popular culture stressed the importance of women as the safe keepers of life whose form should be admired as a thing of natural beauty. The caricature presented here of 'Miss America Femininity' constitutes the absolute antithesis of Aryan female beauty which was defined by its perfection in nature.

While the monster includes female elements as a whole the figure is gendered male. Its left male formed leg is presented in the form of a bomb that is suspended like a sword of Damocles over the monuments of Western civilisation. It is through these references that it also represents the Allied war machine complete with the wings of a bomber. As the monster stands suspended before trampling over Europe the caption reads: 'The "liberators" will save European culture from its downfall'. Reference to a common European culture is being invoked in an attempt to summon sympathy and support within the occupied territories. The use of cultural references here are significant because as we have shown similar forms of pseudo-cultural logic became a core feature of the 'new racisms' of the late twentieth century.

These examples of Nazi propaganda demonstrate the role that racism played managing periods of crisis where control was being lost over the occupied lands of Western Europe. They also show the clear vocabulary of race that was at the disposal of these propagandists. Beyond this, new technologies, such as photography, enabled the mass character of Nazism to be captured in unprecedented ways. Walter Benjamin in his classic essay on 'Art in the Age of Mechanical Reproduction' comments:

> Mass movements are usually discerned more clearly by a camera than by the naked eye. A bird's eye view best captures gatherings of hundreds of thousands. And even though such a view may be accessible to the human eye as it is to the camera, the image received by the eye cannot be enlarged the way a negative is enlarged. (Benjamin, 1968, p. 244)

The spectacular potential of the newsreel, film and other cultural technologies reinforced the mass choreography of moral indolence. Nazism as a social movement was captured on celluloid and circulated so that the German masses could resubmit themselves to its cultural authority.

Racism and representing the black presence in Britain

Throughout the twentieth century the black presence in Britain has been viewed by public commentators as constituting a serious moral and cultural problem; a central anxiety focused on the issue of 'race mixing' and the impact of immigration on the social and cultural fabric of British society. Clive Harris has shown that black people in seaports such as Liverpool and Cardiff posed a serious moral and political problem for the politicians and bureaucrats of the day (Harris, 1988). Documenting the survey conducted in 1935 by the British Social Hygiene Council, Harris demonstrates how this organisation was preoccupied with inquiring into black sailors 'sexual demands' with regard to their white partners, their promiscuity and the suggestion that white women became addicted to the 'black sailor's sex'. In addition to this black men were also connected with the transmission of venereal disease and seen as leading white women into prostitution. Harris goes on to show how the growth in so-called 'half-caste children' became another significant feature of the discourse of state officials, particularly in Cardiff and Liverpool and ultimately at the Home Office. These young people were constructed as being 'marked by a racial trait' and to 'mature sexually at an early age' (ibid., p. 24). This moral panic was to be revisited within a more public arena when, after the Second World War, a number of stories were published about children born to white women and black American and West Indian servicemen. These children were viewed as a 'casualty of war'. One of the Home Office's proposed solutions to 'this problem' was to send these children to America to be brought up with 'other coloured children' (quoted in ibid., p. 37). In the face of opposition from within Britain's black population this proposal was never implemented. There are troubling similarities here between these sentiments and Nazi propagandists' attempts to exploit images of black Allied soldiers in order to engender white panic and anxiety.

Harris argues that what is telling about the preoccupation with miscegenation is the degree to which the racist discourse of this period is preoccupied with skin colour as the prime signifier in the subjectification of black people. The preservation of the English racial character was to be achieved by preserving its hue. Thus racialised Englishness could be: 'Stitched together by exporting the half-caste war babies, by deporting "criminal Negroes" or by repatriating the black population. The black man, or, more accurately, the "Negro", would thus be kept in his place and skin/"race" preserved as a regime of visibility marking the boundary between "cultures"' (ibid., p. 54). The primacy of a colour-coded racism can also be seen within the ways in which post-1945 immigration from the New Commonwealth was constructed within the pages of newspapers and other media. We have noted elsewhere that during the 1950s the geography of Birmingham was represented in news coverage through associating particular districts with racialised characteristics (Solomos and Back, 1995). The mention of particular districts within this discursive formation metonymically triggered a range of associated racial attributes (miscegenation/conflict) and cultural pathologies (drugs, vice, crime). These types of stories were also combined with pieces that criticised the emergence of a 'colour bar' and crudely expressed racial bigotry. Birmingham's geography became defined in terms of 'black areas' and 'white areas', despite the fact that the highest concentrations of minority settlement were rarely above 50 per cent of the total population. This imagined geography provided a core repertoire of racial attributes that were in turn used to interpret events (Back, 1994). Comparable processes were occurring within all of Britain's major cities where there were significant concentrations of minority settlement (Keith, 1993).

During the 1970s media discourses produced a significant shift away from a preoccupation with miscegenation and the early more clearly colour coded racisms, and became centrally preoccupied with covering emerging forms of 'racial crime'. The most sophisticated critique of this conjuncture was produced by Stuart Hall and his associates in their book entitled *Policing the Crisis* (Hall *et al.*, 1978). This study attempted to demonstrate among other things how the moral crisis over the street crime that became known as 'mugging' was related to managing a wider crisis in British society. Hall *et al.* argue that the designation of mugging as a black crime provides a vehicle for engendering divisions:

> [Mugging] ... provides the separation of the class into black and white with a material basis, since, in much black crime (as in much white working-class crime), one part of the class materially 'rips off' another. It provides the separation with its ideological figure, for it transforms the deprivation of the class, out of which crime arises, into the all too intelligible syntax of race, and fixes a false enemy: the black mugger. (Ibid., p. 395)

They conclude that during the 1970s British society managed a crisis in social hegemony through the twin strategies of creating and amplifying the 'mugging moral panic' and moving towards a more authoritarian law and order ideology. The symbolic location of 'black crime' connects with associated racial discourses that construct black communities as being incompatible with the 'British way of life' (Gilroy, 1987). 'Black youth' are thus defined as constituting a social problem (Solomos, 1988).

While the figure of the 'black mugger' was the dominant motif of racism in the 1970s this was elaborated upon in the 1980s in the aftermath of the widespread urban unrest that took place in a number of cities. In 1981, Britain saw widespread conflict in many of its major cities and this was followed in the summer of 1985 by clashes between young people and police in Birmingham, London, Liverpool and elsewhere. These conflicts were reported in Britain's press as a 'new phenomenon' and associated with an explicit discourse of race and criminality. Sir Peter Emery, MP for Honiton commented in 1985: 'The vast majority of people expect the precepts of Anglo-Saxon behaviour and law and order to be maintained. These standards must be maintained, despite what other ethnic minorities want' (quoted in Benyon and Solomos, 1987, p. 25). Like many other racialised discourses such responses demonstrated a profound historical amnesia. Britain has a long history of civil unrest. The Gordon riots in 1780 resulted in 285 deaths and a further 25 were hanged for taking part in them. During the 1930s there were frequent clashes between the unemployed and the police and during demonstrations against Oswald Mosley's British Union of Fascists. What is distinctive about the press reporting of urban conflict in the 1980s is that these events were represented as 'race riots'. There had been previous incidents during the 1950s that represented disorder through a racial lexicon (Miles, 1984) but this mode of representation hardened during the outbreak of violent protest in 1981 and 1985 (Solomos, 1986).

We have commented elsewhere how the representation of these events invoked a host of racialised attributes connected with black youth. What was new about these images of black criminality was the move away from street crime and 'mugging' to violent disorder and riot: black crime shifted from being against the individual to *crimes against society* (Solomos and Back, 1995). The subtext to this version of these dramatic events was that the black presence in Britain was leading to civil breakdown. The headlines that were run in the aftermath of the confrontations on the Lozells Road in Birmingham, in September 1985, show this development. The *Daily Mirror* proclaimed the event as evidence of 'War on the Streets'. The *Sun* included a photograph of a young black man carrying a petrol bomb with the headline 'Hate of the Black Bomber'. This image was carried on the front pages of the *Daily Express, Daily Mail* and *The Observer*. It became the exemplary portrait of this 'new folk devil'. In this sense we can trace the genealogy of racist constructions in British news media from the stereotype of the 1960s' 'welfare scrounger' to the 1970s' 'mugger' and ultimately the 'rioter'.

We have suggested that media stereotyping of Britain's black population has shifted in the last 60 years. These popular representations have adapted and taken on new characteristics while retaining an interconnected quality. In his study of racism and the news media Teun van Dijk concludes:

> The structure and style of headlines not only subjectively express what journalists or editors see as the major topics of new reports, but also tend to emphasise the negative role of ethnic minorities ... [who] continue to be associated with a restricted number of stereotypical topics, such as immigration problems, crime, violence (especially 'riots'), and ethnic relations (especially discrimination), whereas other topics, such as those in the realm of politics, social affairs, and culture are under-reported. (Van Dijk, 1991, p. 245)

The thing that remains constant in this reporting is that black people are seen as constituting a social problem, while at the same time they are seen as experiencing forms of injustice and discrimination that are 'morally offensive'. Splitting of this type is a central feature of racist cultures and is what Peter Hulme refers to as a 'stereotypical dualism' (Hulme, 1986).

Michael Keith in his insightful discussion of the male Bengali street-rebel has described the operation of this dual process within the contemporary urban setting of London's East End (Keith, 1995). He argues that racist discourses make sense of Bengali youth through cartographies of race and power, which map so called Asian gangs within particular sites of street criminality. This is compensated by a white leftist notion of 'the youth' as an agent of insurrection and street revolt. Keith makes the telling point that both of these urban narratives are respectively the product of fear and desire. The street rebel appears as a remixed and recoded urban insurgent, 'the result of both collective action and the manner in which such actions were framed by the mass media' (ibid., p. 366). There is a direct lineage between the Asian street rebel of the 1990s and the connections made between race, crime and locality in the 1970s and 1980s which produced the black mugger and rioter: it is only the racial patina that is exchanged.

In summary, we have argued that the British news media has represented the black presence through identifiable motifs. These have shifted in terms of their content and this dynamism demonstrates the necessity of understanding racism in its historical moment. However, it is equally important to understand the continuities that are maintained as these media discourses change. The media racism in post-war Britain can be characterised as possessing two core features in that: (i) the black presence is seen to have a racially corrosive effect on British culture; and (ii) the race/cultural difference of black people makes them incompatible with the British way of life. As we have shown this deploys the idea that alien traditions of criminality and association have been imported into the British social formation from the ex-colonial periphery.

From the Nazi propagandist to the newspaper editors the printed and electronic media have provided means whereby racist constructions of social reality are made popular. We have, however, characterised the relationship between popular culture and racism as unstable and dynamic. The racisms we have documented share important similarities but we have also stressed the shifting nature of the discourse of racial power. Malcolm X, calling on an analogy from popular culture, argued: 'Racism is like a Cadillac. The 1960 Cadillac doesn't look like the 1921 Cadillac, but it is still a Cadillac; it has simply changed form' (quoted in Otis, 1993, p. 151). It is this inherent instability within racism that makes it so adaptable but equally this reveals how quickly it might be transformed. In the following section we want to focus on recent examples of how cultural difference is represented within popular culture and the implications this has for understanding contemporary racisms.

Corporate multiculturalism: racism, difference and media images

The increase in films made by black directors both in Europe and the United States has brought new representations of culture and difference (Pines, 1988; Ross, 1996). This has resulted in a heated debate over how to interpret these films and their attendant cultural politics (Dent, 1992; Gilroy, 1995). Jhally and Lewis's recent discussion of *The Cosby Show* provides a good example of the complexity of the politics of current media representation of race. It has achieved unparalleled popularity amongst black and white and now commands a global audience. The show established itself as the most popular television show both in the United States and in South Africa under apartheid (Mercer, 1994). The show focuses on an upper middle-class black family and presents them in a world where social barriers like class and race are of no consequence. Jhally and Lewis argue that this challenges media stereotypes of black people but it has consequences: 'Among white people, the admission of black characters to television's upwardly mobile world gives credence to the idea that racial divisions, whether perpetuated by class barriers or racism, do not exist' (Jhally and Lewis, 1992). From this perspective *The Cosby Show* fits in with a wider trend within American film and cinema which located racial injustice in the past and as a result racism is safely confined to history.

It is also important to note that we have seen quite important transformations in recent years in how race is represented through the popular media. For example, advertisers and other media producers are including images of cultural difference within their repertoire of symbols. Within truly global markets some advertisers have attempted to associate their products with the transcendence of racism and cultural barriers. The result, as Kevin Robins has commented, is that cultural difference is assembled within a new 'cosmopolitan' market place: 'The local and "exotic" are torn out of place and time to be re-packaged for the world bazaar. So-called world culture may reflect the valuation of difference and particularity, but it is also very much about making profit from it' (Robins, 1991, p. 31). This market-driven multiculturalism refigures older themes associated with the fetish for the exotic, albeit mediated by the new technologies' global

integration. However, we cannot easily dismiss the unprecedented level of the enchantment with difference. The impulses
behind these shifts may be no more than a desperate attempt for
the West to recentre itself by possessing Otherness. But this does
not mean that no significant changes have taken place in how the
popular media represents race, 'blackness' and ethnicity. A recent
study of the situation in the United States, which has perhaps
seen the most activity in this field in recent years, notes the
complex ways in which popular racial images have been challenged and transformed in recent years (Turner, 1994).

In advertising we can find some of the most interesting shifts in
media representations of difference. As we showed earlier,
nineteenth-century advertisers used icons of nationhood and scenes
from Empire to bolster the appeal of their products. Pieterse
(1992), in a study of images of Africans in European popular
culture, shows how European advertisers used and played to crass
racist stereotypes of the native. Colonial images and crudely na-
tionalistic emblems are relatively rare in the current period and
where they do appear they are presented almost as a pastiche of
these previous modes of representation. It is telling that John Bull
and Britannia who so dominated nineteenth-century popular
culture in Britain have almost disappeared from the advertisers'
symbolic lexicon. Rather what we have seen in recent times is an
attempt by some multinational corporations to develop a transnational advertising aesthetic. Perhaps the best and most perplexing
example of this is the clothes manufacturer Benetton. Through the
camera of Oliviero Toscani, Benetton have attempted to promote a
message of human unity and harmony in their advertising. Starting
in 1984 they attempted to represent the world's diverse people and
cultures as synonymous with the many colours of Benetton's
produce. Since then their campaigns have provoked unparalleled
controversy, winning them awards and adulation alongside accusations of hypocrisy and opportunism.

One of the striking features of the Benetton campaigns is the
degree to which their message of transcultural unity is predicated
upon absolute images of racial and cultural difference. The initial
campaigns alluded to past and present conflicts through the pre-
sentation of archetypal images of Jews and Arabs embracing the
globe. What is intriguing about this move is that Benetton's
products do not have to be shown in order to convey meanings

about the brand quality; the message is simply resolved by the motif juxtaposed over the images of boundaries and conflicts. The 'United Colors of Benetton' becomes the antithesis of conflict, the expression of unity, the nurturer of internationalism (Back and Quaade, 1993). However, what is more troubling about this strategy is the degree to which it is reliant on racisms very categories of personhood and the stereotypes which run from these. The example reproduced here (Figure 7.6) shows three young people poking their tongues out at the viewer. This advertisement was used in a poster campaign in 1991. The message of transcendence encapsulated in Benettons slogan only makes sense if it is superimposed on a representation of clear difference. These three figures are coded through a grammar of absolute racial difference: the blue-eyed blonde white Aryan figure, flanked respectively by a 'Negroid' black child and an 'Oriental' child. This message of unity can only work if it has a constitutive representation of absolute racial contrast. The danger with such representations is that they rely on a range of racial archetypes that are themselves the product of racism and as a result make racial atavism socially legitimate forms of common-sense knowledge: the concept of race is left unchallenged.

One of the most interesting things about Toscani's photography is the ways in which he plays with ambiguity. The most dramatic example of this included a picture showing the hands of two men, one black and the other white, handcuffed together; and a picture of the torso of a black woman breast-feeding a white baby released in 1989. The reactions to these ads varied according to national context. In the United States, they were withdrawn following public complaint. The later image conjured the historical experience of slavery and the position of black women within a gendered and racialised system of exploitation, including their designation as objects of white sexual desire. In the United States and Britain, the image of handcuffed hands evoked notions of black criminality; far from suggesting two men united in incarceration. The advertisement was associated with the daily reality of young black men arrested by predominantly white law enforcement agencies. In Britain, *The Sun* ran the headline, 'Di's sweaters' firm in "racist ads" row', referring to the fact that Princess Diana had patronised Benetton products for some years. London Transport refused to display the ads on the

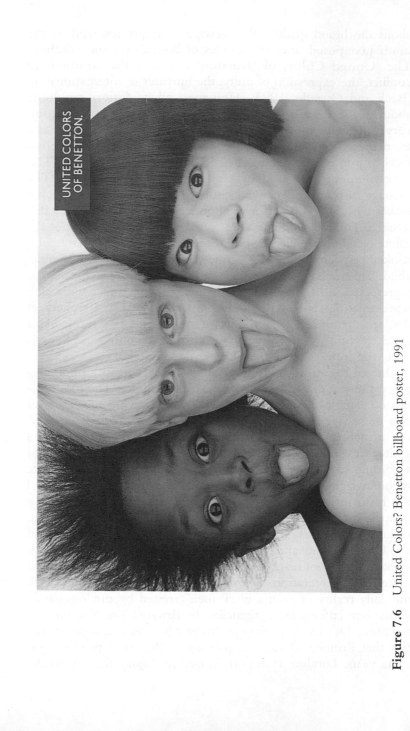

Figure 7.6 United Colors? Benetton billboard poster, 1991

London Underground, justifying their decision by the suggestion that the ads had racist overtones. The most extreme response to the campaign came in France. In Paris, neo-fascist agitators, opposing what they saw as miscegenation, threw a tear-gas canister into a Benetton shop shortly after the posters appeared. While generating controversy these images were embraced by the media more broadly and won prizes in France, Holland, Denmark and Austria. How can we make sense of this diversity of responses? Perhaps the first point to make here is to foreground the importance of understanding these iconic global images within particular contexts. The images invoked different histories of racist discourse in the United States, Britain, France or Japan. The simple point here is that the social composition of the audience affects the range of intertextual reference (histories, representation, symbolic codes, form of racism) that are used to make sense of any particular image (Mercer, 1992). These images are ambiguous because they activate the histories and cultural features of racism through connotation.

While Benetton were very much in the vanguard of this type of imagery during the 1980s, other companies have also embraced the idea of imbuing their brand quality with a transnational ethos. In 1995, British Airways ran a newspaper campaign that presented two brides, a Danish woman in a white long dress alongside an Indian woman in a bridal red sari, the caption read: 'THERE ARE MORE THINGS THAT BRING US TOGETHER THAN KEEP US APART'. The assertion of cultural translation and commensurability – the common reference being that despite ritual differences these two women were both brides – is harnessed to the airline's capacity to bring people together physically. This bears all the hallmarks of the Benetton campaigns of the mid 1980s. One could replace the British Airways' caption with Benetton's and the advertisement would work with equal effect. This intertexual quality can be found in the imagery of other companies too. Philips uses a blonde haired white girl and a black boy alongside the caption 'THE UNIVERSAL LANGUAGE OF PHILIPS'. Again the two children are united through their consumption of the commodity, with a black and white thumb sharing the control panel. This advertisement actually appeared in the newspaper that Benetton produce called *Colors*. *Colors* is an extraordinary publication because it effectively turns news items into Benetton advertising (Back and Quaade, 1993). The intertextual reference made within this advertisement produces a kind of corporate multiculturalism that trades on images of human diversity in order to produce an aesthetic that satisfies and appeals to a global market. This move can be identified within companies as diverse as the drinks magnate Coca-Cola and the Reebok sports shoes manufacturer, reflecting the way in which these companies have embraced a transnational ethos within their imagery to fit in with their global markets. What is common to these campaigns is that they all, in various ways, espouse common humanity and harmony while reinforcing cultural and racial archetypes. At worst they steer a symbolic course that is perilously close to a legacy of crude racist images and associations.

Corporate multiculturalism has not only been confined to the espousal of a saccharin version of internationalism, black style and music have also been used as a means to appeal to a youthful audience. The jeans company Levi Strauss provides a particularly interesting example of this strategy, transforming their 501 jeans from workaday industrial apparel into an essential fashion accessory. From 1984 their campaigns in the United States used black music as a marker of urban authenticity and an expression of individual heartache and freedom. In particular the ads focused on 'the Blues'. Like Benetton, Levi's attempted to blur the commodity forms with an advertising message and also a state of emotional well-being. In Benetton's case the logic of this strategy ran: united colours of people, united colors in garments – 'I wear unity'. Levi's attempted to establish an interplay between the commodity and a message of alienated individualism, and it elided blues jeans with the Blues as a celebration of solitude, alienation and solace. These forms of slippage mean that 501's not only shrink to fit your body but they also convey a kind of identity. This is summed up in their slogan: '501 Blues Shrink to Fit My Body – I got the Blues'. Music becomes the connective device through which social quotations are made and in turn bolster the product's identity with a cultural dowry. A whole range of black artists were used in these campaigns including Taj Mahal, the Neville Brothers, Booby McFerrin and Tiger Haynes. Beyond this the inner city provided the context for staging their story lines often producing romantic images of ghetto life: 'Blacks who appear on the screen seem "connected" and "in tune" with their total social space. Levi's sell the ghetto – a space which transcends social convention, restraint and repressiveness' (Goldman, 1992: p. 191). In some of the advertisements black Americans are presented teaching their white counterparts how to dance, play instruments and express themselves. The 501 advertisements offer their audience instruction in a particular version of blackness via the references to the Blues and the ghetto, where black music is equated with the body, expression, emotionality and ultimately sexuality. Through this 'injection of negritude' young whites in particular are offered a fleeting liberation from the strictures of whiteness.

This fetish for images of urban black America resonates with the association between black culture and youth alienation. Consider this quotation from Jack Kerouac's seminal beat novel *On the Road:*

> At lilac evening I walked with every muscle aching among the lights of 27th and Welton in the Denver coloured section, wishing I were a Negro, feeling that the best the white world had offered was not enough ecstasy for me, not enough life, joy, kicks, darkness, music, not enough night ... I wished I were a Denver Mexican, or even a poor overworked Jap, anything but what I was so drearily, a white man disillusioned. (Kerouac, 1955, p. 148)

What the Levi advertisements do, beyond citing black culture in a very particular fashion, is to invoke the legacy of the youthful 'White Negroes' of the 1950s who aimed to make black modes fit their facts (Mailer, 1961). In Britain the Levi campaigns of the 1980s attempted to reference this phenomenon through staging their advertisements in 1950s America. The key characters in these ads were a youthful male rebel and 'his girl' with classic soul and rhythm and blues providing the soundtrack for the advertisers vignettes. Here black cultural references enter into the mediascapes of the advertisers to perform particular types of work as markers of authenticity, expressiveness, masculinity and sexuality. In a curious way these images are not about reflecting cultural diversity at all, but rather they market a male form of 'rebel whiteness' that can be 'shrunk to fit' along with the Levi 501's and worn or cast off depending on the whims of the consumer.

As we noted earlier, racist constructions of difference can quite easily allow contradictory elements to coexist. The valuation of exotic difference can go hand in hand within racism. This process of coupling the veneration and repression of otherness actually has a long history in the West. James Clifford (1993) has shown how nineteenth-century Parisian Negrophilia was intimately tied up with modernist artistic movements. In this context the Negro stood as the cipher for everything that was pristine and sublime. This fascination and its attendant desire for otherness was used by European intellectuals as an emblem that escaped the emotional and intellectual shackles of modernity. These notions of exotic innocence are no less stereotypical than the idea that the Negro is less civilised and more barbaric. This kind of identification is locked within the discourse of absolute difference which renders blackness exotic and reaffirms black people as a 'race apart'. It was this danger which Frantz Fanon outlined when he argued that those Europeans who blindly adore the difference of the other are as racially afflicted as those who vilify it (Fanon, 1986). Similarly, Bernard Wolfe, who cowrote the biography of the legendary white jazz musician Mezz Merrow, comments on the interconnection of racial longing and hatred:

> It follows that with us, Negrophilia and Negrophobia are not, or not just, polar opposites. We may have seen them, before we're through, as two sides of one coin, a coin we're forever flipping. We can't help ourselves. By the law of averages, it comes up now heads, now tails. By the law of association, every time one side shows up, were acutely aware of the presence of the other just below. (Wolfe (1947/8), 1993, p. 400)

The lesson offered here is as relevant today as it was in the 1940s. The advertisers' current preoccupation may be little more than a reworking of the syndrome that Wolfe outlined, and we need to be vigilantly critical of the ways in which these images are constructed and whom they are directed towards.

We can find plenty of contemporary examples of oscillation between racial adulation and racism. If we look at the ways in which black sporting figures – particularly men – are constructed, we can find the ease with which yesterday's national hero can be transformed into today's racial villain. One of the most extreme examples of this process is the way in which the heavyweight boxer Mike Tyson was transformed from an example of the American dream to dangerous sexual marauder in the aftermath of his conviction for rape. The details of Tyson's case are not at issue here, rather the press reporting of this incident demonstrates how quickly the flip which Wolfe refers to can take place. A less extreme example of this process can be found in the press treatment of another black athlete, this time Britain's Linford Christie. Christie is perhaps the most outstanding sprinter ever to run for Britain and for a long time the men's captain of the British Athletics Team. Christie is undoubtedly a national hero. For many he is the symbol of a new multicultural Britain and along with a collection of other black sporting figures he has established a cultural space in which it possible to be both black and British (Gilroy, 1993b). For the most part, Christie has been represented within the media as embodying Britain's new-found status in the world of athletics. However, something else lies just below the surface on the other side of Wolfe's metaphorical coin.

In the aftermath of Christie's gold medal triumph at the Barcelona Olympic games in 1992 *The Sun* ran a story asking its readers to guess what was in Christie's LUNCH BOX:

> Linford Christie is way out in front in every department and we don't just mean the way he stormed to victory in the 100 metres ... His skin tight lycra shorts hide little as he pounds down the track and his Olympic-sized talents are a source of delight for women around the world. But the mystery remains – just what does Linford, 32, pack in that famous lunchbox? (*The Sun*, 6 August 1992)

The feature offered ten ways for the reader to pack his Lunchbox to look like Linford and included a bizarre range of suggestions from a whole continental liver sausage to four Duracell long life batteries. The story is directed clearly at a male audience that is by implication white. The incident might be seen as innocent fun, and Christie himself after an initial outrage dismissed the story as harmless. What lurks here is a whole series of white male ambivalences about the bodies of black men, their sexuality and ultimately their genitals. The humour of *The Sun* feature invoked – if only partially – the long European history of viewing black men as hypersexual beings that are simultaneously irresistible and threatening to white women. This is reminiscent of the portrayal of black Allied soldiers in Nazi propaganda and the moral panic in Britain about the sexuality of black seamen in the 1930s. In whatever measure the cultural inheritance of racism always makes it possible for the coin to be spun again, exposing the contingent nature of the inclusion of prominent black public figures. It is this contingency and ambivalence within racist culture that is particularly a symptom of our current situation in which complex combinations of national inclusion and vilification can coexist without any necessary contradiction.

Before moving on we want to clarify our argument. We are making two related points. First, what we have referred to as corporate multiculturalism possesses a dual quality. While it espouses the goal of transcultural unity it does so through reinforcing crude cultural and racial archetypes. These images operate within what Stuart Hall (1981) called a 'grammar of race'. The overpowering reference point is that race is real: racial archetypes provide the vehicle for the message, and racial common sense is overbearingly present such that the reality of race is legitimated within this media discourse. Second, the valuation and repackaging of cultural difference within contemporary media result in little more than a process of market driven recolonisation, where the fetish for the exotic reaffirms these various 'global others' as distinct and separate types of humankind. In this context the veneration of difference need not be in any contradiction with white supremacy. Quite the contrary: it can be integrally connected with the formation of contemporary cultures of racism. Yet, we also want to argue that these shifts do create important ambivalences and tensions which can unsettle the valence of racism within popular culture.

Kobena Mercer has explored the ambivalences found in racial fetishism through an analysis of the white gay photographer Robert Mapplethorpe (Mercer, 1994). In his initial reading of the photographs of black nude men found in *Black Males* and *Black Book,* Mercer offers an analysis of Mapplethorpe's 'line of sight' in which:

> Black + Male = Erotic/ Aesthetic Object. Regardless of the sexual preferences of the spectator, the connotation is that the 'essence' of black male identity lies in the domain of sexuality ... black men are confined and defined in their very being as

sexual and nothing but sexual, hence hyper sexual. (Mercer, 1994, p. 174)

He argues that the regulative function of stereotypes polices the potential for generating meanings, and as a result the spectator is fixed within the position of the 'white male subject'. However, in a later rereading Mercer changes his mind and points to the ways in which these images actually undermine the conventions of the spectator and the stereotypes which furnish this way of seeing. Mercer argues that once we understand the political specificity of Mapplethorpe's practice, we can see in his aesthetic use of irony disruptive elements which challenge Eurocentred representative regimes. Black men constitute perhaps the most social and politically marginalised group in the United States, but in Mapplethorpe's photographs the men who come from this social location are raised 'onto the pedestal of the transcendental western aesthetic ideal. Far from reinforcing the fixed beliefs of the white supremacist imaginary, such a deconstructive move begins to undermine the foundational myth of the pedestal itself' (ibid., p. 200). Mercer's argument suggests that through the use of subversion and aesthetic irony racist regimes of representation are propelled into a state of crisis and erasure. It is with these suggestive comments in mind that we want to return to the iconography of Benetton advertising.

Our intention here is not to merely reproduce a parallel argument to Kobena Mercer's insightful and reflective reading of Mapplethorpe's photography. However, if we look closely at Toscani's photography we can see similar – although not comparable – ambivalences at work. In this sense we need to revise partially the analysis offered earlier (Back and Quaade, 1993) and suggest that there are moments within Benetton's advertising imagery when the racial grammar of these representations is unsettled. Toscani has specialised in blurring photographic conventions, turning news photographs into advertising and advertising into the news. Both he and Luciano Benetton have also indulged in self-parody. In the spring 1992 edition of *Colors* their own faces are superimposed on to one of their ads. This notorious image represented two children embracing, one depicted as a white cherub angel and the other a black child devil. In this reworked version Luciano Benetton is cast as the angel and Toscani as the devil. Returning to the original image one might think of it as a moment where racial anxieties are being displayed. Is Toscani forcing the viewer to confront the racist connotations of such an image or is he merely reproducing and activating these racial ideologies? This question captures the core ambivalence found within Toscani's photography. McKenzie Wark has argued that the Benetton campaigns open up a wealth of meaning and that to reduce these advertisements to a moral narrative or any one meaning does more violence than the image itself (Wark, 1992).

In the aftermath of the Los Angeles riots, in an atmosphere of heightened fears of the possibility of further racial conflict, a whole edition of *Colors* was given over to the issue of race. The editorial captured the impulse to deal with this issue: 'If there's one topic COLORS was destined to address, it's racism and the devastation caused by racism. Not just in Los Angeles, Germany or South Africa but everywhere that people are assaulting and killing each other over genetic, linguistic or cultural differences' (*Colors*, no. 4, 1993, p. 68). What is remarkable about this publication is its complete deconstruction of the 'idea of race'. The journal undermined the racial categories so abundantly deployed in the 'United Colors' campaigns since 1984, concluding:

> Finally it occurred to us that while the physical differences between peoples and individuals are real ... the monoliths called races are a purposeful invention, once used to make Europe's slavery and colonial conquests seem moral and inevitable ... What's going on, we believe, is that people continue to live their lives as if the myths about race were fact. Why? Because it's simpler for those in positions of power if those without power vent all their anger on others without power ... As long as our actions are guided by fear, as long as we regard the myths of race and racism as truth none of us is truly safe. (Ibid, p. 70)

The special issue tackled questions ranging from racial harassment, phenotypic difference, neo-Nazi youth culture and mixed relationships. The reflexive and quite extraordinary deconstructivist turn is also embodied within the imagery used in this edition. In a section entitled 'What if...?' Toscani presented a series of famous people with transformed racial characteristics, these included a black Arnold Schwarzenegger, a Semitic Spike Lee, an

Oriental John Paul II, and an Aryan Michael Jackson. This striking image challenges the common sense of race and nation which
in Britain has constructed blackness and Britishness as mutually
exclusive categories. The photograph challenges the reader to ask
why s\he finds it implausible. What is exposed is the association
between race and nation within the ideology of British, or more
precisely, English nationalism.

The 'What If...' photograph of the 'Black Queen' (Figure 7.7)
identifies the mutually inclusive nature of the relationship of
whiteness and Englishness. Through this 'altered image' racial
common-sense is unsettled and the implicit, 'taken for granted
quality' of what it means to look 'English' phenotypically is rendered obvious. In the terms of this ideology the Queen cannot be
'black' because to be English is to be 'white'. Toscani's playful
cosmetic surgery may also strike unwittingly an important historical chord with regard to the descendents of the Monarch. The
controverstial African American scholar J. A. Rogers has claimed
that Queen Charlotte Sophia, Consort of George III, and grand-
mother of Queen Victoria was of German and African decent
(Rogers, 1952). The accurancy of these claims are hard to substantiate but it is not completely impausible that the Queen of
England could have an African lineage. However, the ideologies
of race and nation make the recognition of such heterogeneity
impossible, ridiculous and out of question. What is asserted
instead within the language of nationalism is the compulsory
whiteness of English identity. The photograph of the black
Queen invites the reader to ridicule these associations and opens
up a representational space which challenges the othordoxies of
race and nation.

The ambivalences and traces of anti-racism found within these
examples are important for us to appreciate when evaluating the
contemporary politics of race. In many respects these examples
force us to move beyond the dualism of 'good and bad images'
and challenge us to think through the complex interplay of
meaning and the ambivalences registered within the representation of race and difference. What we have shown is that any sophisticated understanding of the contemporary relationship
between popular culture and racism needs to be alert to the coupling of fear and desire that produces the complex representations
of difference we have analysed here.

Figure 7.7 Altered Image: Toscani's portrait of a black Queen Elizabeth, spring 1993. This image was created for *Colors 4,* the first magazine dedicated entirely to racism. Courtesy of Colors.

Popular culture and difference

We began this chapter by asking the question of how is racism made popular? We have attempted to show how both printed and electronic media have been crucially implicated in providing the technical infrastructure for the creation and dissemination of the cultures of racism. Racism is connected integrally to the history of modernity and modern technologies have provided a key means in the establishment of racial supremacy. Popular culture provided the means whereby the masses within any particular modern social formation participated in the domination of others. We have also argued that racist formulations and ways of seeing can also be challenged within these representational spaces. Popular culture has provided a key means for reproducing racism but this is not inevitably the case. The instability of historically inflected racisms makes it important to stress the ideological battles that are being waged within this domain of vernacular culture. Before ending this chapter we want to revisit some of the main points in our argument.

We have argued that the evident racial discourses found in imperial propaganda, Nazi popular culture, the British news media and contemporary advertising need to be understood within particular historical conditions. While the formations of racism shared some important key features, each of the cases needs to be explained in the context of their specific social, political and historical contexts. Having said this there are some important similarities to be identified within these cases. For example, popular racism is closely connected with establishing cultural definitions of nationhood and belonging. Constructions of national identity operate through an interplay between images of race, gender and culture and the iconic representations which as a result produce models of the human subject that are both racialised and gendered. The propaganda of imperial Britain and Nazi Germany used the emerging forms of mass communication to achieve a political consensus. Through printed materials like cigarette cards and advertising or the electronic allure of the newsreel, racism was enshrined within everyday culture. Consequently, the British and German masses could submit themselves to the moral and political authority of imperialism and Nazism through these forms of leisure and consumption. Manifestations of racism in popular culture are as concerned with the construction of national culture and identity as they are with representing images of difference. The citizens of imperial Britain and Nazi Germany were offered an image of themselves and their place in the world through these popular images. Picking up on Walter Benjamin's insightful comments we have attempted to show how racist and imperial popular culture dissolves politics into aesthetics.

The impact of racism within popular culture also involved the vilification of the presence of others who are constructed as culturally incompatible with particular national territories. This process can also be closely linked with establishing political hegemony in periods of crisis. The use of 'black Allied soldiers' and 'black muggers' by Nazi propagandists and the British news media, respectively, provides two clear examples of the deployment of racist folk demons in order to manage political crises and to enact consent through invoking racial fears. Initially, racial moral panics focused on the question of miscegenation that constructs white women as the threatened emblem of national purity. Such images were not fixed and unchanging. In Britain, for example, they were superseded by a cultural discourse that constructed the black presence as incompatible with the British way of life through the attribution of criminality and cultural pathology to black communities. What remains constant within these new racisms is the enduring intertwining of sex, gender, race and nation within the discourses of racism. Within racist cultures a mutual interconnection exists between the ideological couplets of sex/gender and race/nation.

While we have argued that there are clear continuities of form within popular culture with regard to racism, we have also stressed that important changes have occurred in recent times, partly as a result of the emergence of black film-makers and media producers and a more general interest in representing cultural diversity. In particular we highlighted the pluralist incorporation of images of cultural difference within commercial cultures. The cultural politics of this corporate multiculturalism is complex. Transcendent and radical rhetoric can coexist with crude representations of cultural difference that flirt with the historic legacy of racism. We have argued that the ambivalences that are produced in this situation are important and have potentially disruptive effects. Any contemporary analysis of the relationship between racism and popular culture needs to be alert to the ways in which current vernacular forms connect with the legacy if racism. At the same time, it is important to be sensitive to the potential that popular culture has for conveying critical discourses that unsettle and undermine racist regimes of representation.

In this chapter we have tried to analyse the shifting relationship between popular culture and racism. Various racisms continue to feature prominently within European and American commercial media cultures but the hold these forms of representation have is far from total or secure. The complex and changing forms of racial discourse and racism forms the focus of our final chapter. It is with the questions raised in the last two chapters in mind that we now turn to the broader context of racial structuring and the contemporary cultural politics of race and racism.

8 Shifting Meanings of Race and Racism

In *Racism and Society* we have explored what we see as some of the key features of contemporary academic and political debates about racism in the changing social and global environment in which we live. It is appropriate that for a series such as this one we have attempted to cover both ongoing theoretical debates as well as political and policy dilemmas. We have also chosen to cover a broad canvas and this has necessitated that we develop an analytical framework for the analysis of the changing forms of racism that goes beyond the narrow confines of much current sociological writing on this topic. In doing so we hope we have been able to show that there is a need to broaden our horizons somewhat if we are to provide an understanding of contemporary racisms that helps us to understand what is after all a complex phenomenon, and one that cannot be tackled simply through a narrow analytical or disciplinary framework. It is for this reason that we have not attempted to stay within the rather narrow confines of current intellectual fashions and focus instead on a set of issues and questions that will hopefully lead to more substantive research in the future. We have also attempted to break through some of the limits of recent political and policy debates, in order to address the fundamental question of what we can do to tackle the dangers and the evils of racism as an ideology and a destructive social and political force. Rather than assume that we know what needs to be done we have attempted throughout to maintain a critical perspective on the role of anti-racist ideas and movements, and to raise questions about the limits and contradictions which seem inherent in the conduct of contemporary struggles and mobilisations about racism.

We are very aware that we ourselves have only travelled part of the route that we wanted to follow at the beginning of this project, but we see this book as a beginning rather than an end. In places we realise that our discussion in this volume is limited and we have not been able to cover all the range of approaches that have emerged in recent years. We have sought above all to outline the key analytical questions and discuss them at some length rather than attempt to cover all possible approaches. In addition, some of the arguments we have outlined in this volume need to be investigated more substantively from both a historical and an empirical perspective. Perhaps the main failing of recent research in this field has been precisely the failure to link up theoretical debates with detailed research on specific aspects of race and racism in both national and local contexts. This has meant that we are still some way off from developing a clear understanding of the processes which have helped to produce and reproduce racist movements and ideas both in the past and in the present.

As we have argued in the core chapters of this study, any account of the role of racism in contemporary societies needs to cover a rather broad and constantly shifting terrain. Our main concern has been to produce an analysis of the role of racism in contemporary societies and to account for the changing forms of interaction between racism and other features of contemporary social relations. In addition, however, we have had to situate the key issues we have looked at in this volume within a historical framework and to deal with the terms of theoretical and political debate about what it is that we are looking at under the broad category of racism. We have also become acutely aware during the process of producing this book that any rounded analysis of racism and racial relations requires a theoretical framework that is capable of explaining processes of change and transformation. In their different ways this is what each chapter seeks to do, though it is also the case that there is a need for more conceptual clarification and empirical research before we can deal adequately with all the complex issues raised. In exploring the main themes covered we have outlined, at least in general terms, our own theoretical framework for conceptualising racism in its various forms. This has allowed us to tackle some of the main problems we face in conceptualising the changing morphology of contemporary

racisms and to provide an analytical framework for understanding
how racism helps to structure social relations in a wide variety of
societies.

A number of issues remain to be explored further, however,
and it is to these that we now turn in this final chapter. Rather
than retrace the arguments already discussed in previous chapters
we shall be primarily concerned with teasing out and exploring
some of the key problems that we have touched upon in a more
reflective mode than was possible in earlier chapters. In particular
we want to map out some of the main problems involved in:

- the question of how constructions of race take shape in the
  context of social and political change;
- the analysis of what are called 'new' forms of racism;
- the issue of how contemporary debates about citizenship,
  multiculturalism and anti-racism deal with the question of
  difference.

These are all issues that have led to extensive debates in recent
years and they are at the heart of any analysis of the role of racism
as a social relation. For this reason we want to round off this
volume by returning to some of the dilemmas raised by these
questions.

As should become clear in the following pages we do not
think that there are any easy answers to these dilemmas and we
make no claim to providing an account that resolves them.
Rather we suggest that it is of some importance in the present
social and political climate that we reflect with some seriousness
on the complex range of processes and mobilisations that go
into the formation of racist and anti-racist politics and movements in Britain, Europe and elsewhere. In order that we can
go beyond this process of reflection and attempt to situate the
kinds of responses to racism that may be necessary and appropriate in the present political environment, we have to question
some of the dominant assumptions that have guided research in
this field for some time. We need, in other words, to come to
terms with the limitations of existing theoretical perspectives
and develop new conceptual tools and approaches that can help
us to understand contemporary processes of social and political
mobilisation.

Such tools are not easy to come by, as can be seen from the difficulties contemporary social theorists have in accounting for processes of social change more generally. Cornelius Castoriadis has argued persuasively that one of the major lacunae in contemporary social theory is the relative absence of theories which can tackle the issue of how social and political institutions actually change over time (Castoriadis, 1991, 1993). This absence is all the more evident in the context of theories of race and ethnic relations where there is a dearth of accounts of how racialised social relations are formed and transformed over space and time (Carter *et al.*, 1993).

For the purposes of this chapter we shall concentrate on two key issues. First, we explore the shifting meanings of race and racism in the contemporary social and political environment. Recent debates have focused particularly on the articulation of new forms of racial discourses, and whether we are seeing a fundamental transformation in the language of race within contemporary societies. But the question of what is new about these discourses has not been adequately discussed. Second, we turn to the issue of the prospects for the future and the likely avenues of social and political change. While there are obvious limitations to the predictive value of the arguments that we have developed in this book, it is still important to address the question of what are the likely outcomes of the trends that we have looked at in previous chapters.

Constructions of race

At the heart of contemporary debates about race and racism there are a number of key questions that have guided debate, even if we are no nearer to resolving them. Perhaps the most important of these questions are the following: how can we understand the mobilising power of contemporary racisms? What counter-ideologies can be developed to undermine the appeal of racist ideas and movements? Is it possible for communities that are socially defined by 'differences' of race, ethnicity, religion or other signifiers to live together in societies which are able to ensure equality, justice and civilised tolerance? We have in one way or another touched upon various aspects of these questions throughout this volume, and they lie at the heart of many of the key debates in contemporary social and political theory (I. M. Young, 1990). We have tried above all to emphasise that the social and political impact of ideas about race needs to be seen in the context of the experience of modernity and postmodernity which has shaped our societies over the past two centuries (Habermas, 1987, 1994; Toulmin, 1990). But if modern racism has its foundations in the period since the late eighteenth century, there is little doubt that it has had a major impact on the course of historical development during the twentieth century and seems destined to continue to do so. It seems clear as we move towards the twenty-first century that racist ideas and movements are continuing to have an impact on a range of contemporary societies in a variety of ways (Winant, 1994). What is more we have seen in recent years the growth and genocidal impact of new forms of racial and ethnically based ideologies in many parts of the globe, including most notably in the 1990s in both Western and Eastern Europe and parts of Africa. It is almost impossible to read a newspaper or watch television news coverage without seeing the contemporary expressions of racist ideas and practices, whether in terms of the rise of neo-fascist movements in some societies or the implementation of policies of genocide and what is euphemistically called 'ethnic cleansing'.

Recent developments in Western and Eastern European societies are a case in point. The rise of extreme right-wing and neo-fascist movements and parties has resulted in the development of new forms of racist politics and in the articulation of popular racism and violence against migrant communities. At the same time, we have seen a noticeable rise in anti-Semitism in both Western and Eastern Europe, evident in both physical and symbolic threats to Jewish communities. In this environment it is perhaps not surprising that questions about immigration and race have assumed a new importance, both politically and socially, helping to construct an environment in which the future of both settled migrant communities and new groups of migrants and refugees is very much at the heart of public debate (Habermas, 1994; Miles, 1994).

Developments such as these show why it is impossible in the present political and social environment to ignore the impact of racism and racial discrimination on the social and political institutions of most advanced industrial societies. Whereas until the 1980s it was still relatively common to treat questions about racism, ethnicity and nationalism as relatively marginal to the agenda of both social scientists and policy-makers, it is perhaps no exaggeration to say that in many ways these issues have moved right to the core of public debate. Indeed, as we have tried to show in the previous chapters, almost every aspect of contemporary social and political relations is deeply inflected with a racial or ethnic dimension. In this context, as we move ever closer towards the next century, it is vital that we develop a grounded and historically based view of the role that racialised social relations play in contemporary societies and are likely to play in the future.

As we hope we have shown in the substantive chapters of this book this objective is by no means easy to achieve. This is partly because the terms of both official and popular discourses about race and racism are in a constant state of flux. The recent changes we have seen in European societies are perhaps the most clear example of this volatility, represented both by the development of new racist political movements and by intense official debate about what kinds of policies should be pursued to deal with such issues as immigration and the political and social rights of migrants (Ford, 1992; Wrench and Solomos, 1993). But it is also the case that similar transformations are evident in other parts of the globe. Castles and Miller's (1993) account of the changing politics of migration in various parts of the world illustrates the complex variety of factors that have helped to construct political understandings of the position of migrant communities in quite disparate geographical and social contexts. Numerous other accounts have shown how ideas about 'race, 'nation' and 'ethnicity' are constantly changing as a result of both governmental regulation and popular mobilisation.

We hope we have shown that categories such as race and ethnicity are best conceived as political resources, that are used by both dominant and subordinate groups for the purposes of legitimising and furthering their own social identities and social interests. In this context it is important to remember that identities based on race and ethnicity are not simply imposed, since they are also often the outcome of resistance and political struggle in which racialised minorities play a key and active role. As we have

shown throughout this volume it is important to pay close attention to the political power struggles that are at the heart of social
relations.

In the contemporary social and political environment such struggles are inherently very complex and are structured by specific
configurations of identity-based politics (Huyssen, 1986). An interesting example of this complexity was the debate that took place
in the United States during 1991 about the nomination of Clarence
Thomas, a black judge of conservative political views, to the US
Supreme Court. The nomination was controversial from the start,
but it became more so during the Senate hearings when Thomas
was accused of sexual harassment by Anita Hill, a black woman
and former junior colleague of his. The hearing became a *cause
célèbre* and symbolised the way in which American society had
become polarised around specific racial, ethnic and gender identities. While some blacks supported Thomas on racial grounds,
others opposed him on gender grounds. Black women were
divided on how to respond to the debate about Thomas and
specifically on how to deal with the way in which he sought to
defend himself by comparing his treatment to the role of lynching
in the history of American racial relations. At the same time, there
were some notable differences in the responses of black feminists
and intellectuals to the case, and it came to symbolise some of the
tensions and contradictions that underlay the politics of identity in
American society (Morrison, 1992).

Such trends need to be situated within the changing socio-
economic environment of contemporary societies. But as we
have emphasised it is also important to view them within
processes of cultural and social change. By this we mean that it is
of some importance not to lose sight of the complex social, political and cultural determinants that shape contemporary racist discourses and movements and other forms of racialised discourse
and mobilisation. Indeed, what is clear from recent accounts of
the growth of new forms of cultural racism is that within the language of contemporary racist movements there is both a certain
flexibility about what is meant by race as well as an attempt to re-
constitute themselves as movements whose concern is with defending their 'nation' rather than attacking others as such. It is
perhaps not surprising in this context that within the contemporary languages of race one finds a combination arguments in

favour of cultural difference along with negative images of the 'other' as a threat and as representing an 'impure' culture (Gilman, 1985; Enzensberger, 1994).

Much of the recent theoretical work has argued that racism needs to be conceptualised through a sensitivity to the historical context in which it is expressed and its changing character. David Goldberg, for example, comments that the theoretical analysis of racism:

> Entails not only that there is no single characteristic form of racism, but also that the various racisms have differing effects and implications. Racisms assume their particular characters, they are exacerbated. And they have different entailments and ramifications in relation to specific considerations of class constitution, gender, national identity, region, and political structure. But the character and implicature of each racism are also set in terms of its own historical legacy and the related conception of race. (Goldberg, 1993, p. 91)

However, as he rightly goes on to point out, the impulse to specify racisms spatially and historically may overlook the consideration of what processes tie different racisms together (ibid., p. 96). In this study we have attempted to bear in mind both the need for specificity as well as the connections that tie different kinds of racism together. As we argued in Chapter 6, it is clear that within a range of contemporary neo-fascist cultures symbols and cultural items are being exchanged on both a national and a transnational basis. We need to bear these processes in mind when developing theoretical frameworks to analyse the differential development of racist discourses.

It is this flexibility of racist discourses that can help us to understand their workings in specific social and political contexts. It is also perhaps the main problem that we face in carrying out research on the relationship between contemporary racism and social relations, since it is increasingly difficult to situate contemporary notions of 'race' within fixed boundaries. In this sense Collette Guillaumin is quite correct when she argues that the 'idea of race' is neither rigid nor fixed. Its boundaries and its meanings are flexible, even though the 'core may remain the same' (Guillaumin, 1991, p. 5). Yet it is precisely this aspect of the 'idea of race' that helps us to understand the seemingly endless ability for the reinvention of new forms of racism and social movements which attempt to use racial and ethnic boundaries as a basis for political action.

It follows from the above argument that although at its root racism may involve clear and simple images, it is by no means uniform or without contradictions. Indeed, what is really interesting about racism as a set of ideas and political practices is that it is able to provide images of the 'other' which are simple and unchanging and at the same time to adapt to the changing social and political environment. Thus contemporary racist ideas are able to maintain a link with the mystical values of classical racism and to adopt and use cultural and political symbols that are part of contemporary societies. In this sense Mosse perceptively captured a key feature of contemporary racisms when he argued that part of the reason for the power and influence of racism in the modern world is the way in which it manages to combine mystical ideas about race and myths of origin, with the appropriation of scientific discourses about racial classification (Mosse, 1985a, pp. 77–8). It is precisely this combination of the mystical and the scientific that lies at the heart of the attempts by contemporary racist movements to reinvent their ideas as those which are attempting to protect the cultural and ethnic boundaries of race and nation. The language of 'national identity' becomes in the present environment yet another way of fashioning what some writers have called a 'postmodern racism', which defines itself as against both racism and multiculturalism (Žižek, 1993; Goldberg, 1994; Robertson *et al.*, 1994).

This ability of racist ideologies constantly to reinvent themselves has, of course, been a feature of racism over the past two centuries, and it has certainly characterised the period that we have focused on in this study. It is clear, for example, that within the context of the 1990s the political discourses that are classified under the general label of racism are connected to, but at the same time quite distinct from, the racist political discourses that characterised, the Nazi period, for instance. But what we clearly need to know much more about are the processes which have brought about these changes and the likely impact of these new forms of racist politics on the patterns of social and political mobilisation in contemporary societies.

What is also interesting is that in times of crisis and sociopolitical change it is precisely racial ideologies that seek to provide in one way or another the 'simple answers' demanded by popular opinion. Although Balibar may be correct in warning against the dangers of too simple a reduction of racism to 'crisis situations' (Balibar and Wallerstein, 1991, pp. 217–18), it is important to recognise the complex interrelationships that can develop between wider processes of change and the growth of racist movements and ideas. As Goldberg has perceptively argued in times of fundamental social and political change:

> Race extends a tremulous identity in a social context marked by uncertainty – the uncertainty of a future beyond this life, the uncertainty of situatedness, or at least of its lack, and the uncertainties of self-assertion and assertiveness in a world of constant flux, power shifts, neighbours and nations next door one day and gone the next. Identities like race, especially of race, offer a semblance of order, an empowerment, or at minimum an affectation of power. (Goldberg, 1993, p. 210)

This aspect of racial ideologies, namely their claim to offer a 'semblance of order' in periods of social and economic change, has been noted in a variety of historical and political contexts. Writing in relation to the history of anti-Semitism, for example, Gilman and Katz (1991) have noted the ways in which 'times of crisis' and uncertainty over the course of social and economic change have often proved to be the periods in which new racist ideas and movements have emerged and provided a basis for social mobilisation and exclusion.

Žižek (1993) also notes the role of contemporary racism and nationalism in providing a basis of certainty and identity, as against 'foreigners' and 'others' who are different and who do not belong to the 'community' or the 'nation'. Addressing in particular the situation in Eastern Europe he warns against the tendency to see events in the ex-Yugoslavia as 'irrational' or as a 'ridiculous anachronism' which is out of place in the modern world. On the contrary, argues Žižek, we should see such events as the 'first clear taste of the twenty-first century, the prototype of the post-cold war conflicts' (ibid., p. 223). Interestingly enough for writers such as Žižek, events in places such as the ex-Yugoslavia are not a left-over of the past but a premonition of what lies ahead. He warns against the tendency to situate events in the ex-Yugoslavia as a return to the past, precisely because such arguments have a tendency to forget the contemporary forces that produce the conditions for genocide and 'ethnic cleansing'.

Such arguments present what may be seen as a rather pessimistic scenario about the future. But given recent developments in various parts of the globe, it is perhaps timely that such arguments are being articulated and that we are forced to come to terms with them. One of the lessons of our experience during most of the twentieth century is that it is not possible to assume that racism is merely a passing phenomenon. The tenacity of racist ideas and movements, in a variety of specific historical contexts, points to the need to see racism as an ever changing social phenomenon which recreates itself in new forms all the time (Huyssen, 1995).

New forms of racism

One of the themes we have tried to explore in the course of this study is the development of new patterns of racial reasoning around key aspects of social relations in contemporary societies. This is not to say that what is at work is simply a process of linear evolution towards what is sometimes called 'new racism' or 'cultural racism'. For what is clear is that the framing of racialised discourses as 'new' does not necessarily help us to understand the complex variety of arguments and ideas that are to be found within contemporary racist discourses. Nor for that matter does it tell us much about what is new and what is old in the racial politics that confronts us in the present environment.

While it is important to be clear about the differences between contemporary and traditional forms of racism, it does seem that some of the arguments about this issue do not really add much analytical clarity to this complex issue. Henry Giroux, for example, argues for the emergence of a 'new racism' in the following terms: 'We are now witnessing in the United States (and Europe) the emergence of a new racism and politics of cultural difference both in the recognition of the relations between Otherness and difference, on the one hand, and meaning and the politics of representation on the other' (Giroux, 1993, p. 8). From rather different perspectives other recent writings have talked of the emergence of meta-racism, new racism or more descriptively new cultural forms of racial discourse (Todorov, 1986; Taguieff, 1990; Balibar and Wallerstein, 1991; Bhabha, 1994). While there is, as we have argued in the course of this book, something valuable and important about these arguments, it seems important to emphasise that what some writers have called new racism is not a uniform social entity as such. There is strong evidence that racial discourses are increasingly using a new cultural and social language to justify their arguments, but the search for a uniform definition of new racism has proved intractable, and has again emphasised the slippery nature of contemporary racisms. A key problem is that in a very real sense what some writers today call *new racism* has in some sense always been with us. While it is true that in the nineteenth and early twentieth centuries there was an emphasis in much racial thinking on the 'biological' superiority of some races over others, it is also the case that racial thinking has also always been about idealised and transcendent images of culture, landscape and national identity (Huyssen, 1995).

An important feature of racism over the years has been the various ways it has managed to combine different, and often contradictory, elements within specific social and political contexts. In this sense we would agree with Mosse that racism is not a coherent set of propositions that has remained the same in the period since the eighteenth century, but can best be conceived as a scavenger ideology, which gains its power from its ability to pick out and utilise ideas and values from other sets of ideas and beliefs in specific socio-historical contexts (Mosse, 1985a, p. 234). There is, in other words, no essential notion of race that has remained unchanged by wider political, philosophical, economic and social transformations (Gilman, 1993).

The characterisation of racism as a 'scavenger ideology' does not mean, however, that there are no continuities in racial thought across time and spatial boundaries. Indeed, it seems obvious that when one looks at the various elements of racial discourses in contemporary societies there are strong continuities in the articulation of images of the 'other', as well as in the we-images which are evident in the ways in which racist movements define the boundaries of 'race' and 'nation'. The evident use of images of the past and evocations of popular memory in the language of contemporary racist and nationalist movements points to the need to understand the complex ways in which these movements are embedded in specific images of landscape and territory (Huyssen, 1995).

Citizenship, multiculturalism and anti-racism

As we look towards the next century one of the main questions that we face is the issue of 'citizenship rights' in societies that are becoming increasingly multicultural. Within both popular and academic discourse there is growing evidence of concern about how questions of citizenship need to be reconceptualised in the context of multicultural societies. Indeed, in contemporary European societies this can be seen as in some sense the main question which governments of various kinds are trying to come to terms with. Some important elements of this debate are the issue of the political rights of minorities, including the question of representation in both local and national politics, and the position of minority religious and cultural rights in societies which are becoming more diverse. Underlying all of these concerns is the much more thorny issue of what, if anything, can be done to protect the rights of minorities and develop extensive notions of citizenship and democracy that include those minorities that are excluded on racial and ethnic criteria.

There are clearly quite divergent perspectives in the present political environment about how best to deal with these concerns. There is, for example, a wealth of discussion about what kind of measures are necessary to tackle the inequalities and exclusions which confront minority groups. At the same time there is clear evidence that existing initiatives are severely limited in their impact. A number of commentators have pointed to the limitations of legislation and public policy interventions in bringing about a major improvement in the socio-political position of minorities.

This raises a number of questions. First, what kind of policies could tackle discrimination and inequality more effectively? Second, what links could be made between policies on immigration and policies on social and economic issues? What kind of positive social policy agenda can be developed to deal with the position of both established communities and new migrants in the

1990s and beyond? All of these questions are at the heart of contemporary debates and have given rise to quite divergent policy prescriptions. It is quite clear that in the present political environment it is unlikely that any sort of agreement about how to develop new policy regimes in this field will be easy to achieve. On the contrary, it seems likely that this will remain an area full of controversy and conflict for some time to come.

But it is also the case that some key issues are coming to the fore in public debate. A case in point is the whole question of citizenship in relation to race and ethnicity. Policy debates in Britain, unlike other European societies, have not often looked seriously at the issue of political and citizenship rights of migrants and their descendants. This is partly because it is widely assumed that such issues are not as relevant in this country. But it also clear that ethnic minorities in Britain and elsewhere are questioning whether they are fully included in and represented through political institutions. It is not surprising, therefore, that an important concern in recent years has been with the issue of citizenship and the rights of minorities in British society. This is partly because there is a growing awareness of the gap between formal citizenship and the *de facto* restriction of the economic and social rights of minorities as a result of discrimination, economic restructuring and the decline of the welfare state.

The controversies about the Rushdie affair and a number of other similar cases across Europe have highlighted the increased prominence of these issues in current political debates. The growing public interest about the role of fundamentalism among sections of the Muslim communities in various countries has given a new life to debates about the issue of cultural differences and processes of integration (Asad, 1990, 1993). By highlighting some of the most obvious limitations of multiculturalism and anti-racism in shaping policy change in this field, such controversies have done much to bring about a much more critical debate about the role and impact of policies which are premised on notions such as multiculturalism. But they have also highlighted the ever changing terms of political and policy agendas about these issues and the fact that there is little agreement about what kind of strategies for change should be pursued.

The full impact of current debates on the future of immigration is not as yet clear, but it seems likely that they will have an influence on how such issues as multiculturalism and anti-racism are seen in the future. In the context of national debates about the position of ethnic minority communities the impact is already evident. In Britain, for example, there are already signs that the Rushdie affair has given a new impetus to debates about issues such as immigration, integration and public order. The hostile media coverage of the events surrounding the political mobilisations around the Rushdie affair also served to reinforce the view that minorities who do not share the dominant political values of British society pose a threat to social stability and cohesion. Some commentators have argued that as a result of the Rushdie affair more attention needed to be given to the divergent political paths seemingly adopted by sections of the African–Caribbean and Asian communities. Whatever the merit of such arguments it is clear that in the current environment one cannot develop any analysis of contemporary racial and ethnic relations without accounting for differentiation within both majority and minority communities.

Prospects for the future

There seems little doubt that one of the key questions we shall have to confront in the future is how to understand and tackle the social and political impact of racism, both as a set of ideas and as a form of political mobilisation. In broad terms we shall (i) need to be able to explain both the roots of contemporary racist ideas and movements and the source of their current appeal, and (ii) consider what kinds of counter-strategies can be adopted to challenge new types of racist mobilisation. Yet it is precisely on this issue that current research seems to be least enlightening, since researchers have not, by and large, had much to say about the reasons why we have seen a resurgence of racist ideas in recent times.

Simplistic and monolithic accounts of racism will in the final analysis do little to enlighten us as to why it is that in particular social and political contexts millions of people respond to the images, promises and hopes which are at the heart of mass racist movements. Additionally, they tell us little about the possibilities and limits of political strategies and policies that aim to challenge institutionalised racial inequalities. As Moon has persuasively argued in relation to the long-running debate about differentiated citizenship rights, 'we must be alert to the ways in which the effort to identify and respond to differences among people may turn into a process of reification, leading to a false imputation of essentialist qualities to the members of some group, ignoring important variations within groups' (Moon, 1993, p. 188). As we have tried to show in previous chapters, one of the limitations of anti-racist politics as it has developed is precisely this pattern of reifying minority communities as static and unchanging cultural and political collectivities. There is a need to confront the reality that in the present environment we have, in one way or another, to move beyond the certainties both of racism and simplistic multiculturalism and anti-racism.

The preoccupation in much of the recent literature in this field with issues of identity, and the assertion of the relevance and importance of understanding the role of 'new ethnicities', has not resolved the fundamental question of how to balance the quest for ever more specific identities with the need to allow for broader and less fixed cultural identities. Indeed, if anything, this quest for a politics of identity has helped to highlight one of the key dilemmas of liberal political thought (Moon, 1993; Squires, 1993). Amy Gutmann captures this contradiction well when she argues:

> One reasonable reaction to questions about how to recognise the distinct cultural identities of members of a pluralistic society is that the very aim of representing or respecting differences in public institutions is misguided. An important strand in contemporary liberalism lends support to this reaction. It suggests that our lack of identification with institutions that serve public purposes, the impersonality of public institutions, is the price that citizens should be willing to pay for treating us all as equals, regardless of our particular ethnic, religious, racial or sexual identities. (Gutmann, 1992, p. 4)

Yet what is quite clear is that the quest for ever more specific as opposed to universal identities is becoming more pronounced in the present political environment. The search for national, ethnic and racial has become a pronounced, if not dominant, feature of political debate within both majority and minority communities in the 'postmodern' societies of the 1990s.

One of the dilemmas we face in the present environment is that there is a clear possibility that new patterns of segregation could establish themselves and limit everyday interaction between racially defined groups. Hazel Carby, writing of the situation in the United States, argues that many suburban middle-class white Americans are effectively cut off from contact with inner city blacks. She contrasts this with the explosion in the number of books published by black women and men which provide narratives of black lives, and which are often read by these same middle-class whites. She makes the poignant point:

> For white suburbia, as well as for white middle-class students in universities, these texts are becoming a way of gaining knowledge of the 'other', a knowledge that appears to satisfy and replace the desire to challenge existing frameworks of segregation. Have we, as a society, successfully eliminated the need for achieving integration through political agitation for civil rights and opted instead for knowing each other through cultural texts? (Carby, 1992, p. 198)

The growing evidence of a 'crisis of race' and of racialised class inequalities in the United States is a timely reminder that the Civil Rights Movement and other movements since then have had at best a partial impact on established patterns of racial inequality and have not stopped the development of new patterns of exclusion and segregation.

The arguments developed by Carby and others have to be situated carefully in the rather specific context of the racial politics that have shaped American society in the post Civil Rights Movement era. But it is also clear that there is evidence that within contemporary European societies there is the danger of institutionalising new forms of exclusion as a result of increased racial violence and racist mobilisations by the extreme right. It is no surprise in the present environment of fear, violence and physical attacks on foreigners that commentators such as Hans Magnus Enzensberger warns of the danger of violence and 'civil war' becoming an endemic feature of many cities in contemporary Europe, unless the conditions which produce racism and xenophobic nationalism are fully understood (Enzensberger, 1994). Yet others warn of the dangers faced by liberal democracies in the context of the growth of 'corporate national populism' and 'postmodern racism' (Žižek, 1993, pp. 224–6; see also Žižek, 1989).

Pronouncements such as these are, of course, intentionally melodramatic and they are meant to be both a warning as well as a description of the present situation. But given our recent experiences in quite diverse local and national political environments who would argue with any real faith that we can ignore them? Can we be sure that the resurgence of racist nationalism does not pose a very real danger for the possibility of civilised coexistence between groups defined as belonging to different racial, ethnic and national identities?

The arguments developed above point to the need to see racism as a flexible and constantly changing ideology. In this sense contemporary racisms are not some throwback to the past, they are an integral element of present day social relations. It is interesting to note, for example, that the genocidal policies pursued in the former Yugoslavia in recent years have been presented in much of the media as a return to values and ideas which somehow were out of place in the late twentieth century. Yet it is also during this century that we saw the attempt by the Nazi regime to use modern technology and the power of the state as a tool for the genocide of a particular 'race'. It is one of the ironies of modernity, as writers such as Mosse and Bauman have shown, that the Holocaust was very much the product of modernity: 'The holocaust could not have taken place without the application of modern technology, without the modern centralised state with its card files and communication systems, and without the brutalisation of men's minds by the experience of the First World War' (Mosse, 1985a, p. 232). This is, of course, not to say that the Holocaust or other attempts at genocide were the inevitable product of modernity and of modern state power. But it is important to recognise that the events in the former Yugoslavia need to be situated very much in the present and not constructed as some timeless expression of ethnic and religious hatred.

As we have argued throughout this volume, it is important to remember that there is no single monolithic racism which structures ideas and values in all societies, or which shapes social relations in all social environments. Rather there are quite distinct racisms that are constructed and reconstructed through time and space by social action. This helps to explain the complex forms which the racisms that we see around us today take, both in terms of their theoretical justifications and the political mobilisations associated with them. It is only by understanding the full implications of this rather simple point that we can begin to develop a better and relevant approach to the question of how it is that we can counter the dangers of contemporary racisms and construct alternative models of democracy that can allow for the representation of difference.

The key concerns of this book have converged around the argument that it is essential that we break once and for all with deterministic and fixed notions about the relationship between race and racism and broader sets of social relations. We have to develop an analysis of contemporary racisms that is capable of understanding and explaining the power of the rather diverse racisms that have taken shape in the contemporary environment. In the present environment of political turmoil and tension it has become easy in quite diverse societies, such as Germany, Britain and France, to see migrants and racial minorities as the principal threat to order and social stability. Before we can successfully challenge the hegemony of such ideas we must be able to understand both why they have arisen at the present time and why it is that they have managed to attract sizeable political support. In order to do this we must develop an analysis of racism in the present that is adequate to the task of telling us something about the future as well as the past.

Guide to Further Reading

In *Racism and Society* we have sought to provide a critical and innovative account of the role of racial relations and racism in contemporary societies. In doing so we have inevitably touched on issues, ideas and events that ideally need fuller exploration. It is for this reason that we want in this guide to give some direction as to the key texts that provide an in-depth insight into the issues discussed in specific chapters. We do not aim to list all the main contributions that have been made over the years, or even the ones that have helped to influence us, but rather to indicate some key critical contributions that have helped to structure contemporary debates and research. In addition to the texts cited here and the references a number of journals are important reading for all concerned with issues of race and ethnicity, notably *Ethnic and Racial Studies, New Community, Patterns of Prejudice, Sage Race Relations Abstracts* and *Social Identities*. It is in these journals that the findings of recent research are published and it is therefore important to look at them as well as the texts we suggest here. It is also increasingly the case that mainstream journals in sociology, politics, geography and other disciplines publish relevant articles and research papers.

1 Theoretical Perspectives

This chapter covers a wide range of theoretical and conceptual debates and it is therefore difficult to suggest general texts which cover the whole field. Some of the most relevant texts to look at are Arendt, 1973; Banton, 1987a; Benedict, 1943; Gates Jr, 1986; Goldberg, 1990 and 1993; Hall, 1980; LaCapra, 1991; Miles, 1989; Rex and Mason, 1986; Winant, 1994. On the interface between race and gender it is useful to look at: Anthias and Yuval-Davis, 1992; Carby, 1982 and 1987; Collins, 1990; hooks, 1981; Minh-ha, 1989; Spivak, 1987 and 1993; Wallace, 1990a; Ware, 1992; Williams, 1991.

2 Historical Perspectives

The historical literature on race and racism is both vast and concerned with a variety of national historical perspectives. It may be best to start by looking at some comparative historical texts such as Banton, 1977; Cox, 1970; Fredrickson, 1981; Kiernan, 1969; Mosse, 1985a; Stepan, 1982. Other key texts of direct relevance to this chapter are: Banton and Harwood, 1975; Barkan, 1992; Biddiss, 1970; Jordan, 1968; Snowden, 1970. On the history of anti-Semitism see in particular: Cohn, 1970; Gilman and Katz, 1991; Poliakov,

1974a and 1974b; Pulzer, 1988; Rose, 1990. Other challenging attempts to develop a historical perspective towards the study of racism can be found in: Barzun, 1938; Fredrickson, 1988; Montagu, 1964; Pieterse, 1992; Young, 1995.

3   Social Relations and Inequality

The analysis of racism and social relations is a relatively underdeveloped area, though it has begun to attract more attention in recent years. There are few texts which provide a rounded overview of the main trends but it is worth going through some of the following for an overview: Banton, 1992; Blauner, 1989; Heisler, 1991; Orfield, 1988; Weir, 1993; Wilson, 1987. For some of the recent social trends in contemporary European societies see the papers in Wrench and Solomos, 1993. For some of the more recent trends and debates in the United States see: Fainstein, 1993; Jencks, 1992; Katz, 1989; Sawhill, 1989; Wacquant, 1994.

4   Racism, Class and Political Action

There is a wide range of studies of the politics of race and racism, exploring the experience of a number of different societies as well as offering comparative perspectives. Some of the most relevant texts in this field include: Omi and Winant, 1994; Smith, 1994; Solomos, 1993; Solomos and Back, 1995. Additionally, there are a number of accounts which focus more specifically on an analysis of the impact of race and ethnicity on the political system. See in particular: Anwar, 1986; Layton–Henry, 1992; Saggar, 1992. For broader trends and developments in contemporary Europe see Wrench and Solomos, 1993.

5   Racism and Anti-Racism

This is an area that has led to much debate in recent years, though there is surprisingly little research that addresses the general field as opposed to the experience in specific policy arenas, such as education, local government and social welfare. Some interesting accounts of the controversies surrounding anti–racism can be found in: Cambridge and Feuchtwang, 1990; Palmer, 1986; Sivanandan, 1990b. Additionally, it is useful to explore some of the conceptual and ethical dilemmas about this issue. See for example: Bhatt, 1994a; Bonnett, 1993; Cohen, 1991; Gilroy, 1990b; Goldberg, 1993; Guillaumin, 1991; Jacoby, 1994; Rattansi, 1992; Taguieff, 1990; Taylor, 1992a; Todorov, 1986; I.M. Young, 1990.

6   Identity, Hybridity and New Ethnicities

Over the years these topics have simulated controversy, and in recent times are still subject to intense debate. On anthropological accounts of ethnicity see in particular: Barth, 1959 and 1969; Jenkins, 1986; Wallman, 1979. Some of the best critical overviews of the issues covered by recent debates can be found in: Back, 1991 and 1995; Bhabha, 1994; Brah, 1993; CCCS, 1982; Chambers, 1994; Fanon, 1986; Giddens, 1991; Gilroy, 1987, 1993a and 1993b; Hall, 1991a and 1992; Hewitt, 1986; Jenkins, 1986; Modood, 1988; Mosse, 1966 and 1987; Smith, 1991; Winant, 1994. On hybridity and fascist symbols see: Griffin, 1991; Pulzer, 1988; Quinn, 1994. On the role of diasporic cultures see: Apter, 1991; Boyarin and Boyarin, 1993; Safran, 1991.

7 Race, Racism and Popular Culture

The analysis of racism and popular culture has become an important area of research in recent years, and this has resulted in a number of important and innovative studies. Some of the key works are: Asad, 1990; Brantlinger, 1988; Cheyette, 1993; Cohen, 1988b; Dirks, 1992; Dyer, 1988; Gates, 1988; Gilman 1985 and 1991; Gilroy, 1993b; MacKenzie, 1986; Said, 1993; Van Deburg, 1992; van Dijk, 1991; Wallace, 1990b; Williams, 1991. On the role of popular culture and racism in Nazi Germany see: Adam, 1992; Hinz, 1979; Peukert, 1987. On the interactions between culture and popular memory see Huyssen, 1995.

8 Shifting Meanings of Race and Racism

Some of the main themes discussed in this chapter have not been analysed in any great detail in the existing literature. Some of the texts that relate to our own thinking on these issues are: Balibar and Wallerstein, 1991; Connolly, 1991; Enzensberger, 1992 and 1994; Mercer, 1994; Moon, 1993; Mosse, 1985a and 1985b; Solomos and Back, 1995; Taylor, 1992a and 1992b; Todorov, 1986; Williams, 1991; Winant, 1994; Zizek, 1993. Because key aspects of contemporary racial relations and racism are in a constant state of flux there are few texts which provide an adequate conceptual or empirical point of reference. But see the various accounts in Wrench and Solomos, 1993, for contemporary trends and developments in Europe, and Omi and Winant, 1994, for an account of the situation in the United States. A number of challenging accounts of the ethical and political dilemmas raised by the meanings attached to race in contemporary American society are also worth looking at: Gooding-Williams, 1993; Morrison, 1992; Roediger, 1994; Terkel, 1992; Wellman, 1993.

References

Adam, P. (1992) *The Arts of the Third Reich* (London: Thames and Hudson).

Adorno, T. W. and Horkheimer, M. (1986) *Dialectic of Enlightenment* (London: Verso).

Ahmad, A. (1992) *In Theory: Classes, Nations, Literatures* (London: Verso).

Al-Azmeh, A. (1993) *Islams and Modernities* (London: Verso).

Allen, T. W. (1994) *The Invention of the White Race. Volume One: Racial Oppression and Social Control* (London: Verso).

Ålund, A. and Schierup, C.-U. (1991) *Paradoxes of Multiculturalism: Essays on Swedish Society* (Aldershot: Avebury).

Anderson, B. (1991) *Imagined Communities: Reflections on the Origin and Spread of Nationalism*, revised edition (London: Verso).

Anderson, E. (1976) *A Place on the Corner* (Chicago: University of Chicago Press).

Anderson, N. (1923) *The Hobo* (Chicago: University of Chicago Press).

Anderson, P. (1992) *A Zone of Engagement* (London: Verso).

Anthias, F. (1992) 'Connecting "race" and ethnic phenomena', *Sociology*, 26, 3: 421–38.

Anthias, F. and Yuval-Davis, N. (1992) *Racialized Boundaries* (London: Routledge).

Anwar, M. (1979) *The Myth of Return: Pakistanis in Britain* (London: Heinemann).

Anwar M. (1986) *Race and Politics: Ethnic Minorities and the British Political System* (London: Tavistock).

Appadurai, A. (1990) 'Disjuncture and Difference in the Global Cultural Economy', *Public Culture*, 2, 2: 1–24.

Appiah, K. A. (1992) *In My Father's House: Africa in the Philosophy of Culture* (London: Methuen).

Appiah, K. A. and Gates, H. L. Jr (1992) 'Multiplying Identities', *Critical Inquiry* 18: 624–29

Apter, A. (1991) 'Herskovits's Heritage: Rethinking Syncretism in the African Diaspora', *Diaspora*, 1, 3: 235–60

Arbuthnot, J. (1976) *The History of John Bull*, edited by A. W. Bower and R. A. Erickson (Oxford: Clarendon Press).

Arendt, H. (1973) *The Origins of Totalitarianism*, new edition (San Diego: Harcourt Brace).

Asad, T. (1990) 'Ethnography, Literature, and Politics: Some Readings and Uses of Salman Rushdie's *The Satanic Verses*', *Cultural Anthropology*, 5, 3: 239–69.

Asad, T. (1993) *Genealogies of Religion: Discipline and Reasons of Power in Christianity and Islam* (Baltimore: Johns Hopkins University Press).

Asante, M. K. (1987) *The Afrocentric Idea* (Philadelphia: Temple University Press).

Asante, M. K. (1994) 'Finally, Afrocentricty Operationalised', *African People's Review*, 3, 3.

Aschenbrenner, J. (1975) *Life Lines: Black Families in Chicago* (New York: Holt, Rinehart and Winston).

Atherton, H. M. (1974) *Political Prints in the Age of Hogarth: A Study of the Ideographic Representation of Politics* (Oxford: Oxford University Press).

Back, L. (1991) 'Social Context and Racist Name Calling: An Ethnographic Perspective on Racist Talk Within a South London Adolescent Community', *European Journal of Intercultural Studies*, 1, 3: 19–39.

Back, L. (1993a) 'Race, Identity and Nation Within an Adolescent Community in South London', *New Community*, 19, 2: 217–33

Back, L. (1993b) 'Cultures of Racism, Rituals of Masculinity: Mutual Crossings of Racism and Gender', in N. Lindisfarne and A. Cornwall (eds), *The Meanings of Masculinity* (London: Routledge).

Back, L. (1993c) 'The African Heritage of White Europeans', in L. Back and A. Nayak, (eds) *Invisible Europeans: Black People in the 'New Europe'* (Birmingham: AFFOR Press).

Back, L. (1994) 'The Sounds of the City', *Anthropology in Action*, 1, 1: 11–16.

Back, L. (1995) *New Ethnicities, Multiple Racisms: Young People and Transcultural Dialogue* (London: UCL Press).

Back, L. and Nayak, A. (eds) (1993) *Invisible Europeans?: Black People in the 'New Europe'* (Birmingham: AFFOR Press).

Back, L. and Quaade, V. (1993) 'Dream Utopias, Nightmare Realities: Imaging Race and Culture with the World of Benetton Advertising', *Third Text*, 22: 65–80.

Back, L. and Solomos, J. (1993) 'Doing Research, Writing Politics: The Dilemmas of Political Intervention in Research on Racism', *Economy and Society*, 22, 2: 178–99

Balibar, E. and Wallerstein, I. (1991) *Race, Nation, Class: Ambiguous Identities* (London: Verso).

Ball, W. and Solomos, J. (eds) (1990) *Race and Local Politics* (London: Macmillan).

Banton, M. (1967) *Race Relations* (New York: Basic Books).

Banton, M. (1977) *The Idea of Race* (London: Tavistock).

Banton, M. (1980) 'The Idiom of Race: A Critique of Presentism', *Research in Race and Ethnic Relations*, vol. 2: 21–42.

Banton, M. (1983) *Racial and Ethnic Competition* (Cambridge: Cambridge University Press).

Banton, M. (1987a) *Racial Theories* (Cambridge: Cambridge University Press).

Banton, M. (1987b) 'The Battle of the Name', *New Community*, XIV, 1/2: 170–5.

Banton, M. (1991) 'The Race Relations Problematic', *British Journal of Sociology*, 42, 1: 115–30.

Banton, M. (1992) 'The Nature and Causes of Racism and Racial Discrimination', *International Sociology*, 7, 1: 69–84.

Banton, M. and Harwood, J. (1975) *The Race Concept* (Newton Abbot: David and Charles).
Barkan, E. (1992) *The Retreat of Scientific Racism* (Cambridge: Cambridge University Press).
Barker, M. (1981) *The New Racism* (London: Junction Books).
Barley, N. (1989) *Native Land* (London: Viking).
Barth, F. (1959) *Political Leadership Among Swat Pathans* (London: Athlone Press).
Barth, F. (1969) *Ethnic Groups and Boundaries: The Social Organisation of Cultural Difference* (London: George Allen and Unwin).
Barthes, R. (1973) *Mythologies* (London: Granada).
Barthes, R. (1985) *The Grain of the Voice* (New York: Hill and Wang).
Barzun, J. (1938) *Race: A Study in Modern Superstition* (London: Methuen).
Bauman, Z. (1989) *Modernity and the Holocaust* (Oxford: Blackwell).
Bauman, Z. (1991) *Modernity and Ambivalence* (Cambridge: Polity Press).
Bauman, Z. (1992) *Intimations of Postmodernity* (London: Routledge).
Bauman, Z. (1993) *Postmodern Ethics* (Oxford: Blackwell).
Beck, U. (1992) *Risk Society: Towards a New Modernity* (London: Sage).
Benedict, R. (1983) *Race and Racism* (London: Routledge and Kegan Paul).
Benjamin, W. (1968) 'The Work of Art in the Age of Mechanical Reproduction', in W. Benjamin, *Illuminations* (London: Harcourt, Brace and World).
Benyon, J. and Solomos, J. (eds) (1987) *The Roots of Urban Unrest* (Oxford: Pergamon Press).
Berman, M. (1983) *All That Is Solid Melts Into Air* (London: Verso).
Bernal, M. (1987) *Black Athena: The Afroasiatic Roots of Classical Civilisation. Volume I, The Fabrication of Ancient Greece 1785–1985* (London: Free Association Books).
Bernal, M. (1991) *Black Athena: The Afroasiatic Roots of Classical Civilisation. Volume II, The Archaeological and Documentary Evidence* (London: Free Association Books).
Bhabha, H. K. (ed.) (1990) *Nation and Narration* (London: Routledge).
Bhabha, H. K. (1994) *The Location of Culture* (London: Routledge).
Bhachu, P. (1985) *Twice Migrants: East African Settlers in Britain* (London: Tavistock).
Bhachu, P. (1991) 'Culture, Ethnicity and Class Amongst Punjabi Sikh Women in 1990s Britain', *New Community*, 17, 3: 401–12.
Bhatt, C. (1994a) *Race, Ethnicity and Religion: Agency, Translocality and New Political Movements*, unpublished Ph.D. thesis, Birkbeck College, University of London.
Bhatt, C. (1994b) 'New Foundations: Contingency, Indeterminacy and Black Translocality', in J. Weeks (ed.), *The Lesser Evil and the Greater Good: The Theory and Politics of Social Diversity* (London: Rivers Oram Press).
Biddiss, M. (1970) *Father of Racist Ideology: The Social and Political Thought of Count Gobineau* (London: Weidenfeld and Nicolson).
Biddiss, M. (1975) 'European Racist Ideology 1850–1945', *Patterns of Prejudice*, 9, 5: 11–19.
Biddiss, M. (1979) *Images of Race* (Leicester: Leicester University Press).
Björgo, T. and Witte, R. (eds) (1993) *Racist Violence in Europe* (London: Macmillan).

Blackburn, R. (1988) *The Overthrow of Colonial Slavery* (London: Verso).

Blackburn, R. (ed.) (1991) *After the Fall: The Failure of Communism and the Future of Socialism* (London: Verso).

Blauner, R. (1989) *Black Lives, White Lives: Three Decades of Race Relations in America* (Berkeley: University of California Press).

Bloom, A. (1987) *The Closing of the American Mind* (Harmondsworth: Penguin).

Bolt, C. (1971) *Victorian Attitudes to Race* (London: Routledge and Kegan Paul).

Bonnett, A. (1993) *Radicalism, Anti-racism and Representation* (London: Routledge).

Boston, T. D. (1988) *Race, Class and Conservatism* (Boston: Unwin Hyman).

Bottomley, G. (1991) 'Culture, Ethnicity, and the Politics/Poetics of Representation', *Diaspora*, 1, 3: 303–20.

Bourdieu, P. (1991) *Language and Symbolic Power* (Cambridge: Polity Press).

Bourne, J. (1980) 'Cheerleaders and Ombudsmen: The Sociology of Race Relations in Britain', *Race and Class*, 21, 4: 331–52.

Boyarin, D. and Boyarin, J. (1993) 'Diaspora: Generation and the Ground of Jewish Identity', *Critical Inquiry*, 19, 693–725.

Brah, A. (1993) 'Difference, Diversity, Differentiation', in J. Wrench and J. Solomos (eds), *Racism and Migration in Western Europe* (Oxford: Berg).

Brah, A. (1994) 'Time, Place, and Others: Discourses of Race, Nation, and Ethnicity', *Sociology*, 28, 3: 805–13.

Brantlinger, P. (1988) *Rule of Darkness: British Literature and Imperialism, 1830–1914* (Ithaca: Cornell University Press).

Brantlinger, P. (1990) *Crusoe's Footprints: Cultural Studies in Britain and America* (New York: Routledge).

Brooks, R. L. (1990) *Rethinking the American Race Problem* (Berkeley: University of California Press).

Brown, C. (1984) *Black and White Britain: The Third PSI Survey* (Cambridge: Cambridge University Press).

Brown, C. (1992) 'Same Difference: The Persistence of Racial Disadvantage in the British Employment Market', in P. Braham, A. Rattansi and P. Skellington (eds), *Racism and Antiracism: Inequalities, Opportunities and Policies* (London: Sage).

Brubaker, R. (1992) *Citizenship and Nationhood in France and Germany* (Cambridge, Mass.: Harvard University Press).

Bryan, B., Dadzie, S. and Scafe, S. (1985) *The Heart of the Race: Black Women's Lives in Britain* (London: Virago).

Buck-Morss, S. (1991) *The Dialectics of Seeing: Walter Benjamin and the Arcades Project* (Cambridge, Mass.: MIT Press).

Burleigh, M. and Wippermann, W. (1991) *The Racial State: Germany, 1933–1945* (Cambridge: Cambridge University Press).

Calhoun, C. (ed.) (1994) *Social Theory and the Politics of Identity* (Oxford: Blackwell).

Cambridge, A. X. and Feuchtwang, S. (eds) (1990) *Antiracist Strategies* (Aldershot: Avebury).

Carby, H. (1982) 'White Woman Listen! Black Feminism and the Boundaries of Sisterhood', in CCCS, *The Empire Strikes Back: Race and Racism in 70s Britain* (London: Hutchinson).

Carby, H. (1987) *Reconstructing Womanhood* (New York: Oxford University Press).

Carby, H. (1992) 'The Multicultural Wars', in G. Dent (ed.), *Black Popular Culture* (Seattle: Bay Press).

Carter, E., Donald, J. and Squires, J. (eds) (1993) *Space and Place: Theories of Identity and Location* (London: Lawrence and Wishart).

Cashmore, E. E. (1979) *Rastaman: The Rastafarian Movement in Britain* (London: George Allen and Unwin).

Castells, M. (1977) *The Urban Question: A Marxist Approach* (Cambridge: MIT Press).

Castells, M. (1983) *The City and the Grassroots* (London: Edward Arnold).

Castles, S. and Miller, M. J. (1993) *The Age of Migration* (London: Macmillan).

Castoriadis, C. (1991) *Philosophy, Politics, Autonomy* (New York: Oxford University Press

Castoriadis, C. (1993) *Political and Social Writings: Volume 3, 1961–1979: Recommencing the Revolution: From Socialism to the Autonomous Society* (Minneapolis: University of Minnesota Press).

Catholic University of America (1967) *New Catholic Encyclopaedia* (Washington DC: Catholic University of America).

CCCS (Centre for Contemporary Cultural Studies) (1982) *The Empire Strikes Back: Race and Racism in 70s Britain* (London: Hutchinson).

Chambers, I. (1990) *Border Dialogues* (New York: Routledge).

Chambers, I. (1994) *Migrancy, Culture, Identity* (London: Routledge).

Chapman, M. (1978) *The Gaelic Vision in Scottish Culture* (London: Croom Helm).

Chapman, M. (1982) ' "Semantics" and the "Celts"', in D. Parkin (ed.), *Semantic Anthropology*, ASA Monograph 22, (London: Academic Press).

Cheyette, B. (1993) *Constructions of 'the Jew' in English Literature and Society: Racial Representations, 1875–1945* (Cambridge: Cambridge University Press).

Child, H. and Colles, D. (1971) *Christian Symbols Ancient and Modern: A Handbook for Students* (London: G. Bell).

Clifford, J. (1993) 'Negrophilia', in D. Hollier (ed.), *The New History of French Literature* (Cambridge, Mass.: Harvard University Press).

Clifford, J. 1994) 'Diasporas', *Cultural Anthropology*, 9, 3: 302–38.

Cock, J. (1989) *Maids and Madams: Domestic Workers Under Apartheid* (London: The Women's Press).

Cohen, A. (1974) 'Introduction: The Lesson of Ethnicity', in A. Cohen (ed.), *Urban Ethnicity* (London: Tavistock).

Cohen, A. (1980) 'Drama and Politics in the Development of a London Carnival', *Man*, 15: 65–87.

Cohen, A. (1982) 'A Polyethnic London Carnival as a Contested Cultural Performance', *Ethnic and Racial Studies*, 5, 1: 25–41.

Cohen, A. (1993) *Masquerade Politics: Explorations in the Structure of Urban Cultural Movements* (Oxford: Berg).

Cohen, A. P. (1985) *The Symbolic Construction of Community* (London: Tavistock).

Cohen, A. P. (ed.) (1982) *Belonging: Identity and Social Organisation in British Rural Cultures* (Manchester: Manchester University Press).

Cohen, P. (1972) 'Subcultural Conflict and Working-Class Community', *Working Papers in Cultural Studies*, 2, University of Birmingham.

Cohen, P. (1988a) 'Popular Racism, Unpopular Education', *Youth and Policy*, 24: 8–12.

Cohen, P. (1988b) 'Tarzan and the Jungle Bunnies': Class, Race and Sex in Popular Culture', *New Formations*, 5: 25–30.

Cohen, P. (1991) 'Monstrous Images, Perverse Reasons: Cultural Studies in Anti-Racist Education', Centre for Multicultural Education, Institute of Education, University of London, Working Papers, No. 11.

Cohen, P. (1992) ' "It's Racism What Dunnit" ' : Hidden Narratives in Theories of Racism', in J. Donald and A. Rattansi (eds), '*Race*', *Culture and Difference* (London: Sage).

Cohen, P. (1993) *Home Rules: Some Reflections on Racism and Nationalism in Everyday Life* (London: University of East London).

Cohen, P. and Bains, H. (eds) (1988) *Multi-racist Britain* (London: Macmillan).

Cohn, N. (1970) *Warrant for Genocide: The Myth of the Jewish World – Conspiracy and the Protocols of the Elders of Zion* (Harmondsworth: Penguin).

Cole, M. (1989) 'Race and Class or 'Race', Class, Gender and Community?: A Critical Appraisal of the Racialised Fraction of the Working Class Thesis', *British Journal of Sociology*, 40, 1: 118–29.

Colley, L. (1992) *Britons: Forging the Nation, 1707–1837* (New Haven: Yale University Press).

Collins, P. H. (1990) *Black Feminist Thought* (London: Unwin Hyman).

Collinson, S. (1993) *Medicine, Race and Gender: An Examination of Medical Theory and Practice*, unpublished Ph.D. thesis, Birkbeck College, University of London.

Commission of the European Communities (1989) *Living in Europe: A Handbook for Europeans* (Brussels: ECSC).

Condry, E. (1976) 'The Impossibility of Solving the Highland Problem', *Journal of the Anthropological Society of Oxford*, VII, 3: 138–50.

Connolly, W. E. (1991) *Identity/Difference: Democratic Negotiations of Political Paradox* (Ithaca: Cornell University Press).

Coombes, A. (1994) *Reinventing Africa* (London: Yale University Press).

Cottrell, S. (1989) 'The Devil on Two Sticks: Franco-phobia in 1803', in R. Samuel (ed.), *Patriotism: The Making and Unmaking of British National Identity. Volume 1: History and Politics* (London: Routledge).

Cox, O. C. (1970) *Caste, Class and Race* (New York: Monthly Review Press).

Craton, M. (1980) *Testing the Chains: Resistance to Slavery in the British West Indies* (Ithaca: Cornell University Press).

Cross, M. (1989) 'Moving Targets: The Changing Face of Racism', *New Statesman and Society*, 7 April: 35.

Curtin, P. (1964) *Image of Africa: British Ideas and Action 1780–1850*, 2 vols, (Madison: University of Wisconsin Press).

Dahya, B. (1974) 'The Nature of Pakistani Ethnicity in Industrial Cities in Britain', in A. Cohen (ed.), *Urban Ethnicity*, ASA Monograph 12 (London: Tavistock).

Davis, D. B. (1966) *The Problem of Slavery in Western Culture* (New York: Oxford University Press).

Daye, S. (1994) *Middle-Class Blacks in Britain* (London: Macmillan).
Dengler, C. N. (1991) *In Search of Human Nature: The Decline and Revival of Darwinism in American Social Thought* (New York: Oxford University Press).
Dent, G. (ed.) (1992) *Black Popular Culture* (Seattle: Bay Press).
Diawara, M. (1991) 'The Nature of Mother Dreaming Rivers', *Third Text*, 13: 73–84.
Dikötter, F. (1992) *The Discourse of Race in Modern China* (London: Hurst).
Dirks, N. B. (ed.) (1992) *Colonialism and Culture* (Ann Arbor: University of Michigan Press).
Drake, St C. and Cayton, H. R. (1993) *Black Metropolis: A Study of Negro Life in a Northern City* (Chicago: University of Chicago Press).
Drescher, S. (1987) *Capitalism and Antislavery: British Mobilisation in Comparative Perspective* (New York: Oxford University Press).
Du Bois, W. E. B. (1989) *The Souls of Black Folk* (New York: Bantam).
Duffield, M. (1988) *Black Radicalism and the Politics of De-industrialisation* (Aldershot: Avebury).
Dyer, R. (1988) 'White', *Screen*, 29, 4: 44–5.
Ekwe-Ekwe, H. (1994a) 'The Idiocy and Tragedy of a Euroassimiliationist Illusion', *African People's Review*, 3, 2: 16–17.
Ekwe-Ekwe, H. (1994b) 'Retrieval, Recasting, Reconstruction', *African People's Review*, 3, 3: 4–5.
Engerman, S. L. and Genovese, E. D. (1975) *Race and Slavery in the Western Hemisphere: Quantitative Studies* (Princeton: Princeton University Press).
Enzensberger, H. M. (1992) 'The Great Migration', *Granta*, 42: 15–51.
Enzensberger, H. M. (1994) *Civil War* (London: Granta Books).
Epstein, A. L. (1958) *Politics in an Urban African Community* (Manchester: Manchester University Press).
Fainstein, N. (1993) 'Race, Class and Segregation: Discourses about African–Americans', *International Journal of Urban and Regional Research*, 17, 3: 304–403.
Fanon, F. (1967a) *Towards the African Revolution* (New York: Monthly Review Press).
Fanon, F. (1967b) *The Wretched of the Earth* (Harmondsworth: Penguin).
Fanon, F. (1986) *Black Skin, White Masks* (London: Pluto Press).
Farley, R. and Allen, W. R. (1989) *The Color Line and the Quality of Life in America* (New York: Oxford University Press).
Ferguson, R. (1992) 'Introduction: Invisible Center', in R. Ferguson, M. Gever, T. Minh-ha, C. West (eds), *Out There: Marginalization and Contemporary Cultures* (Cambridge, Mass.: MIT Press).
Feuchtwang, S. (1990) 'Racism: Territoriality and Ethnocentricity', in A. X. Cambridge and S. Feuchtwang (eds), *Antiracist Strategies* (Aldershot: Avebury).
Finley, M. I. (1980) *Ancient Slavery and Modern Ideology* (Harmondsworth: Penguin).
Finley, M. I. (1983) *Economy and Society in Ancient Greece* (Harmondsworth: Penguin).
Fisher, G. and Joshua, H. (1982) 'Social Policy and Black Youth', in E. E. Cashmore and B. Troyna (eds), *Black Youth in Crisis* (London: George Allen and Unwin).

Fitzgerald, M. (1984) *Political Parties and Black People: Participation, Representation and Exploitation* (London: Runnymede Trust).

Fitzgerald, M. (1988) 'Different Roads? The Development of Afro-Caribbean and Asian Political Organisation in London', *New Community*, XIV, 3: 385–96.

Foner, N. (1979) *Jamaica Farewell: Jamaican Migrants in London* (London: Routledge and Kegan Paul).

Ford, G. (1992) *Fascist Europe: The Rise of Racism and Xenophobia* (London: Pluto Press).

Forsythe, D. (1989) 'German Identity and the Problem of History', in E. Tonkin, M. McDonald and M. Chapman (eds), *History and Ethnicity*, ASA Monographs 27, (London: Routledge).

Foster, R. F. (1993) *Paddy & Mr Punch: Connections in English and Irish History* (London: Allen Lane).

Fox, R. (1973) *Encounter with Anthropology* (New York: Harcourt Brace Jovanovich).

Frankenberg, R. (1957) *Village on the Border* (London: Cohen and West).

Frankenberg, R. (1993) *White Women, Race Matters: The Social Construction of Whiteness* (London: Routledge).

Frankenberg, R. and Mani, L. (1993) 'Crosscurrents, Crosstalk: Race, "Postcoloniality" and the Politics of Location', *Cultural Studies*, 7, 2: 292–310.

Fredrickson, G. M. (1971) *The Black Image in the White Mind* (New York: Harper and Row).

Fredrickson, G. M. (1981) *White Supremacy: A Comparative Study in American and South African History* (New York: Oxford University Press).

Fredrickson, G. M. (1988) *The Arrogance of Race* (Middletown: Wesleyan University Press).

Gaber, I. and Aldridge, J. (eds) (1994) *In the Best Interests of the Child: Culture, Identity and Trans-racial Adoption* (London: Free Association Books).

Gans, H. J. (1962) *The Urban Villagers* (New York: Free Press).

Garrison, L. (1979) *Black Youth, Rastafarianism and Identity Crisis in Britain* (London: Afro-Caribbean Educational Project).

Gates Jr, H. L. (1988) *The Signifying Monkey* (New York: Oxford University Press).

Gates Jr, H. L. (ed.) (1986) *'Race', Writing and Difference* (Chicago: University of Chicago Press).

Genovese, E. D. (1967) *The Political Economy of Slavery* (New York: Vintage). (1972) *Roll, Jordan, Roll: The World the Slaves Made* (New York: Vintage).

Gerhart, G. M. (1978) *Black Power in South Africa: The Evolution of an Ideology* (Berkeley: University of California Press).

Giddens, A. (1991) *Modernity and Self-Identity* (Cambridge: Polity Press).

Gilbert, M. (1986) *The Holocaust* (London: Fontana).

Gilman, S. L. (1985) *Difference and Pathology: Stereotypes of Sexuality, Race and Madness* (Ithaca: Cornell University Press).

Gilman, S. L. (1991) *The Jew's Body* (New York: Routledge).

Gilman, S. L. (1993) *The Case of Sigmund Freud: Medicine and Identity at the Fin De Siècle* (Baltimore: Johns Hopkins University Press).

Gilman, S. L. and Katz, S. T. (eds) (1991) *Anti-Semitism in Times of Crisis* (New York: New York University Press).

Gilroy, P. (1987) *There Ain't No Black in the Union Jack* (London: Hutchinson).

Gilroy, P. (1990a) 'One Nation Under a Groove: The Cultural Politics of "Race" and Racism in Britain', in D. T. Goldberg (eds), *Anatomy of Racism* (Minneapolis: University of Minnesota Press).

Gilroy, P. (1990b) 'The End of Anti-Racism' in W. Ball and J. Solomos (eds), *Race and Local Politics* (London: Macmillan).

Gilroy, P. (1991) 'It Ain't Where You're From, It's Where You're At ... The Dialectics of Diasporic Identification', *Third Text*, 13: 3–16.

Gilroy, P. (1992a) 'Cultural Studies and Ethnic Absolutism', in L. Grossberg, C. Nelson and P. Treichler (eds), *Cultural Studies* (London: Routledge).

Gilroy, P. (1992b) It's a Family Affair', in G. Dent (ed.), *Black Popular Culture* (Seattle: Bay Press).

Gilroy, P. (1993a) *The Black Atlantic: Modernity and Double Consciousness* (London: Verso).

Gilroy, P. (1993b) *Small Acts: Thoughts on the Politics of Black Cultures* (London: Serpent's Tail).

Gilroy, P. (1994a) ' "After the Love Has Gone": Bio-politics and Etho-poetics in the Black Public Sphere', *Public Culture*, Fall: 1–27.

Gilroy, P. (1994b) 'Diaspora', *Paragraph*, 17, 3: 207–12

Gilroy, P. (1995) 'Unwelcome: Review of Welcome II the Terrordrome', *Sight and Sound*, 2: 18–19.

Giroux, H. A. (1993) 'Living Dangerously: Identity, Politics and the New Cultural Racism', *Cultural Studies*, 7, 1: 1–27.

Glazer, N. (1988) *The Limits of Social Policy* (Cambridge, Mass.: Harvard University Press).

Gluckman, M. (1961) 'Anthropological Problems Arising from the African Industrial Revolution', in A. Southall (ed.), *Social Change in Modern Africa* (London: Oxford University Press).

Goldberg, D. T. (1992) 'The Semantics of Race', *Ethnic and Racial Studies*, 15, 4: 543–69.

Goldberg, D. T. (1993) *Racist Culture* (Oxford: Blackwell).

Goldberg, D. T. (ed.) (1990) *Anatomy of Racism* (Minneapolis: University of Minnesota Press).

Goldberg, D. T. (ed.) (1994) *Multiculturalism: A Critical Reader* (Oxford: Blackwell).

Goldman, R. (1992) *Reading Ads Socially* (London: Routledge).

Gooding-Williams, R. (ed.) (1993) *Reading Rodney King, Reading Urban Uprising* (New York: Routledge).

Gorer, G. (1982) 'English Identity Over Time and Empire', in G. De Vos and L. Romanucci-Ross (eds), *Ethnic Identity: Cultural Continuities and Change* (Chicago: University of Chicago Press).

Graff, G. (1992) *Beyond the Culture Wars* (New York: W. W. Norton).

de Grazia, E. and Newman, R. K. (1982) *Banned Films: Movies, Censors and the First Amendment* (New York: R. R. Bowker).

Gregory, S. (1993) 'Thinking Empowerment Through Difference: Race and the Politics of Identity', *Diaspora*, 2, 3: 401–10.

Griffin, R. (1991) *The Nature of Fascism* (London: Pinter).

Grimshaw, A. (ed.) (1992) *The C. L. R. James Reader* (Oxford: Blackwell).

Guillaumin, C. (1980) 'The Idea of Race and its Elevation to Autonomous Scientific and Legal Status', in UNESCO, *Sociological Theories: Race and Colonialism* (Paris: UNESCO).

Guillaumin, C. (1988) 'Race and Nature: The System of Marks', *Feminist Studies*, 8, 2: 25–44.

Guillaumin, C. (1991) '"Race" and Discourse', in M. Silverman (ed.), *Race, Discourse and Power in France* (Aldershot: Avebury).

Guillaumin, C. (1995) *Racism, Sexism, Power and Ideology* (London: Routledge).

Gutman, A. (1992) 'Introduction', in C. Taylor *et al.*, *Multiculturalism and 'The Politics of Recognition'* (Princeton: Princeton University Press).

Habermas, J. (1987) *Two Philosophical Discourse of Modernity* (Cambridge: Polity Press).

Habermas, J. (1994) *The Past as Future* (Cambridge: Polity Press).

Hacker, A. (1992) *Two Nations: Black and White, Separate, Hostile, Unequal* (New York: Scribners).

Hall, C. (1992) *White, Middle Class and Male: Explorations in Feminism and History* (Cambridge: Polity Press).

Hall, S. (1980) 'Race Articulation and Societies Structured in Dominance', in UNESCO, *Sociological Theories: Race and Colonialism* (Paris: UNESCO).

Hall, S. (1981) 'The Whites of Their Eyes: Racist Ideologies and the Media', in G. Bridges and R. Brunt (eds), *Silver Linings: Some Strategies for the Eighties* (London: Lawrence and Wishart).

Hall, S. (1987) 'Minimal Selves', in L. Appignanesi (ed.), *The Real Me: Postmodernism and the Question of Identity* (London: Institute of Contemporary Arts).

Hall, S. (1988) 'New Ethnicities', in K. Mercer (ed.), *Black Film/British Cinema* (London: Institute of Contemporary Arts).

Hall, S. (1989) 'After Dread and Anger', BBC Radio 4.

Hall, S. (1990) 'Cultural Identity and Diaspora', in J. Rutherford (ed.), *Identity: Culture, Community, Difference* (London: Lawrence and Wishart).

Hall, S. (1991a) 'The Local and the Global', in A. D. King (ed.), *Culture, Globalisation and the World System* (London: Macmillan).

Hall, S. (1991b) 'Old and New Identities, Old and New Ethnicities', in A. D. King (ed.), *Culture, Globalisation and the World System* (London: Macmillan).

Hall, S. (1992) 'The Question of Cultural Identity', in S. Hall, D. Held and T. McGrew (eds), *Modernity and its Futures* (Cambridge: Polity Press).

Hall, S., Critcher, C., Jefferson, T., Clarke, J. and Roberts, B. (1978) *Policing the Crisis: Mugging, the State, and Law and Order* (London: Macmillan).

Hall, S. and Jacques, M. (eds) (1989) *New Times: The Changing Face of Politics in the 1990s* (London: Lawrence and Wishart).

Hannerz, U. (1969) *Soulside: Inquiries into Ghetto Culture and Community* (New York, Columbia University Press).

Hannerz, U. (1980) *Exploring the City: Inquiries Towards an Urban Anthropology* (New York: Columbia University Press).

Hannerz, U. (1989a) 'Culture Between Centre and Periphery: Towards a Macroanthropology', *Ethnos*, 54, III–V: 200–16.

Hannerz, U. (1989b) *Five Nigerians and the Global Ecumene*, paper given to the SSRC Symposium on 'Public Culture in India and Its Global Problematics', Carmel, California, 26–30, April 1989.

Haraway, D. J. (1991) *Simians, Cyborgs, and Women: The Reinvention of Nature* (London: Free Association Books).

Haraway, D. J. (1992) 'The Promises of Monsters: A Regenerative Politics for Inappropriate/d Others', in L. Grossberg, C. Nelson and P. Treichler (eds), *Cultural Studies* (London: Routledge).

Harding, S. (ed.), (1993) *The 'Racial' Economy of Science: Toward a Democratic Future* (Bloomington: Indiana University Press).

Harding, V. (1981) *There is a River: The Black Struggle for Freedom in America* (New York: Vintage).

Harris, C. (1988) 'Images of Blacks in Britain: 1930–60', in S. Allen and M. Macey (eds), *Race and Social Policy* (London: Economic and Social Research Council).

Harvey, D. (1989) *The Condition of Postmodernity* (Oxford: Blackwell).

Hebdige, D. (1981) 'Skinheads and the Search for a White Working Class Identity', *New Socialist*, September 1981: 38.

Heisler, B. S. (1991) 'A Comparative Perspective on the Underclass: Questions of Urban Poverty, Race and Citizenship', *Theory and Society*, 20, 4: 455–83.

Henriques, J. (1984) 'Social Psychology and the Politics of Racism', in J. Henriques, W. Hollway, C. Urwin, C. Venn and V. Walkerdine, *Changing the Subject* (London: Methuen).

Henriques, J., Hollway, W., Urwin, C., Venn, C., Walkerdine, V. (1984) *Changing the Subject: Psychology, Social Regulation and Subjectivity* (London: Methuen).

Heskett, J. (1990) 'Modernism and Archaism in Design in the Third Reich' in B. Taylor and W. van der Will (eds), *The Nazification of Art: Art, Design, Music, Architecture and Film in the Third Reich* (Winchester: Winchester Press).

Hewitt, R. (1986) *White Talk, Black Talk: Inter-racial Friendship and Communication Amongst Adolescents* (Cambridge: Cambridge University Press).

Hewitt, R. (1991) 'Language, Youth and the Destabilisation of Ethnicity', paper given at the Conference on Ethnicity in Youth Culture: Interdisciplinary Perspectives, Fittjagard, Botkyrka, Sweden, 3–6 June 1991.

Hill, R. A. (ed.) (1987) *Marcus Garvey: Life and Lessons* (Berkeley: University of California Press).

Hinz, B. (1979) *Art in the Third Reich* (Oxford: Blackwell).

Hitler, A. (1992) *Mein Kampf* (London: Pimlico).

Hobsbawm, E. and Ranger, T. (eds) (1983) *The Invention of Tradition* (Cambridge: Cambridge University Press).

hooks, b. (1981) *Ain't I A Woman: Black Women and Feminism* (Boston: South End Press).

hooks, b. (1991) *Yearning: Race, Gender, and Cultural Politics* (London: Turnaround).

hooks, b. (1992) 'Representing Whiteness in the Black Imagination', in L. Grossberg, C. Nelson and P. Treichler (eds), *Cultural Studies* (London: Routledge).

Howe, S. (1993) *Anticolonialism in British Politics* (Oxford: Clarendon Press).

Hughes, R. (1993) *Culture of Complaint: The Fraying of America* (New York: Oxford University Press).

Hulme, P. (1986) *Colonial Encounters: Europe and the Native Caribbean* (London: Methuen).

Husband, C. (1977) 'News, Media, Language and Race Relations: A Case Study in Identity Maintenance', in H. Giles (ed.), *Language, Ethnicity and Intergroup Relations* (London: Academic Press).

Huyssen, A. (1986) *After the Great Divide: Modernism, Mass Culture and Postmodernism* (London: Macmillan).

Huyssen, A. (1995) *Twilight Memories: Marking Time in a Culture of Amnesia* (New York: Routledge).

Hyam, R. (1990) *Empire and Sexuality: The British Experience* (Manchester: Manchester University Press).

Institute of Jewish Affairs (1994) *Antisemitism: World Report* (London: Institute of Jewish Affairs).

Jacoby, R. (1987) *The Last Intellectuals: American Culture in the Age of Academe* (New York: Noonday Press).

Jacoby, R. (1994) *Dogmatic Wisdom: How the Culture Wars Divert Education and Distract America* (New York: Doubleday).

James, S. and Busia, A. (eds) (1993) *Theorizing Black Feminisms* (London: Routledge).

James, W. and Harris, C. (eds) (1993) *Inside Babylon: The Caribbean Diaspora in Britain* (London: Verso).

JanMohamed, A. R. and Lloyd, D. (eds) (1990) *The Nature and Context of Minority Discourse* (New York: Oxford University Press).

Jencks, C. (1992) *Rethinking Social Policy: Race, Poverty, and the Underclass* (Cambridge, Mass: Harvard University Press).

Jencks, C. and Peterson, P. (eds) (1991) *The Urban Underclass* (Washington DC: Brookings Institution).

Jenkins, R. (1986) 'Social Anthropological Models of Inter-ethnic Relations', in J. Rex and D. Mason (eds), *Theories of Race and Ethnic Relations* (Cambridge: Cambridge University Press).

Jhally, S. and Lewis, J. (1992) *Enlightened Racism: The Cosby Show, Audiences, and the Myth of the American Dream* (Boulder: Westview Press).

Jones, G. (1980) *Social Darwinism and English Thought: The Interaction Between Biological and Social Theory* (New Jersey: Humanities Press).

Jones, S. (1988) *Black Culture, White Youth: The Reggae Tradition from JA to UK* (London: Macmillan).

Jordan, W. (1968) *White Over Black: American Attitudes Towards the Negro, 1550–1812* (New York: W. W. Norton).

Kaldor, M. (ed.) (1991) *Europe from Below: An East–West Dialogue* (London: Verso).

Kaplan, A. and Pease, D. E. (eds) (1993) *Cultures of United States Imperialism* (Durham: Duke University Press).

Kater, M. H. (1992) *Different Drummers: Jazz in the Culture of Nazi Germany* (New York: Oxford University Press).

Katz, M. B. (1989) *The Undeserving Poor* (New York: Pantheon Books).

Keith, M. (1993) *Race, Riots and Policing: Lore and Disorder in a Multi-racist Society* (London: UCL Press).

Keith, M. (1995) 'Ethnic Entrepreneurs and Street Rebels: Looking Inside the Inner City', in S. Pile and N. Thrift (eds), *Mapping the Subject: Geographies of Cultural Transformation* (London: Routledge).

Keith, M. and Pile, S. (eds) (1993) *Place and the Politics of Identity* (London: Routledge).

Kennedy, P. (1993) *Preparing for the Twenty-first Century* (London: HarperCollins).

Kennedy, P. and Nicholls, A. (eds) (1981) *Nationalist and Racialist Movements in Britain and Germany Before 1914* (London: Macmillan).

Kerouac, J. (1955) *On the Road* (New York: Signet).

Khan, V. S. (1976) 'Pakistanis in Britain: Perceptions of a Population', *New Community*, 5, 1/2: 222–9.

Khan, V. S. (1979) 'South Asian Women in South London', in S. Wallman (ed.), *Ethnicity at Work* (London: Macmillan).

Kiernan, V. G. (1969) *The Lords of Humankind: Black Man, Yellow Man, and White Man in the Age of Empire* (Harmondsworth: Penguin).

Kisch, J. and Mapp, E. (1992) *A Separate Cinema: Fifty Years of Black-Cast Posters* (New York: Noonday Press).

Kristeva, J. (1991) *Strangers to Ourselves* (New York: Columbia University Press).

Kristeva, J. (1993) *Nations without Nationalism* (New York: Columbia University Press).

LaCapra, D. (ed.), (1991) *The Bounds of Race: Perspectives on Hegemony and Resistance* (Ithaca: Cornell University Press).

Laclau, E. (1990) *New Reflections on the Revolution of Our Time* (London: Verso).

Laclau, E. (ed.), (1994) *The Making of Political Identities* (London: Verso).

Lamont, M. and Fournier, M. (eds) (1992) *Cultivating Differences: Symbolic Boundaries and the Making of Inequality* (Chicago: University of Chicago Press).

Lash, S. and Friedman, J. (eds) (1992) *Modernity & Identity* (Oxford: Blackwell).

Lash, S. and Urry, J. (1994) *Economies of Signs and Space* (London: Sage).

Lawrence, E. (1981) 'White Sociology, Black Struggle', *Multi-Racial Education*, 9: 3–17.

Lawrence, E. (1982) 'In the Abundance of Water the Fool is Thirsty: Sociology and Black "Pathology"', in CCCS (1982) *The Empire Strikes Back* (London: Hutchinson).

Layton-Henry, Z. (1992) *The Politics of Immigration: Immigration, 'Race' and 'Race' Relations in Post-war Britain* (Oxford: Blackwell).

Liebow, E. (1967) *Tally's Corner: A Study of Negro Street Corner Men* (Boston: Little, Brown).

Lipsitz, G. (1990) *Time Passages: Collective Memory and American Popular Literature* (Minneapolis: University of Minnesota Press).

Long, E. (1774) *History of Jamaica* (London).

Lorimer, D. A. (1978) *Colour, Class and the Victorians* (Leicester: Leicester University Press).

Lovejoy, A. O. (1964) *The Great Chain of Being* (Cambridge, Mass.: Harvard University Press).

Lovejoy, P. E. (1983) *Transformations in Slavery: A History of Slavery in Africa* (Cambridge, Mass.: Harvard University Press).

Lowe, L. (1991) *Critical Terrains: French and British Orientalisms* (Ithaca: Cornell University Press).

Lyon, M. H. (1972–3) 'Ethnicity in Britain: The Gujarati Tradition', *New Community*, 2, 1: 1–11.

Lyon, M. H. (1973) 'Ethnic Minority Problems: An Overview of Some Recent Research', *New Community*, 2, 4: 329–50.

Lyotard, J.-F. (1984) *The Postmodern Condition: A Report on Knowledge* (Manchester: Manchester University Press).

McDonald, M. (1986) 'Culture and Ethnic Kinship and the Problem of Being English', *Current Anthropology*, 27, 4: 333–48.

McAdam, D. (1982) *Political Process and the Development of Black Insurgency, 1930–1970* (Chicago: University of Chicago Press).

McCole, J. (1993) *Walter Benjamin and the Antinomies of Tradition* (Ithaca: Cornell University Press).

McCrudden, C., Smith, D. J. and Brown, C. (1991) *Racial Justice at Work* (London: Policy Studies Institute).

Mack, J. (1992) *Heil Herbie* broadcast in the *Without Walls* series for Channel Four Television, United Kingdom.

MacKenzie, J. M. (1984) *Propaganda and Empire: The Manipulation of British Public Opinion 1880–1960* (Manchester: Manchester University Press).

MacKenzie, J. M. (ed.), (1986) *Imperialism and Popular Culture* (Manchester: Manchester University Press).

McLuhan, M. (1964) *Understanding Media* (London: Routledge and Kegan Paul).

Maier, C. S. (ed.), (1988) *The Unmasterable Past: History, Holocaust, and German National Identity* (Cambridge, Mass.: Harvard University Press).

Mailer, N. (1961) 'The White Negro: Superficial Reflections on the Hipster', in N. Mailer, *Advertisements for Myself* (London: Andre Deutsch).

Mann, M. (1993) *The Sources of Social Power. Volume II: The Rise of Classes and Nation States, 1760–1914* (Cambridge: Cambridge University Press).

Manning, P. (1990) *Slavery and African Life* (Cambridge: Cambridge University Press).

Mannoni, O. (1964) *Prospero and Caliban: The Psychology of Colonisation* (New York: Fredrick A. Praeger).

Marks, S. and Trapido, S. (eds) (1987) *The Politics of Race, Class and Nationalism in Twentieth Century South Africa* (London: Longman).

Marshall, T. H. (1950) *Citizenship and Social Class* (Cambridge: Cambridge University Press).

Martin, T. (1976) *Race First: The Ideological and Organisational Struggles of Marcus Garvey and the Universal Negro Improvement Association* (Dover: Majority Press).

Martin, T. (ed.), 1991) *African Fundamentalism: A Literary and Cultural Anthology of Garvey's Harlem Renaissance* (Dover: Majority Press).

Melucci, A. (1989) *Nomads of the Present* (London: Radius).

Memmi, A. (1969) *The Coloniser and the Colonised* (Boston: Beacon Press).

Mercer, K. (1992) 'Skin Head Sex Thing: Racial Difference and Homoerotic Imagery', *New Formations*, 16: 1–23.

Mercer, K. (1994) *Welcome to the Jungle: New Positions in Black Cultural Studies* (London: Routledge).

Miles, R. (1982) *Racism and Migrant Labour* (London: George Allen and Unwin).

Miles, R. (1984a) 'Marxism Versus the "Sociology of Race Relations"?', *Ethnic and Racial Studies*, 7, 2: 217–37.

Miles, R. (1984b) 'The Riots of 1958: Notes on the Ideological Construction of "Race Relations" as a Political Issue in Britain', *Immigrants and Minorities*, 3, 3: 252–75

Miles, R. (1986) 'Labour Migration, Racism and Capital Accumulation in Western Europe', *Capital and Class*, 28: 49–86.

Miles, R. (1988) 'Racism, Marxism and British Politics', *Economy and Society*, 17, 3: 428–60.

Miles, R. (1989) *Racism* (London: Routledge).

Miles, R. (1993) *Racism After 'Race Relations'* (London: Routledge).

Miles, R. (1994) 'A Rise of Racism in Contemporary Europe?: Some Sceptical Reflections on its Nature and Extent', *New Community*, 20, 4: 547–62.

Miles, R. and Phizacklea, A. (1979) 'Some Introductory Observations on Race and Politics in Britain', in R. Miles and A. Phizacklea (eds), *Racism and Political Action in Britain* (London: Routledge and Kegan Paul).

Miles, R. and Phizacklea, A. (1984) *White Man's Country: Racism in British Politics* (London: Pluto Press).

Miller, C. L. (1990) *Theories of Africans* (Chicago: University of Chicago Press).

Minh-ha, T. (1989) *Woman, Native, Other: Writing Postcoloniality and Feminism* (Bloomington: Indiana University Press).

Mirza, H. (1992) *Young, Female and Black* (London: Routledge).

Modood, T. (1988) '"Black", Racial Equality and Asian Identity', *New Community*, XIV, 3: 397–404.

Modood, T. (1990) 'Catching Up with Jesse Jackson: Being Oppressed and Being Somebody', *New Community*, 17, 1: 85–96.

Modood, T. (1992) *Not Easy Being British: Colour, Culture and Citizenship* (London: Runnymede Trust and Trentham Books).

Mohanty, C., Russo, A., and Torres, L. (eds) (1991) *Third World Women and the Politics of Feminism* (Bloomington: Indiana University Press).

Montagu, A. (ed.), (1964) *The Concept of Race* (New York: Free Press).

Moon, J. D. (1993) *Constructing Community: Moral Pluralism and Tragic Conficts* (Princeton: Princeton University Press).

Morris, J. (1973) 'The Popularisation of Imperial History', *Journal of Imperial and Commonwealth History*, 1: 113–18.

Morrison, T. (1988) *Beloved* (London: Picador).

Morrison, T. (1992) *Playing in the Dark: Whiteness and the Literary Imagination* (Cambridge, Mass.: Harvard University Press).

Morrison, T. (ed.), (1992) *Race-ing Justice, En-gendering Power: Essays on Anita Hill, Clarence Thomas, and the Construction of Social Reality* (New York: Pantheon).

Moses, W. J. (1978) *The Golden Age of Black Nationalism: 1850–1925* (New York: Oxford University Press).

Mosse, G. (1966) *The Crisis of German Ideology: Intellectual Origins of the Third Reich* (London: Weidenfeld and Nicolson).

Mosse, G. (1985a) *Toward the Final Solution: A History of European Racism* (Madison: University of Wisconsin Press).

Mosse, G. (1985b) *Nationalism and Sexuality: Middle-Class Morality and Sexual Norms in Modern Europe* (Madison: University of Wisconsin Press).

Mosse, G. (1987) *Masses and Man: Nationalist and Fascist Perceptions of Reality* (Detroit: Wayne State University Press).

Mouffe, C. (1993) *The Return of the Political* (London: Verso).

Mouffe, C. (ed.), (1992) *Dimensions of Radical Democracy: Pluralism, Citizenship, Community* (London: Verso).

Mudimbe, V. Y. (1988) *The Invention of Africa: Gnosis, Philosophy and the Order of Knowledge* (Bloomington: Indiana University Press).

Mudimbe, V. Y. (1994) *The Idea of Africa* (Bloomington: Indiana University Press).

Mullard, C. (1982) 'The State's Response to Racism: Towards a Relational Explanation', in A. Ohri, B. Manning and P. Curno (eds), *Community Work and Racism* (London: Routledge and Kegan Paul).

Murray, C. (1984) *Losing Ground: American Social Policy, 1950–1980* (New York: Basic Books).

Myrdal, G. (1962) *Challenge to Affluence* (New York: Pantheon Books).

Newman, G. (1987) *The Rise of English Nationalism: A Cultural History, 1740–1830* (London: Weidenfeld and Nicolson).

Newnham, A. (1986) *Employment, Unemployment and Black People* (London: Runnymede Trust).

Offe, C. (1985) *Disorganised Capitalism* (Cambridge: Polity Press).

O'Hara, L. (1992) 'Notes from the Underground: British Fascism, 1974–92. Part 1, 1974–83', *Lobster*, 23: 15–20.

O'Hara (1993) 'Notes from the Underground: British Fascism. Part 4, 1983–6', *Lobster*, 26: 13–18.

Omi, M. and Winant, H. (1994) *Racial Formation in the United States: From the 1960s to the 1990s*, 2nd edition (New York: Routledge).

Opie, R. (1985) *Rule Britannia: Trading on the British Image* (Harmondsworth: Viking).

Opitz, M., Oguntoye, K. and Schultz, D. (eds) (1992) *Showing Our Colours: Afro-German Women Speak Out* (London: Open Letters Press).

Orfield, G. (1985) 'Ghettoization and its Alternatives', in P. Peterson (ed.), *The New Urban Reality* (Washington DC: The Brookings Institution).

Orfield, G. (1988) 'Race and the Liberal Agenda: The Loss of the Integrationist Dream, 1965–1974', in M. Weir, A. S. Orloff and T. Skocpol (eds), *The Politics of Social Policy in the United States* (Princeton: Princeton University Press).

Otis, J. (1993) *Upside Your Head!: Rhythm and Blues on Central Avenue* (Hanover: Wesleyan University Press).

Palmer, F. (ed.) (1986) *Anti-Racism – An Assault on Education and Value* (London: Sherwood Press).

Park, R. E. (1925) 'The City: Suggestions for the Investigation of Human Behaviour in the Urban Environment', in R. E. Park and E. W. Burgess and R. D. McKenzie, *The City* (Chicago: UNC).

Parker, A., Russo, M., Sommer, D., and Yaeger, P. (eds) (1992) *Nationalisms and Sexualities* (New York: Routledge).

Parry, B. (1972) *Delusions and Discoveries: Studies on India in the British Imagination, 1880–1930* (London: Allen Lane).

Patterson, O. (1982) *Slavery and Social Death* (Cambridge, Mass.: Harvard University Press).

Peukert, D. J. K (1987) *Inside Nazi Germany: Conformity, Opposition and Racism in Everyday Life* (London: Penguin).

Phizacklea, A. and Miles, R. (1980) *Labour and Racism* (London: Routledge and Kegan Paul).

Pieterse, J. N. (1992) *White on Black: Images of Africa and Blacks in Western Popular Culture* (New Haven and London: Yale University Press).

Pines, J. (1988) 'The Cultural Context of Black British Cinema', in M. Chan and C. Ardrade-Walking (eds), *Critical Perspectives in Black Independent Cinema* (California: MIT Press).

Pinkney, A. (1984) *The Myth of Black Progress* (Cambridge: Cambridge University Press).

Pointon, M. (1994) '"A Latter Day Siegfried": Ian Botham at the National Gallery, 1986', *New Formations*, 21: 131–45.

Poliakov, L. (1974a) *The Aryan Myth* (Brighton: University of Sussex Press).

Poliakov, L. (1974b) *The History of Anti-Semitism*, 4 vols (London: Routledge and Kegan Paul).

Poliakov, L. (1982) 'Racism from the Enlightenment to the Age of Imperialism', in R. Ross (ed.), *Racism and Colonialism* (The Hague: Martinus Nijhoff).

Porter, R. (ed.), (1993) *Myths of the English* (Cambridge: Cambridge University Press).

Pratt, M. L. (1992) *Imperial Eyes: Travel Writing and Transculturation* (London: Routledge).

Proctor, R. N. (1988) *Racial Hygiene: Medicine under the Nazis* (Harvard: Harvard University Press).

Pryce, K. (1979) *Endless Pressure* (Harmondsworth: Penguin).

Pulzer, P. (1988) *The Rise of Political Anti-Semitism in Germany and Austria* (London: Peter Halban).

Quinn, M. (1994) *The Swastika: Constructing the Symbol* (London: Routledge).

Rampton, M. B. H. (1989) *Evaluations of Black Language Crossing and the Local Sociocultural Order*, Adolescence and Language Use Working Paper, No. 3, Institute of Education, University of London.

Rattansi, A. (1992) 'Changing the Subject? Racism, Culture and Education', in J. Donald and A. Rattansi (eds), *'Race', Culture & Difference* (London: Sage).

Rattansi, A. and Westwood, S. (eds) (1994) *Racism, Modernity and Identity: On the Western Front* (Cambridge: Polity Press).

Reeves, F. (1983) *British Racial Discourse: A Study of British Political Discourse about Race and Race Related Matters* (Cambridge: Cambridge University Press).

Reich, W. (1970) *The Mass Psychology of Fascism* (London: Condor Books).

Renan, E. (1990) 'What is a Nation?', in H. Bhabha (ed.), *Nation and Narration* (London: Routledge).

Rex, J. (1968) 'The Sociology of the Zone of Transition', in R. Pahl (ed.), *Readings in Urban Sociology* (London: Pergamon Press).

Rex, J. (1973) *Race, Colonialism and the City* (London: Routledge and Kegan Paul).

Rex, J. (1979) 'Black Militancy and Class Conflict', in R. Miles and A. Phizacklea (eds), *Racism and Political Action in Britain* (London: Routledge and Kegan Paul).

Rex, J. (1986a) *Race and Ethnicity* (London: Open University Press).

Rex, J. (1986b) 'The Role of Class Analysis in the Study of Race Relations – a Weberian Perspective', in J. Rex and D. Mason (eds), *Theories of Race and Ethnic Relations* (Cambridge: Cambridge University Press).

Rex, J. (1988) *The Ghetto and the Underclass: Essays on Race and Social Policy* (Aldershot: Avebury).

Rex, J. (1989) 'Some Notes on the Development of the Theory of Race and Ethnic Relations in Britain', unpublished discussion document, University of Warwick: Centre for Research in Ethnic Relations.

Rex, J. (1990) 'The Relationship Between Theoretical and Empirical Work in the Centre', unpublished discussion document, University of Warwick: Centre for Research in Ethnic Relations.

Rex, J. (1991) *Ethnic Identity and Ethnic Mobilisation in Britain,* Monographs in Ethnic Relations No 5, University of Warwick: Centre for Research in Ethnic Relations.

Rex, J. and Mason, D. (eds) (1986) *Theories of Race and Ethnic Relations* (Cambridge: Cambridge University Press).

Rex, J. and Moore, R. (1967) *Race, Community and Conflict* (London: Oxford University Press).

Rex, J. and Tomlinson, S. (1979) *Colonial Immigrants in a British City* (London: Routledge and Kegan Paul).

Rhodes, A. (1976) *Propaganda: The Art of Persuasion in World War II* (London: Angus Robertson).

Rhodes, P. J. (1992) *'Racial Matching' in Fostering* (Aldershot: Avebury).

Richards, T. (1990) *The Commodity Culture of Victorian England: Advertising and Spectacle* (London: Verso).

Roberts, R. (1973) *The Classic Slum* (Manchester: Manchester University Press).

Robertson, G., Mash, M., Tickner, L., Bird, J., Curtis, B. and Putnam, T. (eds) (1994) *Travellers' Tales: Narratives of Home and Displacement* (London: Routledge).

Robins, K. (1991) 'Tradition and Translation: National Culture in its Global Context', in J. Corner and S. Harvey (eds), *Enterprise and Heritage: Crosscurrents in National Culture* (London: Routledge).

Roediger, D. (1991) *The Wages of Whiteness: Race and the Making of the American Working Class* (London: Verso).

Roediger, D. (1994) *Towards the Abolition of Whiteness: Essays on Race, Politics, and Working Class History* (London: Verso).

Rogers, J. A. (1952) *Nature Knows No Color-Line: Research into the Negro Ancestry in the White Race* (St Petersburg, Florida: Helda M. Rogers).

Roosens, E. E. (1989) *Creating Ethnicity: The Process of Ethnogenesis* (London: Sage).

Rose, A. L. (1990) *German Question/Jewish Question: Revolutionary Antisemitism in Germany from Kant to Wagner* (Princeton: Princeton University Press).

Ross, K. (1996) *Black and White Media: Black Images in Popular Film and Television* (Cambridge: Polity Press).

Ross, R. (ed.) (1982) *Racism and Colonialism* (The Hague: Martinus Nijhoff).

Rowe, M. (ed.) (1991) *So Very English* (London: Serpent's Tail).

Rushdie, S. (1989) *The Satanic Verses* (London: Viking).

Rushdie, S. (1991) *Imaginary Homelands* (London: Granta Books).
Safran, W. (1991) 'Diasporas in Modern Societies: Myths of Homeland and Return', *Diaspora*, 1, 1: 83–99.
Saggar, S. (1992) *Race and Politics in Britain* (Hemel Hempstead: Harvester Wheatsheaf).
Said, E. W. (1985) *Orientalism* (Harmondsworth: Peregrine).
Said, E. W. (1993) *Culture and Imperialism* (London: Chatto and Windus).
Samuel, R. (ed.) (1989) *Patriotism: The Making and Unmaking of British National Identity*, 3 vols (London: Routledge).
Sartre, J.-P. (1976) *Anti-Semite and Jew* (New York: Schocken Books).
Sawhill, I. V. (1989) 'The Underclass: An Overview', *Public Interest*, 96: 3–15.
Schlesinger Jr, A. M. (1992) *The Disuniting of America: Reflections on a Multicultural Society* (New York: W. W. Norton).
Servos, N. (1990) 'Pathos and propaganda?: On the Mass Choreography of Fascism', *Ballet International Handbook*: 63–6.
Sharpe, J. (1993) *Allegories of Empire: The Figure of Woman in the Colonial Text* (Minneapolis: University of Minnesota Press).
Simmons, S. (1993) *The Films of D.W. Griffith* (Cambridge: Cambridge University Press).
Sivanandan, A. (1982) *A Different Hunger* (London: Pluto Press).
Sivanandan, A. (1983) 'Challenging Racism: Strategies for the Eighties', *Race and Class*, 25: 1–12.
Sivanandan, A. (1988) 'The New Racism', *New Statesman and Society*, 2 February.
Sivanandan, A. (1990a) 'All that Melts into Air is Solid: The Hokum of New Times', *Race and Class*, 31, 3: 1–30.
Sivanandan, A. (1990b) *Communities of Resistance* (London: Verso).
Sluga, H. (1993) *Heidegger's Crisis: Philosophy and Politics in Nazi Germany* (Cambridge, Mass.: Harvard University Press).
Small, S. (1994) *Racialized Barriers: The Black Experience in the United States and England in the 1980s* (London: Routledge).
Smith, A. D. (1986) *The Ethnic Origins of Nations* (Oxford: Blackwell).
Smith, A. D. (1991) *National Identity* (Harmondsworth: Penguin).
Smith, A. M. (1994) *New Right Discourse on Race and Sexuality: Britain, 1968–1990* (Cambridge: Cambridge University Press).
Smith, D. J. (ed.) (1992) *Understanding the Underclass* (London: Policy Studies Institute).
Snowden Jr, F. M. (1970) *Blacks in Antiquity: Ethiopians in the Greco-Roman Experience* (Cambridge, Mass.: Belknap Press).
Snowden Jr, F. M. (1983) *Before Color Prejudice: The Ancient View of Blacks* (Cambridge, Mass.: Harvard University Press).
Solomos, J. (1986) 'Polititical Language and Violent Protest: Ideological and Policy Responses to the 1981 and 1985 Riots', *Youth and Policy*, 18: 12–24.
Solomos, J. (1988) *Black Youth, Racism and the State* (Cambridge: Cambridge University Press).
Solomos, J. (1993) *Race and Racism in Britain*, 2nd edition (London: Macmillan).
Solomos, J. (ed.) (1982) *Migrant Workers in Metropolitan Cities* (Strasbourg: European Science Foundation).

Solomos, J. and Back, L. (1995) *Race, Politics and Social Change* (London: Routledge).

Solomos, J., Findlay, B., Jones, S. and Gilroy, P. (1982) 'The Organic Crisis of British Capitalism and Race: The Experience of the Seventies', in CCCS (Centre for Contemporary Cultural Studies) *The Empire Strikes Back* (London: Hutchinson).

Solomos, J. and Wrench, J. (1993) 'Race and Racism in Contemporary Europe', in J. Wrench and J. Solomos (eds), *Racism and Migration in Western Europe* (Oxford: Berg).

Solow, B. L. and Engerman, S. L. (eds) (1987) *British Capitalism and Caribbean Slavery: The Legacy of Eric Williams* (Cambridge: Cambridge University Press).

Sontag, S. (1990) 'Fascinating Fascism', in B. Taylor and W. van der Will (eds), *The Nazification of Art: Art, Design, Music, Architecture and Film in the Third Reich* (Winchester: Winchester Press).

Sowell, T. (1981) *Markets and Minorities* (Oxford: Blackwell).

Sowell, T. (1983) *The Economics and Politics of Race: An International Perspective* (New York: Quill).

Squires, J. (ed.) (1993) *Principled Positions: Postmodernism and the Rediscovery of Value* (London: Lawrence and Wishart).

Spivak, G. C. (1987) *In Other Worlds* (London: Methuen).

Spivak, G. C. (1993) *Outside in the Teaching Machine* (New York: Routledge).

Spurr, D. (1993) *The Rhetoric of Empire* (Durham and London: Duke University Press).

Stack, C. (1974) *All Our Kin: Strategies for Survival in a Black Community* (New York: Harper and Row).

Stanfield II, J. H. (1985) *Philanthropy and Jim Crow in American Social Science* (Westport: Greenwood Press).

Stanfield II, J. H. (ed.) (1993) *A History of Race Relations Research: First Generation Recollections* (London: Sage).

Stanfield II, J. H. and Dennis, R. M. (eds) (1993) *Race and Ethnicity in Research Methods* (London: Sage).

Stepan, N. (1982) *The Idea of Race in Science* (London: Macmillan).

Stocking Jr, G. (1968) *Race, Culture and Evolution* (Chicago: University of Chicago Press).

Stocking Jr, G. (1987) *Victorian Anthropology* (New York: Free Press).

Stubbs, P. (1987) 'Professionalism and the Adoption of Black Children', *British Journal of Social Work*, 17, 5: 473–92.

Stutley, M. (1973) *The Illustrated Dictionary of Hindu Iconography* (London: Routledge and Kegan Paul).

Sundquist, E. J. (1993) *To Wake the Nations: Race in the Making of American Literature* (Cambridge, Mass.: Belknap Press).

Taguieff, P.-A. (1988) *La Force du Préjugé* (Paris: La Découverte).

Taguieff, P.-A. (1990) 'The New Cultural Racism', *Telos*, 83: 109–22.

Takagi, R. (1993) *A Different Mirror: A History of Multicultural America* (Boston: Little, Brown).

Taussig, M. (1987) *Shamanism, Colonialism, and the Wild Man: A Study in Terror and Healing* (Chicago: University of Chicago Press).

Taussig, M. (1993) *Mimesis and Alterity: A Particular History of the Senses* (New York: Routledge).

Taylor, B. (1990) 'Post-modernism in the Third Reich', in B. Taylor and W. van der Will (eds), *The Nazification of Art: Art, Design, Music, Architecture and Film in the Third Reich* (Winchester: Winchester Press).

Taylor, B. and van der Will, W. (eds) (1990) *The Nazification of Art: Art, Design, Music, Architecture and Film in the Third Reich* (Winchester: Winchester Press).

Taylor, C., Gutmann, A., Rockefeller, S. C., Walzer, M. and Wolf, S. (1992a) *Multiculturalism and 'The Politics of Recognition'* (Princeton: Princeton University Press).

Taylor, C. (1992b) *The Ethics of Authenticity* (Cambridge, Mass.: Harvard University Press).

Terkel, S. (1992) *Race: How Blacks and Whites Think and Feel About the American Obsession* (London: Sinclair-Stevenson).

Thatcher, M. (1988) *Britain and Europe* (London: Conservative Political Centre).

Thompson, L. A. (1989) *Romans and Blacks* (London: Routledge).

Thrasher, F. R. (1927) *The Gang: A Study 1,313 Gangs in Chicago* (Chicago: University of Chicago Press).

Tizard, B. and Phoenix, A. (1989) 'Black Identity and Transracial Adoption', *New Community*, 15, 3: 427–37.

Tizard, B. and Phoenix, A. (1993) *Black, White or Mixed Race? Race and Racism in the Lives of Young People of Mixed Parentage* (London: Routledge).

Todorov, T. (1984) *The Conquest of America: The Question of the Other* (New York: Harper and Row).

Todorov, T. (1986) 'Race, Writing and Culture', in H. L. Gates Jr (ed.), *'Race', Writing and Difference* (Chicago: University of Chicago Press).

Todorov, T. (1993) *On Human Diversity: Nationalism, Racism and Exoticism in French Thought* (Cambridge, Mass.: Harvard University Press).

Toulmin, S. (1990) *Cosmopolis: The Hidden Agenda of Modernity* (Chicago: University of Chicago Press).

Touraine, A. (1981) *The Voice and the Eye: An Analysis of Social Movements* (Cambridge: Cambridge University Press).

Troyna, B. (1977a) 'Angry Youngsters – a Response to Racism in Britain', *Youth in Society*, 26, December: 13–15.

Troyna, B. (1977b) 'The Reggae War', *New Society*, 10 March: 491–2.

Troyna, B. (1979) 'Differential Commitment to Ethnic Identity by Black Youth in Britain', *New Community*, VII, 3: 406–14.

Turner, B. S. (1994) *Orientalism, Postmodernism and Globalism* (London: Routledge).

Turner, P. (1994) *Ceramic Uncles and Celluloid Mammies: Black Images and Their Influence on Culture* (New York: Anchor Books).

Ullah, P. (1987) 'Unemployed Black Youth in a Northern City', in D. Fryer and P. Ullah (eds), *Unemployed People: Social and Psychological Perspectives* (Milton Keynes: Open University Press).

Van Deburg, W. L. (1992) *New Day in Babylon: The Black Power Movement and American Culture* (Chicago: University of Chicago Press).

van Dijk, T. A. (1991) *Racism and the Press* (London: Routledge).

van Dijk, T. A. (1993) *Elite Discourse and Racism* (London: Sage).

Varenne, J. (1973) *Yoga and the Hindu Tradition* (Chicago: University of Chicago Press).

Venediktov, A. (1994) 'Introduction to *A Last Bid for the South*', *Index on Censorship*, 1/2: 61–2.

Verkuyten, M., de Jong, W. and Masson, K. (1994) 'Similarities in Racist and Anti-racist Discourse: Dutch Local Residents Talking about Ethnic Minorities', *New Community*, 20, 2: 253–67.

Wacquant, L. J. D. (1994) 'The New Urban Colour Line: The State and Fate of the Ghetto in PostFordist America', in C. Calhoun (ed.), *Social Theory and the Politics of Identity* (Oxford: Blackwell).

Wallace, M. (1990a) *Black Macho and The Myth of the Superwoman* (London: Verso).

Wallace, M. (1990b) *Invisibility Blues: From Pop to Theory* (London: Verso).

Wallman, S. (1978a) 'The Boundaries of "Race": Processes of Ethnicity in England', *Man*, 13, 2: 200–17.

Wallman, S. (1978b) 'Race Relations or Ethnic Relations?', *New Community*, VI, 3: 306–9.

Wallman, S. (1983) 'Identity Options', in C. Fried (ed.), *Minorities: Community and Identity* (Berlin: Springer-Verlag).

Wallman, S. (1986) 'Ethnicity and the Boundary Process in Context', in J. Rex and D. Mason (eds), *Theories of Race and Ethnic Relations* (Cambridge: Cambridge University Press).

Wallman, S. (ed.) (1979) *Ethnicity at Work* (London: Macmillan).

Wallman, S. in association with Buchanan, I., Dhooge, Y., Gershuny, J. I., Kosmin, B. and Wann, M. (1982) *Living in South London: Perspectives on Battersea, 1871–1981* (Aldershot: Gower).

Walvin, J. (1992) *Black Ivory: A History of British Slavery* (London: HarperCollins).

Walvin, J. (ed.) (1982) *Slavery and British Society, 1776–1846* (London: Macmillan).

Ware, V. (1992) *Beyond the Pale: White Women, Racism and History* (London: Verso).

Wark, M. (1992) 'Still Life Today: The Benetton Campaigns', *Photophile*, 36: 33–6.

Warner, M. (1993) *Indigo* (London: Vintage).

Weeks, J. (ed.) (1994) *The Lesser Evil and the Greater Good: The Theory and Politics of Social Diversity* (London: Rivers Oram Press).

Weindling, P. (1989) *Health, Race and German Politics Between National Unification and Nazism, 1870–1945* (Cambridge: Cambridge University Press).

Weir, M. (1993) 'From Equal Opportunity to "The New Social Contract": Race and the Politics of the American Underclass', in M. Cross and M. Keith (eds), *Racism, the City and the State* (London: Routledge).

Wellman, D. (1993) *Portraits of White Racism*, 2nd edition (Cambridge: Cambridge University Press).

West, C. (1992) 'The New Cultural Politics of Difference', in R. Ferguson, M. Gever, T. Minh-ha and C. West (eds), *Out There: Marginalization and Contemporary Cultures* (Cambridge, Mass.: MIT Press).

West, C. (1993a) *Beyond Eurocentrism and Multiculturalism: Volume I, Prophetic Thought in Postmodern Times* (Monroe: Common Courage Press).

West, C. (1993b) *Beyond Eurocentrism and Multiculturalism: Volume II, Prophetic Reflections: Notes on Race and Power in America* (Monroe: Common Courage Press).

West, C. (1993c) *Keeping Faith: Philosophy and Race in America* (New York: Routledge).

West, C. (1993d) *Race Matters* (Boston: Beacon Press).

Wieviorka, M. (1992) *La France Raciste* (Paris: Seuil).

Wieviorka, M. (1993) 'Tendencies to Racism in Europe: Does France Represent a Unique Case, or it Representative of a Trend?', in J. Wrench and J. Solomos (eds), *Racism and Migration in Western Europe* (Oxford: Berg).

Williams, E. (1944) *Capitalism and Slavery* (London: André Deutsch).

Williams, P. (1991) *The Alchemy of Race and Rights* (Cambridge, Mass.: Harvard University Press).

Williams, P. and Chrisman, L. (eds) (1993) *Colonial Discourse and Post-Colonial Theory: A Reader* (New York: Harvester Wheatsheaf).

Wilson, S. (1982) *Ideology and Experience: Antisemitism in France at the Time of the Dreyfus Affair* (London: Associated University Press).

Wilson, W. J. (1987) *The Truly Disadvantaged: The Inner City, the Underclass and Public Policy* (Chicago: University of Chicago Press).

Wilson, W. J. (1991) 'Studying Inner-city Social Dislocations: The Challenge of Public Agenda Research', *American Sociological Review*, 56, 1: 1–14.

Winant, H. (1994) *Racial Conditions: Politics, Theory, Comparisons* (Minneapolis: University of Minnesota Press).

Wolf, E. (1982) *Europe and the People Without History* (Berkeley: University of California Press).

Wolf, B. [1947/8] (1993) 'Ecstatic in Blackface: The Negro as a Song-and-Dance Man', in M. Mezzrow and B. Wolf, *Really the Blues* (London: Flamingo).

Wrench, J. and Solomos, J. (eds) (1993) *Racism and Migration in Western Europe* (Oxford: Berg).

Young, I. M. (1990) *Justice and the Politics of Difference* (Princeton: Princeton University Press).

Young, R. (1990) *White Mythologies: Writing History and the West* (London: Routledge).

Young, R. (1995) *Colonial Desire: Hybridity in Theory, Culture and Race* (London: Routledge).

Žižek, S. (1989) *The Sublime Object of Ideology* (London: Verso).

Žižek, S. (1993) *Tarrying with the Negative: Kant, Hegel, and the Critique of Ideology* (Durham: Duke University Press).

Index